MEAN Blueprints

Unlock the power of the MEAN stack by creating
attractive and real-world projects

Robert Onodi

[PACKT] open source ✳
PUBLISHING   community experience distilled

BIRMINGHAM - MUMBAI

MEAN Blueprints

First published: May 2016

Production reference: 1240516

Published by Packt Publishing Ltd.
Livery Place
35 Livery Street
Birmingham B3 2PB, UK.

ISBN 978-1-78355-394-5

www.packtpub.com

Credits

Author
Robert Onodi

Reviewer
Dan Shreim

Acquisition Editor
Rahul Nair

Content Development Editor
Mayur Pawanikar

Technical Editor
Vivek Arora

Copy Editor
Vikrant Phadke

Project Coordinator
Nidhi Joshi

Proofreader
Safis Editing

Indexer
Monica Mehta

Graphics
Disha Haria

Production Coordinator
Nilesh Mohite

Cover Work
Nilesh Mohite

About the Author

Robert Onodi has been developing software for close to a decade now. He started working on small applications in Flash, and later moved on to the LAMP stack. For most of his career, he has been working with JavaScript. Having knowledge of both server-side technologies and a passion for JavaScript, he rapidly adopted Node.js in his development stack.

Currently, he works at Evozon, where he shares his dedication for technology and JavaScript with others and develops modern applications using the MEAN stack. Besides his daily programming routine, he is also passionate about mentoring and training.

I rarely have the chance to thank everyone for all their good deeds towards me, probably because we are used to a life lived in fast forward. But this time, I would like to take my time and sincerely thank everyone for their help and support, especially for their trust and sacrifice, making me a better person.

A big thank you to everyone: my family, my loved ones, my friends, my colleagues, everybody at Packt, and all the great people working at Evozon for the support and help they give me each day. There is no greater source of inspiration and motivation in life than doing what you love, with the ones you love.

About the Reviewer

Dan Shreim has worked as a frontend web developer for over 15 years, specializing in AngularJS, user experience, and interface design. He has worked in conjunction with several award-winning agencies on projects for numerous household-name brands around the world crossing the entertainment, financial, security, and business sectors.

He is currently working as an interface developer for a world-leading cybersecurity company in Boulder, Colorado, USA.

He has worked in Toronto, Canada, designing loyalty platforms; and in London, UK, building prototypes for usability testing.

For more information on Dan, please visit his site at `http://snapjay.com`.

I'd like to thank Jasper for his compassion and support over the past few years.

---

www.PacktPub.com

eBooks, discount offers, and more

Did you know that Packt offers eBook versions of every book published, with PDF and ePub files available? You can upgrade to the eBook version at www.PacktPub. com and as a print book customer, you are entitled to a discount on the eBook copy. Get in touch with us at customercare@packtpub.com for more details.

At www.PacktPub.com, you can also read a collection of free technical articles, sign up for a range of free newsletters and receive exclusive discounts and offers on Packt books and eBooks.

https://www2.packtpub.com/books/subscription/packtlib

Do you need instant solutions to your IT questions? PacktLib is Packt's online digital book library. Here, you can search, access, and read Packt's entire library of books.

Why subscribe?

- Fully searchable across every book published by Packt
- Copy and paste, print, and bookmark content
- On demand and accessible via a web browser

Table of Contents

Preface

When learning new technologies or even improving our existing skill set, we are always interested in full-fledged applications: how the application is built from the concept phase to an actual running application, what pain points can different technologies solve, and what guidelines we need to follow to ease our development cycle.

Speaking of technologies, probably the most widespread of them all is JavaScript. I think the good and bad part of JavaScript is its popularity. For decades, we have had no technology that is so widely spread and ready to be integrated on different platforms.

Besides running JavaScript in the browser, which we are all so used to, for a few years we can easily run our JS code on the server using Node.js. It does not stop here, as we can start developing powerful IoT projects using only JavaScript.

For many years, we saw a movement of having a single technology that dominates every platform. I think the JavaScript stack, yes stack, at the moment is big game changer. Probably, you are thinking now that it's not that perfect or colorful; yes, I cannot agree more with you, but the evolution is so rapid — and new things are pushed every day, every minute — that we are on the edge of a technological revolution.

Wait! What? Yes, we can be a part of the revolution, we can be trend setters, we can shape the future of the Web, mobile, and IoT (maybe the universe? But of course). We can push the limits and prove that we can do great things, and we can progressively improve ourselves and the people around us.

The idea behind the book

The idea behind writing this book was to provide a guide and a higher perspective of applications built using the MEAN stack. As I interact with lots of people at the company Evozon, where I'm working, I see a big desire in people to touch and feel how applications are built using different technology stacks.

Especially in popular technologies such as JavaScript, Node.js, and MongoDB. But usually, finding full end-to-end example applications is hard. Don't get me wrong; the Internet is full of great stuff, brilliant people, and so many mind-blowing things, but it is also full of noise and uncertainty, and it's hard to know which path is right or wrong and what should be done in certain scenarios.

That's why we want to showcase different scenarios of building applications using the MEAN stack. Probably it's not the only way of doing things, but it should provide you with a starting point, or give you an insight into how certain parts of an app are built.

This is not a getting started book on Node.js and Angular 2. It will jump right into action and showcase six built-from-the-beginning applications, each with different use cases and solving a high-level problem.

A little bit of twist

Writing a book takes time, a lot of energy, and a little bit of fear. I've feared that I'll never finish this book. It was a long run, and the funniest part was that the first three chapters were written in an earlier version of AngularJS. Don't worry! Everything is shipped using Angular 2.

As you might have guessed, we had a long run and rewrote everything using the currently-in-beta-release Angular 2. Why? Because, as I told you before, we want to push our limits. We want to grow and master new ways of building modern applications.

I've tried to cover a variety of applications built using the MEAN stack, ranging from a simple contact manager and a real-time chat application to a full auction website.

What this book covers

Chapter 1, Contact Manager, will cover the process of building an introductory application to save your contacts in MondoDB. The chapter will introduce you to TDD (short for Test-Driven Development) for your Node.js application. You will learn how to build an Angular 2 app that will access data from the Express API.

Chapter 2, Expense Tracker, is going to dive deep into working with monetary data in JavaScript and storing this data in MongoDB using the exact precision approach. Also, you are going to learn how to add a token for authentication of each request in the client application by extending the built-in HTTP service in Angular. Besides this, you'll see how to use the aggregation framework from MongoDB and display the result in your Angular application.

Chapter 3, Job Board, will focus on building a more consumer-level application that will enable users to define a custom profile with dynamic data. You will use reactive extensions in Angular to create different communication layers in your application. On the backend, we are going to build a RESTful API using Node.js and set up a boilerplate application from the previously built apps that we are going to use further in the book.

Chapter 4, Chat Application, will start reusing the boilerplate built in the previous chapter. But the most fun part will begin when we create a chat service layer that uses SocketIO. This will enable both the backend and the frontend Angular app to communicate in real time to send messages. The chat service will be built in such a way that it's easily extendable with new modules, besides instant messaging, such as when a user is online or goes offline.

Chapter 5, E-Commerce Application, is going to reflect the ease of storing unstructured data in MongoDB. We'll discuss in detail how to store your product catalog in a NoSQL database. Besides this, our initial architecture from the previous chapters is going to get a new form, and we'll experiment with micro-apps, each with its own responsibility. The micro-apps will use the core e-commerce module that encapsulates all the business logic. Also, this chapter will cover two client apps, one built with a totally different technology, and an admin application using Angular 2.

Chapter 6, Auction Application, is going to be more of an extension of the previous chapter; in other words, it will use the e-commerce API to fetch product information and authenticate users. This will push us not only to reuse existing code but rely on other services for faster prototyping when building products. Also, we are going to dive deeper into RxJs and see how we can build a real-time bidding system in our Angular auction application using SocketIO on the server side.

What you need for this book

You will require any modern web browser (such as Chrome's latest version or IE 10+), the Node.js platform installed on your machine, and version 3.2 or higher of MongoDB. Optionally, you can install any web server, such as Nginx, Apache, IIS, or lighttpd, to proxy requests to your Node.js application.

Who this book is for

If you are a web developer with a basic understanding of the MEAN stack, experience of developing applications with JavaScript, and basic experience with NoSQL databases, then this book is for you.

Conventions

In this book, you will find a number of text styles that distinguish between different kinds of information. Here are some examples of these styles and an explanation of their meaning.

Code words in text, database table names, folder names, filenames, file extensions, pathnames, dummy URLs, user input, and Twitter handles are shown as follows: "Create a file called app/models/token.js."

A block of code is set as follows:

```
'use strict';

const LEN = 256;
const SALT_LEN = 64;
const ITERATIONS = 10000;
const DIGEST = 'sha256';
const crypto = require('crypto');

module.exports.hash = hashPassword;
module.exports.verify = verify;
```

When we wish to draw your attention to a particular part of a code block, the relevant lines or items are set in bold:

```
require('./config/express').init(app);
require('./config/routes').init(app);
```

Any command-line input or output is written as follows:

```
Authentication
  Basic authentication
    √ should authenticate a user and return a new token
    √ should not authenticate a user with invalid credentials
2 passing
```

New terms and **important words** are shown in bold. Words that you see on the screen, for example, in menus or dialog boxes, appear in the text like this: "It triggers an event when the **Save** button is clicked on and the form is submitted."

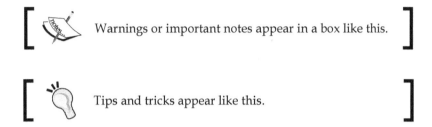

> Warnings or important notes appear in a box like this.

> Tips and tricks appear like this.

Reader feedback

Feedback from our readers is always welcome. Let us know what you think about this book—what you liked or disliked. Reader feedback is important for us as it helps us develop titles that you will really get the most out of.

To send us general feedback, simply e-mail feedback@packtpub.com, and mention the book's title in the subject of your message.

If there is a topic that you have expertise in and you are interested in either writing or contributing to a book, see our author guide at www.packtpub.com/authors.

Customer support

Now that you are the proud owner of a Packt book, we have a number of things to help you to get the most from your purchase.

Downloading the example code

You can download the example code files for this book from your account at `http://www.packtpub.com`. If you purchased this book elsewhere, you can visit `http://www.packtpub.com/support` and register to have the files e-mailed directly to you.

You can download the code files by following these steps:

1. Log in or register to our website using your e-mail address and password.
2. Hover the mouse pointer on the **SUPPORT** tab at the top.
3. Click on **Code Downloads & Errata**.
4. Enter the name of the book in the **Search** box.
5. Select the book for which you're looking to download the code files.
6. Choose from the drop-down menu where you purchased this book from.
7. Click on **Code Download**.

Once the file is downloaded, please make sure that you unzip or extract the folder using the latest version of:

- WinRAR / 7-Zip for Windows
- Zipeg / iZip / UnRarX for Mac
- 7-Zip / PeaZip for Linux

The code bundle for the book is also hosted on GitHub at `https://github.com/PacktPublishing/repository-name`. We also have other code bundles from our rich catalog of books and videos available at `https://github.com/PacktPublishing/`. Check them out!

Errata

Although we have taken every care to ensure the accuracy of our content, mistakes do happen. If you find a mistake in one of our books—maybe a mistake in the text or the code—we would be grateful if you could report this to us. By doing so, you can save other readers from frustration and help us improve subsequent versions of this book. If you find any errata, please report them by visiting `http://www.packtpub.com/submit-errata`, selecting your book, clicking on the **Errata Submission Form** link, and entering the details of your errata. Once your errata are verified, your submission will be accepted and the errata will be uploaded to our website or added to any list of existing errata under the Errata section of that title.

To view the previously submitted errata, go to https://www.packtpub.com/books/content/support and enter the name of the book in the search field. The required information will appear under the **Errata** section.

Piracy

Piracy of copyrighted material on the Internet is an ongoing problem across all media. At Packt, we take the protection of our copyright and licenses very seriously. If you come across any illegal copies of our works in any form on the Internet, please provide us with the location address or website name immediately so that we can pursue a remedy.

Please contact us at copyright@packtpub.com with a link to the suspected pirated material.

We appreciate your help in protecting our authors and our ability to bring you valuable content.

Questions

If you have a problem with any aspect of this book, you can contact us at questions@packtpub.com, and we will do our best to address the problem.

1
Contact Manager

In this chapter, you'll learn how to build a Contact manager application. The application will be divided into two separate parts: one part consisting of the backend, our Node.js API written using Express, and the client application crafted using Angular 2.

Don't worry! This chapter will be more of a guideline, setting up a base project and wrapping your head around TDD (short for **Test-driven development**) in Node.js. We'll also get to see Angular 2 in action. We are not going to write tests on the client side as there are enough things to accumulate in one chapter.

Setting up the base application

The best way to start is with a solid base. That's why we are going to focus on building the base structure of our application. A good base gives you modularity and flexibility and also files should be easily located by you and even your team members.

Always start with something simple and start building around it. As your application grows, you'll probably outgrow your initial application structure, so thinking ahead will bring you big benefits in the long run.

Folder structure

Before jumping in and building your features right away, you should take a moment and sketch out your initial application's structure. In the planning process, a pen and paper should always do it, but I've already saved some time and come up with an initial version:

```
app/
--controllers/
--middlewares/
--models/
```

```
--routes/
config/
--environments/
--strategies/
tests/
--integration/
--unit/
public/
--app/
--src/
--assets/
--typings/
--package.json
--tsconfig.json
--typings.json
package.json
server.js
```

Let's take a look at a more detailed explanation of our folder structure:

- app: This folder contains all the server files used in the application:
  - controllers: This folder is going to store the application controllers, mainly the backend business logic.
  - middlewares: In this folder, we'll store all our pieces of functions that will manipulate the request and response object. A good example would be an authentication middleware.
  - models: This folder will store all the backend models.
  - routes: This folder will contain all the routing files, which is where we are going to define all Express routes.

- config: All application configuration files go here:
  - environments: This folder contains files loaded according to the current environment
  - strategies: All your authentication strategies should go here

- tests: This folder contains all the tests necessary to test the application backend logic:
  - integration: If something uses external modules, it's good practice to create an integration test
  - unit: This should contain tests for small units of code, such as password hashing

- `public`: This should contain all the static files served by our application. I like this separation because it's easy to just tell another web server to handle our static files. Let's say you want nginx to handle static file serving:
    - `app`: This is our client-side application's folder. All compiled TypeScript files will go here. This folder should be automatically populated.
    - `src`: This folder contains all the client-side files used to build our application. We are going to use TypeScript to build our Angular application.
    - `typings`: This contains TypeScript definitions.

Server-side package.json

After setting up the initial folder structure, the next thing to do is to create the `package.json` file. This file will hold all the application's metadata and dependencies. The `package.json` file will be placed at the root of our project folder. The path should be `contact-manager/package.json`:

```json
{
  "name": "mean-blueprints-contact-manager",
  "version": "0.0.9",
  "repository": {
    "type": "git",
    "url": "https://github.com/robert52/mean-blueprints-cm.git"
  },
  "engines": {
    "node": ">=4.4.3"
  },
  "scripts": {
    "start": "node app.js",
    "unit": "node_modules/.bin/mocha tests/unit/ --ui bdd --recursive --reporter spec --timeout 10000 --slow 900",
    "integration": "node_modules/.bin/mocha tests/integration/ --ui bdd --recursive --reporter spec --timeout 10000 --slow 900",
    "less": "node_modules/.bin/autoless public/assets/less public/assets/css --no-watch",
    "less-watch": "node_modules/.bin/autoless public/assets/less public/assets/css"
  },
  "dependencies": {
    "async": "^0.9.2",
    "body-parser": "^1.15.0",
```

```
      "connect-mongo": "^1.1.0",
      "express": "^4.13.4",
      "express-session": "^1.13.0",
      "lodash": "^3.10.1",
      "method-override": "^2.3.5",
      "mongoose": "^4.4.12",
      "passport": "^0.2.2",
      "passport-local": "^1.0.0",
      "serve-static": "^1.10.2"
    },
    "devDependencies": {
      "autoless": "^0.1.7",
      "chai": "^2.3.0",
      "chai-things": "^0.2.0",
      "mocha": "^2.4.5",
      "request": "^2.71.0"
    }
  }
```

We added a few scripts to our `package.json` file to run our unit and integration tests and compile the Less files. You can always use npm to directly run different scripts instead of using build tools such as Grunt or Gulp.

At the time of writing this book, we are using the defined dependencies and their versions. This should do it for now. Let's install them using the following command:

$ npm install

You should see npm pulling a bunch of files and adding the necessary dependencies to the `node_modules` folder. Wait patiently until everything is installed and done. You will be returned to Command Prompt. Now you should see the `node_modules` folder created and with all the dependencies in place.

The first application file

Before everything, we need to create a simple configuration file for our environment. Let's create the file in the `config` folder at `contact-manager/config/environments/development.js` and add the following content:

```
    'use strict';

    module.exports = {
      port: 3000,
      hostname: '127.0.0.1',
      baseUrl: 'http://localhost:3000',
```

```
  mongodb: {
    uri: 'mongodb://localhost/cm_dev_db'
  },
  app: {
    name: 'Contact manager'
  },
  serveStatic: true,
  session: {
    type: 'mongo',
    secret: 'u+J%E^9!hx?piXLCfiMY.EDc',
    resave: false,
    saveUninitialized: true
  }
};
```

Now let's create the main `server.js` file for our application. This file will be the heart of our application. The file should be in the root of our folder, `contact-manager/server.js`. Start with the following lines of code:

```
'use strict';

// Get environment or set default environment to development
const ENV = process.env.NODE_ENV || 'development';
const DEFAULT_PORT = 3000;
const DEFAULT_HOSTNAME = '127.0.0.1';

const http = require('http');
const express = require('express');
const config = require('./config');
const app = express();

var server;

// Set express variables
app.set('config', config);
app.set('root', __dirname);
app.set('env', ENV);

require('./config/mongoose').init(app);
require('./config/models').init(app);
require('./config/passport').init(app);
require('./config/express').init(app);
require('./config/routes').init(app);

// Start the app if not loaded by another module
```

```
if (!module.parent) {
  server = http.createServer(app);
  server.listen(
    config.port || DEFAULT_PORT,
    config.hostname || DEFAULT_HOSTNAME,
    () => {
      console.log(`${config.app.name} is running`);
      console.log(`   listening on port: ${config.port}`);
      console.log(`   environment: ${ENV.toLowerCase()}`);
    }
  );
}

module.exports = app;
```

We define some of our main dependencies and initialize the necessary modules of our application. To modularize things, we are going to put each package of our stack into a separate configuration file. These configuration files will have some logic in them. I like to call them smart configuration files.

Don't worry! We are going to go through each config file one by one. Finally, we will export our Express app instance. If our module is not loaded by another module, for example, a test case, then we can safely start listening to incoming requests.

Creating the Express configuration file

We need to create a configuration file for Express. The file should be created in the config folder at contact-manager/config/express.js and we have to add the following lines of code:

```
'use strict';

const path = require('path');
const bodyParser = require('body-parser');
const methodOverride = require('method-override');
const serveStatic = require('serve-static');
const session = require('express-session');
const passport = require('passport');
const MongoStore = require('connect-mongo')(session);
const config = require('./index');

module.exports.init = initExpress;

function initExpress(app) {
  const root = app.get('root');
```

```
const sessionOpts = {
  secret: config.session.secret,
  key: 'skey.sid',
  resave: config.session.resave,
  saveUninitialized: config.session.saveUninitialized
};

//common express configs
app.use(bodyParser.urlencoded({ extended: true }));
app.use(bodyParser.json());
app.use(methodOverride());
app.disable('x-powered-by');

if (config.session.type === 'mongo') {
  sessionOpts.store = new MongoStore({
    url: config.mongodb.uri
  });
}

app.use(session(sessionOpts));
app.use(passport.initialize());
app.use(passport.session());

app.use(function(req, res, next) {
  res.locals.app = config.app;

  next();
});

// always load static files if dev env
if (config.serveStatic) {
  app.use(serveStatic(path.join(root, 'public')));
}
};
```

You should be familiar with many lines from the preceding code by now, for example, setting the desired body parser of our Express application. Also, we set up the session management, and just in case we set to the server static files, we define the path to the server files.

In a production environment, you should use something different from the default in-memory storage for sessions. That's why we added a special session store, which will store data in MongoDB.

A good practice to get the global environment configuration file is to set a root config file that all application files will load, create a new file called `contact-manager/config/index.js`, and add this code to it:

```
'use strict';

var ENV = process.env.NODE_ENV || 'development';
var config = require('./environments/'+ENV.toLowerCase());

module.exports = config;
```

The preceding code will just load the necessary environment configuration file based on the NODE_ENV process environment variable. If the environment variable is not present, a default development state will be considered for the application. This is a good practice so that we don't make mistakes and connect to the wrong database.

Usually, the NODE_ENV variable can be set when you start your node server; for example, under Unix systems, you can run the following command:

```
$ NODE_ENV=production node server.js
```

Setting up mocha for testing

Before we implement any functionality, we are going to write tests for it. Mocha is a testing framework built on Node.js. This approach will give us the advantage of knowing what code we are going to write and testing our Node.js API before even writing a single line of the client application.

If you don't have Mocha, you can install it globally. If you want Mocha to be globally available in your command line, run the following command:

```
$ npm install -g mocha
```

Setting up Mongoose

In order to store data in MongoDB, we are going to use Mongoose. Mongoose provides an easy way to define schemas to model application data. We have already included mongoose in the `package.json` file, so it should be installed.

We need to create a config file for our mongoose library. Let's create our config file `contact-manager/config/mongoose.js`. First, we start by loading the Mongoose library, getting the appropriate environment config, and establishing a connection with the database. Add the following code to the `mongoose.js` file:

```
'use strict';

const mongoose = require('mongoose');
const config = require('./index');

module.exports.init = initMongoose;

function initMongoose(app) {
  mongoose.connect(config.mongodb.uri);

  // If the Node process ends, cleanup existing connections
  process.on('SIGINT', cleanup);
  process.on('SIGTERM', cleanup);
  process.on('SIGHUP', cleanup);

  if (app) {
    app.set('mongoose', mongoose);
  }

  return mongoose;
};

function cleanup() {
  mongoose.connection.close(function () {
    console.log('Closing DB connections and stopping the app. Bye
bye.');
    process.exit(0);
  });
}
```

Also, we are using a `cleanup()` function to close all connections to the MongoDB database. The preceding code will export the necessary `init()` function used in the main `server.js` file.

Managing contacts

Now that we have the files necessary to start development and add features, we can start implementing all of the business logic related to managing contacts. To do this, we first need to define the data model of a contact.

Creating the contact mongoose schema

Our system needs some sort of functionality to store the possible clients or just contact persons of other companies. For this, we are going to create a contact schema that will represent the same collection storing all the contacts in MongoDB. We are going to keep our contact schema simple. Let's create a model file in `contact-manager/app/models/contact.js`, which will hold the schema, and add the following code to it:

```
'use strict';

const mongoose = require('mongoose');
const Schema = mongoose.Schema;

var ContactSchema = new Schema({
  email: {
    type: String
  },
  name: {
    type: String
  },
  city: {
    type: String
  },
  phoneNumber: {
    type: String
  },
  company: {
    type: String
  },
  createdAt: {
    type: Date,
    default: Date.now
  }
});

// compile and export the Contact model
module.exports = mongoose.model('Contact', ContactSchema);
```

The following table gives a description of the fields in the schema:

Field	Description
email	The e-mail of the contact
name	The full name of the contact
company	The name of the company at which the contact person works
phoneNumber	The full phone number of the person or company
city	The location of the contact
createdAt	The date at which the contact object was created

All our model files will be registered in the following configuration file, found under `contact-manager/config/models.js`. The final version of this file will look something like this:

```
'use strict';

module.exports.init = initModels;

function initModels(app) {
  let modelsPath = app.get('root') + '/app/models/';

  ['user', 'contact'].forEach(function(model) {
    require(modelsPath + model);
  });
};
```

Describing the contact route

In order to communicate with the server, we need to expose routes for client applications to consume. These are going to be endpoints (URIs) that respond to client requests. Mainly, our routes will send a JSON response.

We are going to start by describing the CRUD functionality of the contact module. The routes should expose the following functionalities:

- Create a new contact
- Get a contact by ID
- Get all contacts
- Update a contact
- Delete a contact by ID

We are not going to cover bulk insert and delete in this application.

The following table shows how these operations can be mapped to HTTP routes and verbs:

Route	Verb	Description	Data
`/contacts`	`POST`	Create a new contact	`email`, `name`, `company`, `phoneNumber`, and `city`
`/contacts`	`GET`	Get all contacts from the system	
`/contacts/<id>`	`GET`	Get a particular contact	
`/contacts/<id>`	`PUT`	Update a particular contact	`email`, `name`, `company`, `phoneNumber`, and `city`
`/contacts/<id>`	`DELETE`	Delete a particular contact	

Following the earlier table as a guide, we are going to describe our main functionality and test using Mocha. Mocha allows us to describe the features that we are implementing by giving us the ability to use a describe function that encapsulates our expectations. The first argument of the function is a simple string that describes the feature. The second argument is a function body that represents the description.

You have already created a folder called `contact-manger/tests`. In your `tests` folder, create another folder called `integration`. Create a file called `contact-manager/tests/integration/contact_test.js` and add the following code:

```
'use strict';

/**
 * Important! Set the environment to test
 */
process.env.NODE_ENV = 'test';

const http = require('http');
const request = require('request');
const chai = require('chai');
const userFixture = require('../fixtures/user');
const should = chai.should();

let app;
let appServer;
let mongoose;
let User;
let Contact;
```

```
let config;
let baseUrl;
let apiUrl;

describe('Contacts endpoints test', function() {

  before((done) => {
    // boot app
    // start listening to requests
  });

  after(function(done) {
    // close app
    // cleanup database
    // close connection to mongo
  });

  afterEach((done) => {
    // remove contacts
  });

  describe('Save contact', () => {});

  describe('Get contacts', () => {});

  describe('Get contact', function() {});

  describe('Update contact', function() {});

  describe('Delete contact', function() {});
});
```

In our test file, we required our dependencies and used Chai as our assertion library. As you can see, besides the describe() function, mocha gives us additional methods: before(), after(), beforeEach(), and afterEach().

These are hooks and they can be async or sync, but we are going to use the async version of them. Hooks are useful for preparing preconditions before running tests; for example, you can populate your database with mock data or clean it up.

In the main description body, we used three hooks: before(), after(), and afterEach(). In the before() hook, which will run before any of the describe() functions, we set up our server to listen on a given port, and we called the done() function when the server started listening.

The `after()` function will run after all the `describe()` functions have finished running and will stop the server from running. Now, the `afterEach()` hook will run after each `describe()` function, and it will grant us the ability to remove all the contacts from the database after running each test.

The final version can be found in the code bundle of the application. You can still follow how we add all the necessary descriptions.

Creating a contact

We also added four to five individual descriptions that will define CRUD operations from the earlier table. First, we want to be able to create a new contact. Add the following code to the test case:

```
describe('Create contact', () => {
  it('should create a new contact', (done) => {
    request({
      method: 'POST',
      url: `${apiUrl}/contacts`,
      form: {
        'email': 'jane.doe@test.com',
        'name': 'Jane Doe'
      },
      json:true
    }, (err, res, body) => {
      if (err) throw err;

      res.statusCode.should.equal(201);
      body.email.should.equal('jane.doe@test.com');
      body.name.should.equal('Jane Doe');
      done();
    });
  });
});
```

Getting contacts

Next, we want to get all contacts from the system. The following code should describe this functionality:

```
describe('Get contacts', () => {
  before((done) => {
    Contact.collection.insert([
      { email: 'jane.doe@test.com' },
      { email: 'john.doe@test.com' }
```

```
    ], (err, contacts) => {
      if (err) throw err;

      done();
    });
  });

  it('should get a list of contacts', (done) => {
    request({
      method: 'GET',
      url: `${apiUrl}/contacts`,
      json:true
    }, (err, res, body) => {
      if (err) throw err;

      res.statusCode.should.equal(200);
      body.should.be.instanceof(Array);
      body.length.should.equal(2);
      body.should.contain.a.thing.with.property('email',
      'jane.doe@test.com');
      body.should.contain.a.thing.with.property('email',
      'john.doe@test.com');
      done();
    });
  });
});
```

As you can see, we've also added a `before()` hook in the description. This is
absolutely normal and can be done. Mocha permits this behavior in order to easily
set up preconditions. We used a bulk insert, `Contact.collection.insert()`, to add
data into MongoDB before getting all the contacts.

Getting a contact by ID

When getting a contact by ID, we would also want to check whether the inserted ID
meets our `ObjectId` criteria. If a contact is not found, we will want to return a 404
HTTP status code:

```
describe('Get contact', function() {
  let _contact;

  before((done) => {
    Contact.create({
      email: 'john.doe@test.com'
    }, (err, contact) => {
```

```
        if (err) throw err;

        _contact = contact;
        done();
      });
    });

    it('should get a single contact by id', (done) => {
      request({
        method: 'GET',
        url: `${apiUrl}/contacts/${_contact.id}`,
        json:true
      }, (err, res, body) => {
        if (err) throw err;

        res.statusCode.should.equal(200);
        body.email.should.equal(_contact.email);
        done();
      });
    });

    it('should not get a contact if the id is not 24 characters',
(done) => {
      request({
        method: 'GET',
        url: `${apiUrl}/contacts/U5ZArj3hjzj3zusT8JnZbWFu`,
        json:true
      }, (err, res, body) => {
        if (err) throw err;

        res.statusCode.should.equal(404);
        done();
      });
    });
  });
```

We used the `.create()` method. It's more convenient to use it for single inserts, to prepopulate the database with data. When getting a single contact by ID we want to ensure that it's a valid ID, so we added a test which should reflect this and get a `404 Not Found` response if it's invalid, or no contact was found.

Updating a contact

We also want to be able to update an existing contact with a given ID. Add the following code to describe this functionality:

```
describe('Update contact', () => {
  let _contact;

  before((done) => {
    Contact.create({
      email: 'jane.doe@test.com'
    }, (err, contact) => {
      if (err) throw err;

      _contact = contact;
      done();
    });
  });

  it('should update an existing contact', (done) => {
    request({
      method: 'PUT',
      url: `${apiUrl}/contacts/${_contact.id}`,
      form: {
        'name': 'Jane Doe'
      },
      json:true
    }, (err, res, body) => {
      if (err) throw err;

      res.statusCode.should.equal(200);
      body.email.should.equal(_contact.email);
      body.name.should.equal('Jane Doe');
      done();
    });
  });
});
```

Removing a contact

Finally, we'll describe the remove contact operation (DELETE from CRUD) by adding the following code:

```
describe('Delete contact', () => {
  var _contact;

  before((done) => {
```

```
        Contact.create({
          email: 'jane.doe@test.com'
        }, (err, contact) => {
          if (err) throw err;

          _contact = contact;
          done();
        });
      });

      it('should update an existing contact', (done) => {
        request({
          method: 'DELETE',
          url: `${apiUrl}/contacts/${_contact.id}`,
          json:true
        }, (err, res, body) => {
          if (err) throw err;

          res.statusCode.should.equal(204);
          should.not.exist(body);
          done();
        });
      });
    });
```

After deleting a contact, the server should respond with an HTTP 204 No Content status code, meaning that the server has successfully interpreted the request and processed it, but no content should be returned due to the fact that the contact was deleted successfully.

Running our tests

Suppose we run the following command:

```
$ mocha test/integration/contact_test.js
```

At this point, we will get a bunch of HTTP 404 Not Found status codes, because our routes are not implemented yet. The output should be similar to something like this:

```
Contact
  Save contact
    1) should save a new contact
  Get contacts
    2) should get a list of contacts
```

```
Get contact
    3) should get a single contact by id
    √ should not get a contact if the id is not 24 characters
Update contact
    4) should update an existing contact
Delete contact
    5) should update an existing contact


1 passing (485ms)
5 failing

1) Contact Save contact should save a new contact:

    Uncaught AssertionError: expected 404 to equal 201

    + expected - actual


    +201
    -404
```

Implementing the contact routes

Now, we'll start implementing the contact CRUD operations. We'll begin by creating our controller. Create a new file, `contact-manager/app/controllers/contact.js`, and add the following code:

```javascript
'use strict';

const _ = require('lodash');
const mongoose = require('mongoose');
const Contact = mongoose.model('Contact');
const ObjectId = mongoose.Types.ObjectId;

module.exports.create = createContact;
module.exports.findById = findContactById;
module.exports.getOne = getOneContact;
module.exports.getAll = getAllContacts;
module.exports.update = updateContact;
module.exports.remove = removeContact;

function createContact(req, res, next) {
  Contact.create(req.body, (err, contact) => {
```

```
    if (err) {
      return next(err);
    }

    res.status(201).json(contact);
  });
}
```

What the preceding code does is export all methods of the controller for CRUD operations. To create a new contact, we use the `create()` method from the `Contact` schema.

We are returning a JSON response with the newly created contact. In case of an error, we just call the `next()` function with the error object. We will add a special handler to catch all of our errors later.

Let's create a new file for our routes, `contact-manager/app/routes/contacts.js`. The following lines of code should be a good start for our router:

```
'use strict';

const express = require('express');
const router = express.Router();
const contactController = require('../controllers/contact');

router.post('/contacts', auth.ensured, contactController.create);

module.exports = router;
```

Suppose we run our test now using this, like:

```
$ mocha tests/integration/contact_test.js
```

We should get something similar to the following:

```
Contact
  Create contact
      √ should save a new contact
  Get contacts
      1) should get a list of contacts
  Get contact
      2) should get a single contact by id
      √ should not get a contact if the id is not 24 characters
    Update contact
```

```
    3) should update an existing contact
Delete contact
    4) should update an existing contact



2 passing (502ms)
4 failing
```

Adding all endpoints

Next, we will add the rest of the routes, by adding the following code into the
`contact-manager/app/routes/contact.js` file:

```
router.param('contactId', contactController.findById);

router.get('/contacts', auth.ensured, contactController.getAll);
router.get('/contacts/:contactId', auth.ensured, contactController.
getOne);
router.put('/contacts/:contactId', auth.ensured, contactController.
update);
router.delete('/contacts/:contactId', auth.ensured, contactController.
remove);
```

We defined all the routes and also added a callback trigger to the `contactId` route
parameter. In Express, we can add callback triggers on route parameters using the
`param()` method with the name of a parameter and a callback function.

The callback function is similar to any normal route callback, but it gets an extra
parameter representing the value of the route parameter. A concrete example would
be as follows:

```
app.param('contactId', function(req, res, next, id) {
  // do something with the id ...
});
```

Following the preceding example, when `:contactId` is present in a route path, we
can map a contact loading logic and provide the contact to the next handler.

Finding a contact by ID

We are going to add the rest of the missing functionalities in our controller file,
located at `contact-manager/app/controllers/contact.js`:

```
function findContactById(req, res, next, id) {
  if (!ObjectId.isValid(id)) {
```

```
      res.status(404).send({ message: 'Not found.'});
    }

    Contact.findById(id, (err, contact) => {
      if (err) {
        next(err);
      } else if (contact) {
        req.contact = contact;
        next();
      } else {
        next(new Error('failed to find contact'));
      }
    });
}
```

The preceding function is a special case. It will get four parameter, and the last one will be the ID matching the triggered parameters value.

Getting contact information

To get all contacts, we are going to query the database. We will sort our results based on the creation date. One good practice is to always limit your returned dataset's size. For that, we use a MAX_LIMIT constant:

```
function getAllContacts(req, res, next) {
  const limit = +req.query.limit || MAX_LIMIT;
  const skip = +req.query.offset || 0;
  const query = {};

  if (limit > MAX_LIMIT) {
    limit = MAX_LIMIT;
  }

  Contact
  .find(query)
  .skip(skip)
  .limit(limit)
  .sort({createdAt: 'desc'})
  .exec((err, contacts) => {
    if (err) {
      return next(err);
    }

    res.json(contacts);
  });
}
```

To return a single contact, you can use the following code:

```
function getOneContact(req, res, next) {
  if (!req.contact) {
    return next(err);
  }

  res.json(req.contact);
}
```

Theoretically, we'll have the :contactId parameter in a route definition. In that case, the param callback is triggered, populating the req object with the requested contact.

Updating a contact

The same principle is applied when updating a contact; the requested entity should be populated by the param callback. We just need to assign the incoming data to the contact object and save the changes into MongoDB:

```
function updateContact(req, res, next) {
  let contact = req.contact;
  _.assign(contact, req.body);

  contact.save((err, updatedContact) => {
    if (err) {
      return next(err);
    }

    res.json(updatedContact);
  });
}
```

Removing a contact

Removing a contact should be fairly simple, as it has no dependent documents. So, we can just remove the document from the database, using the following code:

```
function removeContact(req, res, next) {
  req.contact.remove((err) => {
    if (err) {
      return next(err);
    }

    res.status(204).json();
  });
}
```

Running the contact test

At this point, we should have implemented all the requirements for managing contacts on the backend. To test everything, we run the following command:

```
$ mocha tests/integration/contact.test.js
```

The output should be similar to this:

```
  Contact


    Save contact
      √ should save a new contact
    Get contacts
      √ should get a list of contacts
    Get contact
      √ should get a single contact by id
      √ should not get a contact if the id is not 24 characters
    Update contact
      √ should update an existing contact
    Delete contact
      √ should update an existing contact



  6 passing (576ms)
```

This means that all the tests have passed successfully and we have implemented all the requirements.

Securing your application routes

You probably don't want to let anyone see your contacts, so it's time to secure your endpoints. There are many strategies that we can use to authenticate trusted users in an application. We are going to use a classic, state-full e-mail and password based authentication. This means that the session will be stored on the server side.

Remember we discussed at the beginning of the chapter how we are going to store our session on the server side? We choose two integrations, one with default in-memory session management and one that stores sessions in MongoDB. Everything is configurable from the environment configuration file.

When it comes to handling authentication in Node.js, a good go-to module is Passport, which is a piece of authentication middleware. Passport has a comprehensive set of authentication strategies using a simple username-and-password combination for Facebook, Google, Twitter, and many more.

We have already added this dependency to our application and made the necessary initializations in the express configuration file. We still need to add a few things, but before that, we have to create some reusable components in our backend application. We are going to create a helper file that will ease our interactions with passwords.

Describing the password helper

Before we dive deeper into the authentication mechanism, we need to be able to store in MongoDB a password hash instead of the plain password. We want to create a helper for this task that enables us to make operations related to passwords.

Create a new folder in the `tests` folder, named `unit`. Add a new file, `contact-manager/tests/unit/password.test.js`, and then add the following code to it:

```
'use strict';

const chai = require('chai');
const should = chai.should();
const passwordHelper = require('../../app/helpers/password');

describe('Password Helper', () => {
});
```

In our main description body, we are going to add segments that represent our features in more detail. Add this code:

```
describe('#hash() - password hashing', () => {
});
describe('#verify() - compare a password with a hash', () => {
});
```

Mocha also provides an `it()` function, which we are going to use to set up a concrete test. The `it()` function is very similar to `describe()`, except that we put only what the feature is supposed to do. For assertion, we are going to use the Chai library. Add the following code to the `tests/unit/password.test.js` file:

```
describe('#hash() - password hashing', () => {
  it('should return a hash and a salt from a plain string',
  (done) => {
    passwordHelper.hash('P@ssw0rd!', (err, hash, salt) => {
```

```
            if (err) throw err;

            should.exist(hash);
            should.exist(salt);
            hash.should.be.a('string');
            salt.should.be.a('string');
            hash.should.not.equal('P@ssw0rd!');
            done();
        });
    });

    it('should return only a hash from a plain string if salt is
    given', (done) => {
        passwordHelper.hash('P@ssw0rd!', 'secret salt', (err, hash,
        salt) => {
            if (err) throw err;

            should.exist(hash);
            should.not.exist(salt);
            hash.should.be.a('string');
            hash.should.not.equal('P@ssw0rd!');
            done();
        });
    });

    it('should return the same hash if the password and salt ar
    the same', (done) => {
        passwordHelper.hash('P@ssw0rd!', (err, hash, salt) => {
            if (err) throw err;

            passwordHelper.hash('P@ssw0rd!', salt, function(err,
            hashWithSalt) {
                if (err) throw err;

                should.exist(hash);
                hash.should.be.a('string');
                hash.should.not.equal('P@ssw0rd!');
                hash.should.equal(hashWithSalt);
                done();
            });
        });
    });
});
```

The `passwordHelper` should also test whether a password matches the given hash and salt combo. For this, we are going to add the following describe method:

```javascript
describe('#verify() - compare a password with a hash', () => {
  it('should return true if the password matches the hash',
  (done) => {
    passwordHelper.hash('P@ssw0rd!', (err, hash, salt) => {
      if (err) throw err;

      passwordHelper.verify('P@ssw0rd!', hash, salt, (err,
      result) => {
        if (err) throw err;

        should.exist(result);
        result.should.be.a('boolean');
        result.should.equal(true);
        done();
      });
    });
  });

  it('should return false if the password does not matches the
  hash', (done) => {
    passwordHelper.hash('P@ssw0rd!', (err, hash, salt) => {
      if (err) throw err;

      passwordHelper.verify('password!', hash, salt, (err,
      result) => {
        if (err) throw err;

        should.exist(result);
        result.should.be.a('boolean');
        result.should.equal(false);
        done();
      });
    });
  });
});
```

Implementing the password helper

We will implement our password helper in the following file: `contact-manager/app/helpers/password.js`.

The first description of our password helper describes a function that creates a hash from a plain password. In our implementation, we will use a key derivation function that will compute a hash from our password, also known as key stretching.

We are going to use the pbkdf2 function from the built-in Node.js crypto library. The asynchronous version of the function takes a plain password and applies an HMAC digest function. We will use sha256 to get a derived key of a given length, combined with a salt through a number of iterations.

We want to use the same hashing function for both cases: when we already have a password hash and a salt and when we have only a plain password. Let's see the final code for our hashing function. Add the following:

```
'use strict';

const crypto = require('crypto');
const len = 512;
const iterations = 18000;
const digest = 'sha256';

module.exports.hash = hashPassword;
module.exports.verify = verify;

function hashPassword(password, salt, callback) {
  if (3 === arguments.length) {
    crypto.pbkdf2(password, salt, iterations, len, digest, (err,
    derivedKey) => {
      if (err) {
        return callback(err);
      }

      return callback(null, derivedKey.toString('base64'));
    });
  } else {
    callback = salt;
    crypto.randomBytes(len, (err, salt) => {
      if (err) {
        return callback(err);
      }

      salt = salt.toString('base64');
      crypto.pbkdf2(password, salt, iterations, len, digest, (err,
      derivedKey) => {
        if (err) {
          return callback(err);
```

```
    }

      callback(null, derivedKey.toString('base64'), salt);
    });
  });
  }
}
```

Let's see what we get if we run our tests now. Run the following command:

```
$ mocha tests/unit/password.test.js
```

The output should be similar to this:

```
Password Helper
  #hash() - password hashing
    √ should return a hash and a salt from a plain string (269ms)
    √ should return only a hash from a plain string if salt is given
(274ms)
    √ should return the same hash if the password and salt are the same
(538ms)


3 passing (2s)
```

As you can see, we have successfully implemented our hashing function. All the requirements from the test case have passed. Notice that it takes up to 2 seconds to run the tests. Don't worry about this; it's because of the key stretching function taking time to generate the hash from the password.

Next, we are going to implement the verify() function, which checks whether a password matches an existing user's password-hash-and-salt combination. From the description in our tests, this function accepts four parameters: the plain password, a hash that was generated using the third salt parameter, and a callback function.

The callback gets two arguments: err and result. The result can be true or false. This will reflect whether the password matches the existing hash or not. Considering the constraints from the tests and the preceding explanation, we can append the following code to our password.helpr.js file:

```
function verify(password, hash, salt, callback) {
  hashPassword(password, salt, (err, hashedPassword) => {
    if (err) {
      return callback(err);
    }
```

```
      if (hashedPassword === hash) {
        callback(null, true);
      } else {
        callback(null, false);
      }
    });
  }
```

By now, we should have implemented all the specifications from our tests.

Creating the user Mongoose schema

In order to grant access to users in the application, we need to store them in a MongoDB collection. We'll create a new file called contact-manager/app/models/ user.model.js and add the following code:

```
'use strict';

const mongoose = require('mongoose');
const passwordHelper = require('../helpers/password');
const Schema = mongoose.Schema;
const _ = require('lodash');

var UserSchema = new Schema({
  email:  {
    type: String,
    required: true,
    unique: true
  },
  name: {
    type: String
  },
  password: {
    type: String,
    required: true,
    select: false
  },
  passwordSalt: {
    type: String,
    required: true,
    select: false
  },
  active: {
    type: Boolean,
```

```
    default: true
  },
  createdAt: {
    type: Date,
    default: Date.now
  }
});
```

The following table gives a description of the fields in the schema:

Field	Description
email	The e-mail of the user. This is used to identify the user. E-mails will be unique in the system.
name	The full name of the user.
password	This is the password provided by the user. It will not be stored in plaintext in the database but in a hashed form instead.
passwordSalt	Every password will be generated using a unique salt for the given user.
active	This specifies the state of the user. It can be active or inactive.
createdAt	The date when the user was created.

Describing the authentication method from the user model

We'll describe a user authentication method. It will check whether a user has valid credentials. The following file, contact-manager/tests/integration/user.model.test.js, should contain all the test cases regarding the User model. These lines of code will test the authenticate() method:

```
it('should authenticate a user with valid credentials', done =>
{
  User.authenticate(newUserData.email, newUserData.password,
  (err, user) => {
    if (err) throw err;

    should.exist(user);
    should.not.exist(user.password);
    should.not.exist(user.passwordSalt);
    user.email.should.equal(newUserData.email);
    done();
  });
});
```

```
  it('should not authenticate user with invalid credentials', done
  => {
    User.authenticate(newUserData.email, 'notuserpassowrd', (err,
    user) => {
      if (err) throw err;

      should.not.exist(user);
      done();
    });
  });
```

Implementing the authentication method

Mongoose lets us add static methods to compiled models from schemas. The
authenticate() method will search for a user in the database by its e-mail and use the
password helper's verify() function to check whether the sent password is a match.

Add the following lines of code to the contact-manager/app/models/user.js file:

```
UserSchema.statics.authenticate = authenticateUser;

function authenticateUser(email, password, callback) {
  this
  .findOne({ email: email })
  .select('+password +passwordSalt')
  .exec((err, user) => {
    if (err) {
      return callback(err, null);
    }

    // no user found just return the empty user
    if (!user) {
      return callback(err, user);
    }

    // verify the password with the existing hash from the user
    passwordHelper.verify(
      password,
      user.password,
      user.passwordSalt,
      (err, result) => {
        if (err) {
          return callback(err, null);
        }
```

```
      // if password does not match don't return user
      if (result === false) {
        return callback(err, null);
      }

      // remove password and salt from the result
      user.password = undefined;
      user.passwordSalt = undefined;
      // return user if everything is ok
      callback(err, user);
    }
  );
});
}
```

In the preceding code, when selecting the user from MongoDB, we explicitly selected the password and `passwordSalt` fields. This was necessary because we set the password and `passwordSalt` fields to not be selected in the query result. Another thing to note is that we want to remove the password and salt from the result when returning the user.

Authentication routes

In order to authenticate in the system we are building, we need to expose some endpoints that will execute the necessary business logic to authenticate a user with valid credentials. Before jumping into any code, we are going to describe the desired behavior.

Describing the authentication routes

We are only going to take a look at a partial code from the integration test of the authentication functionality, found in `contact-manager/tests/integration/authentication.test.js`. It should look something like this:

```
describe('Sign in user', () => {
  it('should sign in a user with valid credentials', (done) => {
    request({
      method: 'POST',
      url: baseUrl + '/auth/signin',
      form: {
        'email': userFixture.email,
        'password': 'P@ssw0rd!'
      },
      json:true
    }, (err, res, body) => {
```

```
      if (err) throw err;

      res.statusCode.should.equal(200);
      body.email.should.equal(userFixture.email);
      should.not.exist(body.password);
      should.not.exist(body.passwordSalt);
      done();
    });
  });

  it('should not sign in a user with invalid credentials',
  (done) => {
    request({
      method: 'POST',
      url: baseUrl + '/auth/signin',
      form: {
        'email': userFixture.email,
        'password': 'incorrectpassword'
      },
      json:true
    }, (err, res, body) => {
      if (err) throw err;

      res.statusCode.should.equal(400);
      body.message.should.equal('Invalid email or password.');
      done();
    });
  });
});
```

So, we've described an `auth/signin` endpoint; it will authenticate a user using an e-mail-and-password combination. We are testing two scenarios. The first one is when a user has valid credentials and the second is when an incorrect password is sent.

Integrating Passport

We mentioned Passport earlier in the chapter and added some basic logic for this purpose, but we still need to make a proper integration. The Passport module should already be installed and the session management is already in place. So next, we need to create a proper configuration file, `contact-manager/config/passport.js`, and add the following:

```
'use strict';

const passport = require('passport');
const mongoose = require('mongoose');
```

```
const User = mongoose.model('User');

module.exports.init = initPassport;

function initPassport(app) {
  passport.serializeUser((user, done) => {
    done(null, user.id);
  });

  passport.deserializeUser((id, done) => {
    User.findById(id, done);
  });

  // load strategies
  require('./strategies/local').init();
}
```

For each subsequent request, we need to serialize and deserialize the user instance to and from the session. We are only going to serialize the user's ID into the session. When subsequent requests are made, the user's ID is used to find the matching user and restore the data in `req.user`.

Passport gives us the ability to use different strategies to authenticate our users. We are only going to use e-mail and password to authenticate a user. To keep everything modular, we are going to move the strategies into separate files. The so-called local strategy, which will be used to authenticate users using an e-mail and a password, is going to be in the `contact-manager/config/strategies/local.js` file:

```
'use strict';

const passport = require('passport');
const LocalStrategy = require('passport-local').Strategy;
const User = require('mongoose').model('User');

module.exports.init = initLocalStrategy;

function initLocalStrategy() {
  passport.use('local', new LocalStrategy({
      usernameField: 'email',
      passwordField: 'password'
    },
    (email, password, done) => {
      User.authenticate(email, password, (err, user) => {
        if (err) {
          return done(err);
```

```
    }

    if (!user) {
      return done(null, false, { message: 'Invalid email or
      password.' });
    }

    return done(null, user);
    });
  }
));
}
```

Implementing the authentication routes

Now that we have passport up and running, we can define our authentication controller logic and a proper route to sign in users. Create a new file called contact-manager/app/controllers/authentication.js:

```
'use strict';

const passport = require('passport');
const mongoose = require('mongoose');
const User = mongoose.model('User');

module.exports.signin = signin;

function signin(req, res, next) {
  passport.authenticate('local', (err, user, info) => {
    if (err) {
      return next(err);
    }

    if (!user) {
      return res.status(400).send(info);
    }

    req.logIn(user, (err) => {
      if (err) {
        return next(err);
      }

      res.status(200).json(user);
    });
  })(req, res, next);
}
```

Here, we use the `.authenticate()` function from Passport to check a user's credentials using the local strategy implemented earlier. Next, we are going to add the authentication route, create a new file called `contact-manager/app/routes/auth.js`, and add the following lines of code:

```
'use strict';

var express = require('express');
var router = express.Router();
var authCtrl = require('../controllers/authentication');

router.post('/signin', authCtrl.signin);
router.post('/register', authCtrl.register);

module.exports = router;
```

Note that we skipped the register user functionality, but don't worry! The final bundled project source code will have all of the necessary logic.

Restricting access to contacts routes

We created all the requirements to authenticate our users. Now it's time to restrict access to some of the routes, so technically we are going to create a simple ACL. To restrict access, we are going to use a piece of middleware that will check whether users are authenticated or not.

Let's create our middleware file, `contact-manager/app/middlewares/authentication.js`. This should contain these lines of carefully crafted code:

```
'use strict';

module.exports.ensured = ensureAuthenticated;

function ensureAuthenticated(req, res, next) {
  if (req.isAuthenticated()) {
    return next();
  }

  res.status(401).json({
    message: 'Please authenticate.'
  });
}
```

We have already added the necessary logic to restrict users to the contact routes; that was when we first created them. We succeeded in adding all the necessary pieces of code to manage contacts and restrict access to our endpoints. Now we can continue and start building our Angular 2 application.

Integrating Angular 2 into our application

The frontend application is going to be built using Angular 2. At the time of writing this book, the project is still in beta, but it will come in handy to start playing around with Angular and have a good understanding of the environment. Most of the code will follow the official docs view of the tooling and integration methods.

When we first described our folder structure, we saw a `package.json` file for the client application too. Let's take a look at it, found under the `contact-manager/public/package.json` path:

```
{
  "private": true,
  "name": "mean-blueprints-contact-manager-client",
  "dependencies": {
    "systemjs": "^0.19.25",
    "es6-shim": "^0.35.0",
    "es6-promise": "^3.0.2",
    "rxjs": "^5.0.0-beta.2",
    "reflect-metadata": "^0.1.2",
    "zone.js": "^0.6.6",
    "angular2": "^2.0.0-beta.14"
  },
  "devDependencies": {
    "typings": "^0.7.12",
    "typescript": "^1.8.9"
  }
}
```

To install the necessary dependencies, just use the following command:

```
$ npm install
```

You will see npm pulling down different packages, specified in the `package.json` file.

As you can see, we'll use TypeScript in our client-side application. If you have installed it globally, you can use the following command to compile and watch for changes to your `.ts` files:

```
$ tsc -w
```

Only the most important parts of the application will be discussed. The rest of the necessary files and folders can be found in the final bundled source code.

Granting access to our application

We have restricted access to our API's endpoints, so now we have to grant users sign-in functionality from the client application. I like to group the Angular 2 application files based on their domain context. So, for example, all our authentication, registration, and business logic should go into a separate folder; we can call it `auth`.

If your module directory grows, it's good practice to break it down into separate folders based on their context by type. There is no magic number for the file count. Usually, you will get a good feeling when it's time to move files around. Your files should always be easy to locate and give you enough information from their placement in a certain context.

AuthService

We are going to use `AuthService` to implement the data access layer and make calls to the backend. This service is going to be the bridge between our API's sign-in and register features. Create a new file called `contact-manager/src/auth/auth.service.ts`, and add the following TypeScript code into it:

```
import { Injectable } from 'angular2/core';
import { Http, Response, Headers } from 'angular2/http';
import { contentHeaders } from '../common/headers';

@Injectable()
export class AuthService {
  private _http: Http;

  constructor(http: Http) {
    this._http = http;
  }
}
```

We import the necessary modules, define the `AuthService` class, and export it. The Injectable marker metadata will mark our class to be available to be injected. In order to communicate with the backend, we use the HTTP service. Don't forget to add the `HTTP_PROVIDERS` when bootstrapping the application so that the service is available to be injected in the whole application.

To sign in a user, we are going to add the following method:

```
public signin(user: any) {
  let body = this._serialize(user);

  return this._http
  .post('/auth/signin', body, { headers: contentHeaders })
  .map((res: Response) => res.json());
}
```

We can use the `.map()` operator to transform the response into a JSON file. When performing HTTP requests, this will return an `Observable`. You have probably already figured it out—we are going to use **RxJs (Reactive Extensions)** heavily, which is a third-party library favored by Angular.

RxJs implements asynchronous observable pattern. In other words, it enables you to work with asynchronous data streams and apply different operators. Observables are used widely in Angular applications. At the time of writing this book, Angular 2 exposes a stripped-down version of the `Observable` module from RxJs.

Don't worry; we'll get familiar with this technique and the benefits of it as we dive further into the book. Now let's continue with the rest of the missing methods we want to expose:

```
public register(user: any) {
  let body = this._serialize(user);

  return this._http
  .post('/auth/register', body, { headers: contentHeaders })
  .map((res: Response) => res.json());
}

private _serialize(data) {
  return JSON.stringify(data);
}
```

We added the `register()` method to our service, which will handle user registration. Also note that we moved our serialization into a separate private method. I've left this method in the same class so that it's easier to follow, but you can move it into a helper class.

User sign-in component

For a start, we are going to implement the sign-in component. Let's create a new file called `contact-manager/public/src/auth/sigin.ts` and add the following lines of TypeScript code:

```typescript
import { Component } from 'angular2/core';
import { Router, RouterLink } from 'angular2/router';
import { AuthService } from './auth.service';

export class Signin {
  private _authService: AuthService;
  private _router: Router;

  constructor(
    authService: AuthService,
    router: Router
  ) {
    this._authService = authService;
    this._router = router;
  }

  signin(event, email, password) {
    event.preventDefault();

    let data = { email, password };

    this._authService
    .signin(data)
    .subscribe((user) => {
      this._router.navigateByUrl('/');
    }, err => console.error(err));
  }
}
```

We still need to add the `Component` annotation before our `Signin` class:

```typescript
@Component({
    selector: 'signin',
    directives: [
      RouterLink
    ],
    template: `
      <div class="login jumbotron center-block">
        <h1>Login</h1>
```

```
          <form role="form" (submit)="signin($event, email.value,
        password.value)">
          <div class="form-group">
            <label for="email">E-mail</label>
            <input type="text" #email class="form-control"
            id="email" placeholder="enter your e-mail">
          </div>
          <div class="form-group">
            <label for="password">Password</label>
            <input type="password" #password class="form-control"
            id="password" placeholder="now your password">
          </div>
          <button type="submit" class="button">Submit</button>
          <a href="#" [routerLink]="['Register']">Click here to
          register</a>
        </form>
      </div>

    })
```

The `Signin` component is going to be our sign-in form and it uses the `AuthService` to communicate with the backend. In the component's template, we are using local variables marked with a # sign for the email and password fields.

As we said earlier, the HTTP service returns an `Observable` when making a request. This is the reason we can subscribe to the response generated by the requests made from our `AuthService`. On successful authentication, the user is redirected to the default home path.

The `Register` component will look similar to the `Signin` component, so there is no need to detail this scenario. The final version of the `auth` module will be available in the source code.

Custom HTTP service

In order to restrict access to our API endpoints, we have to make sure that, if a request is unauthorized, we redirect the user to the sign-in page. Angular 2 has no support for Interceptors and we don't want to add a handler for each request we integrate into our services.

A more convenient solution would be to build our own custom service on top of the built-in HTTP service. We could call it `AuthHttp`, from authorized HTTP requests. Its purpose would be to check whether a request returned a `401 Unauthorized HTTP status` code.

I would like to take this thought even further and bring a hint of reactive programming, because we are already using RxJS. So, we can benefit from the full set of functionalities it provides. Reactive programming is oriented around data. Streams of data propagate in your application and it reacts to those changes.

Let's get to business and start building our custom service. Create a file called `contact-manager/public/src/auth/auth-http.ts`. We are going to add a few lines of code:

```
import { Injectable } from 'angular2/core';
import { Http, Response, Headers, BaseRequestOptions, Request,
RequestOptions, RequestOptionsArgs, RequestMethod } from
'angular2/http';
import { Observable } from 'rxjs/Observable';
import { Subject } from 'rxjs/Subject';
import { BehaviorSubject } from 'rxjs/Subject/BehaviorSubject';

@Injectable()
export class AuthHttp {
  public unauthorized: Subject<Response>;
  private _http: Http;

  constructor(http: Http) {
    this._http = http;
    this.unauthorized = new BehaviorSubject<Response>(null);
  }
}
```

There are a few things we imported at the top of the file. We'll need all of them in this module. We defined a public property named `unauthorized`, which is a Subject. A **Subject** is both an `Observable` and `Observer`. This means that we can subscribe our subject to a backend data source and also all observers can subscribe to the subject.

In our case, the subject will be a proxy between our data source and all the subscribed observers. If a request is unauthorized, all subscribers get notified with the change. This enables us to just subscribe to the subject and redirect the user to the sign-in page when we detect an unauthorized request.

To succeed in doing this, we have to add a few more methods to our `AuthHttp` service:

```
private request(requestArgs: RequestOptionsArgs,
additionalArgs?: RequestOptionsArgs) {
  let opts = new RequestOptions(requestArgs);

  if (additionalArgs) {
```

```
            opts = opts.merge(additionalArgs);
        }

        let req:Request = new Request(opts);

        return this._http.request(req).catch((err: any) => {
            if (err.status === 401) {
                this.unauthorized.next(err);
            }

            return Observable.throw(err);
        });
    }
```

The preceding method creates a new request with the desired `RequestOptions` and invokes the `request` method from the base HTTP service. Additionally, the `catch` method captures all requests with status code not 200-level.

Using this technique, we can send the unauthorized request to all subscribers by using our `unauthorized` subject. Now that we have our private `request` method, we just need to add the rest of the public HTTP methods:

```
    public get(url: string, opts?: RequestOptionsArgs) {
        return this.request({ url: url, method: RequestMethod.Get},
        opts);
    }

    public post(url: string, body?: string, opts?:
    RequestOptionsArgs) {
        return this.request({ url: url, method: RequestMethod.Post,
        body: body}, opts);
    }

    public put(url: string, body?: string, opts?:
    RequestOptionsArgs) {
        return this.request({ url: url, method: RequestMethod.Put,
        body: body}, opts);
    }

    // rest of the HTTP methods ...
```

I've added only the most commonly used methods; the rest is available in the full version. The preceding code calls our request method and sets the necessary options for each request type. Theoretically, we have created a façade to handle unauthorized requests.

I think we've made good progress and it's time to move on to the rest of the modules of our contact manager application.

The Contact module

This module will hold all the necessary files to manage contacts. As we discussed earlier, we are grouping our files by context, related to their domain. The starting point of our module will be the data layer, which means we'll start implementing the necessary service.

Contact service

Our contact service will have basic CRUD operations and Observable streams to subscribe to. This implementation will use the backend API built using Node.js and Express, but it can be converted anytime to a WebSocket-based API with little effort.

Create a new service file called `contact-manager/src/contact/contact.service.ts` and add the following code:

```
import { Injectable } from 'angular2/core';
import { Response, Headers } from 'angular2/http';
import { Observable } from 'rxjs/Observable';
import { contentHeaders } from '../common/headers';
import { AuthHttp } from '../auth/auth-http';
import { Contact } from '../contact';

type ObservableContacts = Observable<Array<Contact>>;
type ObservableContact = Observable<Contact>;

const DEFAULT_URL = '/api/contacts';

@Injectable()
export class ContactService {
  public contact: ObservableContact;
  public contacts: ObservableContacts;

  private _authHttp: AuthHttp;
  private _dataStore: { contacts: Array<Contact>, contact: Contact };
  private _contactsObserver: any;
  private _contactObserver: any;
  private _url: string;

  constructor(authHttp: AuthHttp) {
```

```
      this._authHttp = authHttp;
      this._url = DEFAULT_URL;
      this._dataStore = { contacts: [], contact: new Contact() };
      this.contacts = new Observable(
        observer => this._contactsObserver = observer
      ).share();
      this.contact = new Observable(
        observer => this._contactObserver = observer
      ).share();
    }
  }
```

In the contact service, we have a few moving parts. First we defined our Observables so that any other component or module can subscribe and start getting the streams of data.

Second, we declared a private data store. This is where we are going to store our contacts. This is good practice as you can easily return all resources from memory.

Also, in our service, we are going to keep private the returned Observers when new instances of Observables are generated. Using the Observers, we can push new data streams to our Observables.

In our public methods, we are going to expose the get all contacts, get one, update, and delete functionalities. To get all contacts, we are going to add the following method to our ContactService:

```
    public getAll() {
      return this._authHttp
      .get(`${this._url}`, { headers: contentHeaders} )
      .map((res: Response) => res.json())
      .map(data => {
        return data.map(contact => {
          return new Contact(
            contact._id,
            contact.email,
            contact.name,
            contact.city,
            contact.phoneNumber,
            contact.company,
            contact.createdAt
          )
        });
      })
      .subscribe((contacts: Array<Contact>) => {
```

```
        this._dataStore.contacts = contacts;
        this._contactsObserver.next(this._dataStore.contacts);
    }, err => console.error(err));
}
```

We use our custom build `AuthHttp` service to load data from our Express application. When a response is received, we transform it into a JSON file, and after that, we just instantiate a new contact for each entity from the dataset.

Instead of returning the whole `Observable` from the HTTP service, we use our internal data store to persist all the contacts. After we have successfully updated the data store with the new data, we push the changes to our `contactsObserver`.

Any component that is subscribed to our stream of contacts will get the new values from the `Observable` data stream. In this way, we always keep our components synced using one single point of entry.

Much of our public method's logic is the same, but we still have a few distinct elements, for example, the update method:

```
public update(contact: Contact) {
  return this._authHttp
  .put(
    `${this._url}/${contact._id}`,
    this._serialize(contact),
    { headers: contentHeaders }
  )
  .map((res: Response) => res.json())
  .map(data => {
    return new Contact(
      data._id,
      data.email,
      data.name,
      data.city,
      data.phoneNumber,
      contact.company,
      data.createdAt
    )
  })
  .subscribe((contact: Contact) => {
    // update the current list of contacts
    this._dataStore.contacts.map((c, i) => {
      if (c._id === contact._id) {
        this._dataStore.contacts[i] = contact;
      }
```

```
      });
      // update the current contact
      this._dataStore.contact = contact;
      this._contactObserver.next(this._dataStore.contact);
      this._contactsObserver.next(this._dataStore.contacts);
    }, err => console.error(err));
  }
```

The `update` method is almost the same as the `create()` method, however it takes the contact's ID as the URL param. Instead of pushing new values down a data stream, we return the `Observable` from the `Http` service, in order to apply operations from the caller module.

Now, if we would like to make changes directly on the `datastore` and push the new values through the `contacts` data stream, we could showcase this in the remove contact method:

```
  public remove(contactId: string) {
    this._authHttp
    .delete(`${this._url}/${contactId}`)
    .subscribe(() => {
      this._dataStore.contacts.map((c, i) => {
        if (c._id === contactId) {
          this._dataStore.contacts.splice(i, 1);
        }
      });
      this._contactsObserver.next(this._dataStore.contacts);
    }, err => console.error(err));
  }
```

We simply use the `map()` function to find the contact we deleted and remove it from the internal store. Afterwards, we send new data to the subscribers.

Contact component

As we have moved everything related to the contact domain, we can define a main component in our module. Let's call it `contact-manager/public/src/contact/contact.component.ts`. Add the following lines of code:

```
import { Component } from 'angular2/core';
import { RouteConfig, RouterOutlet } from 'angular2/router';
import { ContactListComponent } from './contact-list.component';
import { ContactCreateComponent } from './contact-create.component';
import { ContactEditComponent } from './contact-edit.component';
```

```
@RouteConfig([
  { path: '/', as: 'ContactList', component: ContactListComponent,
  useAsDefault: true },
  { path: '/:id', as: 'ContactEdit', component:
  ContactEditComponent },
  { path: '/create', as: 'ContactCreate', component:
  ContactCreateComponent }
])
@Component({
    selector: 'contact',
    directives: [
      ContactListComponent,
      RouterOutlet
    ],
    template: `
      <router-outlet></router-outlet>
    `
})
export class ContactComponent {
  constructor() {}
}
```

Our component has no logic associated with it, but we used the `RouterConfig` annotation. The route config decorator takes an array of routes. Each path specified in the config will match the browser's URL. Each route will load the mounted component. In order to reference routes in the template, we need to give them a name.

Now, the most appealing part is that we can take this component with the configured routes and mount it on another component to have `Child`/`Parent` routes. In this case, it becomes nested routing, which is a very powerful feature added to Angular 2.

Our application's routes will have a tree-like structure; other components load components with their configured routes. I was pretty amazed by this feature because it enables us to truly modularize our application and create amazing, reusable modules.

List contacts component

In the previous component, we used three different components and mounted them on different routes. We are not going to discuss each of them, so we will choose one. As we have already worked with forms in the `Signin` component, let's try something different and implement the list contacts functionality.

Create a new file called `contact-manager/public/src/contact/contact-list.component.ts` and add the following code for your component:

```
import { Component, OnInit } from 'angular2/core';
import { RouterLink } from 'angular2/router';
import { ContactService } from '../contact.service';
import { Contact } from '../contact';

@Component({
    selector: 'contact-list',
    directives: [RouterLink],
    template: `
      <div class="row">
        <h4>
          Total contacts: <span
          class="muted">({{contacts.length}})</span>
          <a href="#" [routerLink]="['ContactCreate']">add new</a>
        </h4>
        <div class="contact-list">
          <div class="card-item col col-25 contact-item"
            *ngFor="#contact of contacts">
            <img src="{{ contact.image }}" />
            <h3>
              <a href="#" [routerLink]="['ContactEdit', { id:
              contact._id }]">
                {{ contact.name }}
              </a>
            </h3>
            <p>
              <span>{{ contact.city }}</span>
              <span>·</span>
              <span>{{ contact.company }}</span>
            </p>
            <p><span>{{ contact.email }}</span></p>
            <p><span>{{ contact.phoneNumber }}</span></p>
          </div>
        </div>
      </div>
      `
})
export class ContactListComponent implements OnInit {
  public contacts: Array<Contact> = [];
  private _contactService: ContactService;

  constructor(contactService: ContactService) {
```

```
      this._contactService = contactService;
  }

  ngOnInit() {
    this._contactService.contacts.subscribe(contacts => {
      this.contacts = contacts;
    });
    this._contactService.getAll();
  }
}
```

In our component's `ngOnInit()`, we subscribe to the contacts data stream. Afterwards, we retrieve all the contacts from the backend. In the template, we use `ngFor` to iterate over the dataset and display each contact.

Creating a contact component

Now that we can list contacts in our application, we should also be able to add new entries. Remember that earlier we used the `RouterLink` to be able to navigate to the `CreateContact` route.

The preceding route will load the `CreateContactComponent`, which will enable us to add new contact entries into our database, through the Express API. Let's create a new component file `public/src/contact/components/contact-create.component.ts`:

```
import { Component, OnInit } from 'angular2/core';
import { Router, RouterLink } from 'angular2/router';
import { ContactService } from '../contact.service';
import { Contact } from '../contact';

@Component({
    selector: 'contact-create,
    directives: [RouterLink],
    templateUrl: 'src/contact/components/contact-form.html'
})
export class ContactCreateComponent implements OnInit {
  public contact: Contact;
  private _router: Router;
  private _contactService: ContactService;

  constructor(
    contactService: ContactService,
    router: Router
  ) {
```

```
    this._contactService = contactService;
    this._router = router;
  }

  ngOnInit() {
    this.contact = new Contact();
  }

  onSubmit(event) {
    event.preventDefault();

    this._contactService
    .create(this.contact)
    .subscribe((contact) => {
      this._router.navigate(['ContactList']);
    }, err => console.error(err));
  }
}
```

Instead of using an embedded template, we are using an external template file that is configured using the `templateUrl` property in the component annotation. There are pros and cons for each situation. The benefits of using an external template file would be that you can reuse the same file for more than one component.

The downfall, at the moment of writing the book, in Angular 2 is that it's hard to use relative paths to your template files, so this would make your components less portable. Also I like to keep my templates short, so they can fit easily inside the component, so in most cases I'll probably use embedded templates.

Let's take a look at the template before further discussing the component, `public/src/contact/components/contact-form.html`:

```html
<div class="row contact-form-wrapper">
  <a href="#" [routerLink]="['ContactList']">&lt; back to
  contacts</a>
  <h2>Add new contact</h2>
  <form role="form"
    (submit)="onSubmit($event)">

    <div class="form-group">
      <label for="name">Full name</label>
      <input type="text" [(ngModel)]="contact.name"
        class="form-control" id="name" placeholder="Jane Doe">
    </div>
    <div class="form-group">
```

```
    <label for="email">E-mail</label>
    <input type="text" [(ngModel)]="contact.email"
      class="form-control" id="email"
      placeholder="jane.doe@example.com">
  </div>
  <div class="form-group">
    <label for="city">City</label>
    <input type="text"
      [(ngModel)]="contact.city"
      class="form-control" id="city" placeholder="a nice place ...">
  </div>
  <div class="form-group">
    <label for="company">Company</label>
    <input type="text"
      [(ngModel)]="contact.company"
      class="form-control" id="company" placeholder="working at
...">
  </div>
  <div class="form-group">
    <label for="phoneNumber">Phone</label>
    <input type="text"
      [(ngModel)]="contact.phoneNumber"
      class="form-control" id="phoneNumber" placeholder="mobile
      or landline">
  </div>

  <button type="submit" class="button">Submit</button>
  </form>
</div>
```

In the template we are using a onSubmit() method from the component to piggyback the form submission and in this case create a new contact and store the data in MongoDB. When we successfully create the contact we want to navigate to the ContactList route.

We are not using local variables, instead we are using two-way data binding with the ngModel for each input, mapped to the properties of the contact object. Now, each time the user changes the inputs value, this is stored in the contact object and on submit it's sent across the wire to the backend.

The RouterLink is used to construct the navigation to the ContactList component from the template. I've left a small improvement, the view title will be the same both for creating and editing, more precisely "Add new contact", and I'll let you figure it out.

Editing an existing contact

When editing a contact, we want to load a specific resource by ID from the backend API and make changes for that contact. Lucky for us this is quite simple to achieve in Angular. Create a new file `public/src/contact/components/contact-edit.component.ts`:

```
import { Component, OnInit } from 'angular2/core';
import { RouteParams, RouterLink } from 'angular2/router';
import { ContactService } from '../contact.service';
import { Contact } from '../contact';

@Component({
    selector: 'contact-edit',
    directives: [RouterLink],
    templateUrl: 'src/contact/components/contact-form.html'
})
export class ContactEditComponent implements OnInit {
  public contact: Contact;
  private _contactService: ContactService;
  private _routeParams: RouteParams;

  constructor(
    contactService: ContactService,
    routerParams: RouteParams
  ) {
    this._contactService = contactService;
    this._routeParams = routerParams;
  }

  ngOnInit() {
    const id: string = this._routeParams.get('id');
    this.contact = new Contact();
    this._contactService
    .contact.subscribe((contact) => {
      this.contact = contact;
    });
    this._contactService.getOne(id);
  }

  onSubmit(event) {
    event.preventDefault();

    this._contactService
    .update(this.contact)
```

```
      .subscribe((contact) => {
        this.contact = contact;
      }, err => console.error(err));
    }
  }
```

We are not so far away from the `ContactCreateComponent`, the structure of the class is almost the same. Instead of the `Router`, we are using `RouteParams` to load the ID from the URL and retrieve the desired contact from the Express application.

We subscribe to the contact `Observable` returned by the `ContactService` to get the new data. In other words our component will react to the data stream and when the data is available it will display it to the user.

When submitting the form, we update the contact persisted in MongoDB and change the view's `contact` object with the freshly received data from the backend.

Finishing touch

We have added all the necessary modules into our application. We should also take a final look at our main app component, found under the following path—`contact-manager/public/src/app.component.ts`:

```
import { Component } from 'angular2/core';
import { RouteConfig, RouterOutlet } from 'angular2/router';
import { Router } from 'angular2/router';
import { AuthHttp } from './auth/auth-http';
import { Signin } from './auth/signin';
import { Register } from './auth/register';
import { ContactComponent } from './contact/components/contact.
component';

@RouteConfig([
  { path: '/signin', as: 'Signin', component: Signin },
  { path: '/register', as: 'Register', component: Register },
  { path: '/contacts/...', as: 'Contacts', component:
  ContactComponent, useAsDefault: true }
])
@Component({
    selector: 'cm-app',
    directives: [
      Signin,
      Register,
      ContactComponent,
      RouterOutlet
```

```
    ],
    template: `
      <div class="app-wrapper col card whiteframe-z2">
        <div class="row">
          <h3>Contact manager</h3>
        </div>
        <router-outlet></router-outlet>
      </div>
    `
})
export class AppComponent {
  private _authHttp: AuthHttp;
  private _router: Router;

  constructor(authHttp: AuthHttp, router: Router) {
    this._authHttp = authHttp;
    this._router = router;
    this._authHttp.unauthorized.subscribe((res) => {
      if (res) {
        this._router.navigate(['./Signin']);
      }
    });
  }
}
```

We mount all the components to their specific routes. Also, when we mount the Contact component, we'll bring in all the configured routes from the component.

In order to be notified when a request is unauthorized, we subscribe to the AuthHttp service's unauthorized data stream. If a request needs authentication, we redirect the user to the sign-in page.

The boot file for our application will look something like this:

```
import { bootstrap } from 'angular2/platform/browser';
import { provide } from 'angular2/core';
import { HTTP_PROVIDERS } from 'angular2/http';
import { ROUTER_PROVIDERS, LocationStrategy, HashLocationStrategy }
from 'angular2/router';
import { AuthHttp } from './auth/auth-http';
import { AuthService } from './auth/auth.service';
import { ContactService } from './contact/contact.service';
import { AppComponent } from './app.component';

import 'rxjs/add/operator/map';
```

```
import 'rxjs/add/operator/share';
import 'rxjs/add/operator/debounceTime';
import 'rxjs/add/operator/catch';
import 'rxjs/add/observable/throw';

bootstrap(AppComponent, [
  ROUTER_PROVIDERS,
  HTTP_PROVIDERS,
  AuthService,
  AuthHttp,
  ContactService,
  provide(LocationStrategy, {useClass: HashLocationStrategy})
]);
```

We import and define the necessary providers and also add the operators we used from RxJs. This is because Angular, by default, uses only a stripped-down version of the Observable module.

Through the contact module we used a custom class named `Contact`, which plays the role of a `Contact` model. This will be instantiated any time we want to make sure we are working with a contact entity. Besides, the nice thing about TypeScript is that it enables us to use structured code.

Classes come in handy when we want to have initial values, for example, in our components we used a `contact.image` property to display a contact's profile image. This was not implemented in the backend, so we use a mock URL for an image. Let's see the `Contact` class, `public/src/contact/contact.ts`:

```
export class Contact {
  _id: string;
  email: string;
  name: string;
  city: string;
  phoneNumber: string;
  company: string;
  image: string;
  createdAt: string;

  constructor(
    _id?: string,
    email?: string,
    name?: string,
    city?: string,
    phoneNumber?: string,
    company?: string,
```

```
    createdAt?: string
  ) {
    this._id = _id;
    this.email = email;
    this.name = name;
    this.city = city;
    this.phoneNumber = phoneNumber;
    this.company = company;
    this.image = 'http://placehold.it/171x100';
    this.createdAt = createdAt;
  }
}
```

As you can see we just define what properties a contact instance can have and create a default value for the `image` property. Arguments passed to the `constructor` marked with `?` are optional.

At this moment, we should have everything in place; in case you missed something, you can check out the final version of the code.

The key takeaways from this chapter are as follows:

- Building backend web services using Node.js, Express, and MongoDB
- Writing tests first, before actually implementing functionalities
- Securing our API routes using Passport
- Making Angular 2 and Express communicate and work together
- Getting into Reactive Extensions and reactive programming
- Building a custom Angular HTTP service

Summary

This brings us to the end of this rather introductory chapter.

We went full stack, right from implementing our backend logic to learning to write tests before actual implementations. We exposed a RESTful route for our resources from MongoDB. We also built a small Angular 2 frontend application that interacts with the web server.

In the next chapter, we'll dive deeper into MongoDB and start working with monetary data. It should be a fun ride!

2
Expense Tracker

In this chapter, we will see how to build an expense tracker application. It will store all of our expenses for a given category. We will be able to see an aggregated balance of our expenses, or expenses by category. Each user will have a separate account to manage their expenses.

Some of the interesting topics that we will cover are:

- Creating a multiuser system
- Working with monetary data
- Using the MongoDB aggregation framework
- Different authentication strategies, such as HTTP Basic and token-based authentication

Setting up the base application

Let's set up the base structure and files of our application. The whole source code for the project will be available as a bundle at `https://www.packtpub.com/`. Therefore, we are only going to detail the most important part of setting up the base application.

Installing the dependencies

Let's start by creating our `package.json` file in the root of the project and adding the following code:

```
{
  "name": "mean-blueprints-expensetracker",
  "version": "0.0.1",
  "repository": {
    "type": "git",
```

```
    "url": "https://github.com/robert52/mean-blueprints-
    expensetracker.git"
  },
  "engines": {
    "node": ">=0.12.0"
  },
  "scripts": {
    "start": "node app.js",
    "unit": "mocha tests/unit/ --ui bdd --recursive --reporter
    spec --timeout 10000 --slow 900",
    "integration": "mocha tests/integration/ --ui bdd --recursive
    --reporter spec --timeout 10000 --slow 900"
  },
  "dependencies": {
    "async": "^0.9.0",
    "body-parser": "^1.12.3",
    "express": "^4.12.4",
    "express-session": "^1.11.2",
    "lodash": "^3.7.0",
    "method-override": "^2.3.2",
    "mongoose": "^4.0.2",
    "passport": "^0.2.1",
    "passport-local": "^1.0.0",
    "serve-static": "^1.9.2"
  },
  "devDependencies": {
    "chai": "^2.3.0",
    "chai-things": "^0.2.0",
    "mocha": "^2.2.4",
    "request": "^2.55.0"
  }
}
```

The next step after defining the package.json file is to install the necessary dependencies. Run this command:

```
npm install
```

After npm has pulled all the necessary files, you should be returned to the command prompt.

Creating the base configuration files

We are going to reuse a lot of code from the previous contact manager project. We created a file to load the necessary environment config file based on the current environment node is running. Add a new config file.

Create a file called `config/environments/development.js` and add the following code:

```
'use strict';

module.exports = {
  port: 3000,
  hostname: 'localhost',
  baseUrl: 'http://localhost:3000',
  mongodb: {
    uri: 'mongodb://localhost/expense_dev_db'
  },
  app: {
    name: 'Expense tracker'
  },
  serveStatic: true,
  session: {
    session: {
      type: 'mongo',
      secret: 'someVeRyN1c3S#cr3tHer34U',
      resave: false,
      saveUninitialized: true
    }
  }
};
```

Next, we are going to create the configuration file for Express and add the following lines of code to `config/express.js`:

```
'use strict';

const path = require('path');
const bodyParser = require('body-parser');
const methodOverride = require('method-override');
const serveStatic = require('serve-static');
const session = require('express-session');
const MongoStore = require('connect-mongo')(session);
const passport = require('passport');
```

```
const config = require('./index');

module.exports.init = initExpress

function initExpress(app) {
  const env = app.get('env');
  const root = app.get('root');
  const sessionOpts = {
    secret: config.session.secret,
    key: 'skey.sid',
    resave: config.session.resave,
    saveUninitialized: config.session.saveUninitialized
  };

  app.use(bodyParser.urlencoded({ extended: true }));
  app.use(bodyParser.json());
  app.use(methodOverride());
  app.disable('x-powered-by');

  if (config.session.type === 'mongo') {
    sessionOpts.store = new MongoStore({
      url: config.mongodb.uri
    });
  }

  app.use(session(sessionOpts));
  app.use(passport.initialize());
  app.use(passport.session());

  if (config.serveStatic) {
    app.use(serveStatic(path.join(root, 'public')));
  }
}
```

Finally, we are going to add a file called `config/mongoose.js` to connect to MongoDB, with the following content:

```
'use strict';

const mongoose = require('mongoose');
const config = require('./index');

module.exports.init = initMongoose;

function initMongoose(app) {
```

```
mongoose.connect(config.mongodb.uri);

// If the Node process ends, cleanup existing connections
process.on('SIGINT', cleanup);
process.on('SIGTERM', cleanup);
process.on('SIGHUP', cleanup);

if (app) {
  app.set('mongoose', mongoose);
}

return mongoose;
}

function cleanup() {
  mongoose.connection.close(function () {
    console.log('Closing DB connections and stopping the app. Bye
    bye.');
    process.exit(0);
  });
}
```

Creating the main server.js file

The main entry point for our application is the `server.js` file. Create it in the root of the project. This file starts the web server and bootstraps all of the logic. Add the following lines of code:

```
'use strict';

// Get process environment or set default environment to development
const ENV = process.env.NODE_ENV || 'development';
const DEFAULT_PORT = 3000;
const DEFAULT_HOSTNAME = 'localhost';

const http = require('http');
const express = require('express');
const config = require('./config');
const app = express();
let server;

/**
 * Set express (app) variables
 */
```

```
app.set('config', config);
app.set('root', __dirname);
app.set('env', ENV);

require('./config/mongoose').init(app);
require('./config/models').init(app);
require('./config/passport').init(app);
require('./config/express').init(app);
require('./config/routes').init(app);

app.use((err, req, res, next) => {
  res.status(500).json(err);
});

/**
 * Start the app if not loaded by another module
 */
if (!module.parent) {
  server = http.createServer(app);
  server.listen(
    config.port || DEFAULT_PORT,
    config.hostname || DEFAULT_HOSTNAME,
    () => {
      console.log(`${config.app.name} is running`);
      console.log(`   listening on port: ${config.port}`);
      console.log(`   environment: ${ENV.toLowerCase()}`);
    }
  );
}

module.exports = app;
```

Setting up the user section

In the previous chapter, we also had a user section for the application. In this chapter, we are going to extend those functionalities by adding the register and change password functionalities. We are going to reuse the existing code base and add the new features.

Describing the user model

We will create a test file specifically for the user model. This will come in handy for testing all its functionalities without booting up the entire application. Create a file called `test/integration/user.model.test.js` and add the following content:

```javascript
'use strict';

/**
 * Important! Set the environment to test
 */
process.env.NODE_ENV = 'test';

const chai = require('chai');
const should = chai.should();
consst config = require('../../config/environments/test');

describe('User model', function() {
  const mongoose;
  const User;
  const _user;
  const newUserData = {
    email: 'jane.doe@test.com',
    password: 'user_password',
    name: 'Jane Doe'
  };

  before(function(done) {
    mongoose = require('../../config/mongoose').init();
    User = require('../../app/models/user');
    done();
  });

  after(function(done) {
    User.remove({}).exec(function(err) {
      if (err) throw err;

      mongoose.connection.close(function() {
        setTimeout(function() { done(); }, 1000);
      });
    });
  });
});
```

We have defined the base for our test file. Now we are going to add each test case one by one, before the last closing bracket:

1. A user should be able to register with our system. We can test this with the following lines of code:

```
it('should register a user', function(done) {
  User.register(newUserData, function(err, user) {
    if (err) throw err;

    should.exist(user);
    user.email.should.equal(newUserData.email);
    should.not.exist(user.password);
    should.not.exist(user.passwordSalt);
    should.exist(user.createdAt);
    user.active.should.equal(true);

    _user = user;
    done();
  });
});
```

2. The same user cannot register twice with the same e-mail:

```
it('should not register a user if already exists',
function(done) {
  User.register(newUserData, function(err, user) {
    should.exist(err);
    err.code.should.equal(11000); // duplicate key error
    should.not.exist(user);
    done();
  });
});
```

3. After successful registration, a user should be able to authenticate into our system:

```
it('should authenticate a user with valid credentials',
function(done) {
  User.authenticate(newUserData.email, 'user_password',
  function(err, user) {
    if (err) throw err;

    should.exist(user);
    should.not.exist(user.password);
    should.not.exist(user.passwordSalt);
    user.email.should.equal(newUserData.email);
```

```
        done();
    });
});
```

4. If a user provides invalid credentials, it should not be authenticated successfully:

```
it('should not authenticate user with invalid
credentials', function(done) {
    User.authenticate(newUserData.email, 'notuserpassowrd',
    function(err, user) {
        if (err) throw err;

        should.not.exist(user);
        done();
    });
});
```

5. A user should be able to change the current password:

```
it('should change the password of a user', function(done)
{
    _user.changePassword('user_password',
    'new_user_password', function(err, result) {
        if (err) throw err;

        should.exist(result);
        result.success.should.equal(true);
        result.message.should.equal('Password changed
        successfully.');
        result.type.should.equal('password_change_success');

        // run a check credential with the new password
        User.authenticate(_user.email, 'new_user_password',
        function(err, user) {
            if (err) throw err;

            should.exist(user);
            user.email.should.equal(_user.email);
            done();
        });
    });
});
```

6. An old password challenge must be passed in order to set a new password:

```
it('should not change password if old password does not
match', function(done) {
  _user.changePassword('not_good', 'new_user_password',
  function(err, result) {
    should.not.exist(result);
    should.exist(err);
    err.type.should.equal('old_password_does_not_match');

    // run a check credential with the old password
    User.authenticate(_user.email, 'new_user_password',
    function(err, user) {
      if (err) throw err;

      should.exist(user);
      user.email.should.equal(_user.email);
      done();
    });
  });
});
```

With the preceding test suit, we have described and will test the functionality of our implemented methods.

Implementing the user model

The user model is going to use the same password helper principle as in *Chapter 1, Contact Manager*. Let's create a file called app/helpers/password.js. The file should contain the following code:

```
'use strict';

const LEN = 256;
const SALT_LEN = 64;
const ITERATIONS = 10000;
const DIGEST = 'sha256';
const crypto = require('crypto');

module.exports.hash = hashPassword;
module.exports.verify = verify;
```

Now add the `hashPassword()` function:

```
function hashPassword(password, salt, callback) {
  let len = LEN / 2;

  if (3 === arguments.length) {
    generateDerivedKey(password, salt, ITERATIONS, len, DIGEST,
    callback);
  } else {
    callback = salt;
    crypto.randomBytes(SALT_LEN / 2, (err, salt) => {
      if (err) {
        return callback(err);
      }

      salt = salt.toString('hex');
      generateDerivedKey(password, salt, ITERATIONS, len, DIGEST,
      callback);
    });
  }
}
```

We have added an extra function, called `generateDerivedKey()`, in order not to repeat code blocks:

```
function generateDerivedKey(password, salt, iterations, len,
digest, callback) {
  crypto.pbkdf2(password, salt, ITERATIONS, len, DIGEST, (err,
  derivedKey) => {
    if (err) {
      return callback(err);
    }

    return callback(null, derivedKey.toString('hex'), salt);
  });
}
```

Finally, add the `verify()` function:

```
function verify(password, hash, salt, callback) {
  hashPassword(password, salt, (err, hashedPassword) => {
    if (err) {
      return callback(err);
    }

    if (hashedPassword === hash) {
```

```
        callback(null, true);
      } else {
        callback(null, false);
      }
    });
  }
```

Next, let's create a user schema in the model file. Create a new file, called `app/models/user.js`, and add the following:

```
'use strict';

const _ = require('lodash');
const mongoose = require('mongoose');
const passwordHelper = require('../helpers/password');
const Schema = mongoose.Schema;

const UserSchema = new Schema({
  email:  {
    type: String,
    required: true,
    unique: true
  },
  name: {
    type: String
  },
  password: {
    type: String,
    required: true,
    select: false
  },
  passwordSalt: {
    type: String,
    required: true,
    select: false
  },
  phoneNumber: {
    type: String
  },
  active: {
    type: Boolean,
    default: true
  },
  createdAt: {
    type: Date,
```

```
      default: Date.now
    }
});

UserSchema.statics.register = registerUser;
UserSchema.statics.authenticate = authenticateUser;
UserSchema.methods.changePassword = changeUserPassword;
```

Now, one by one, let's add the required methods from the test. We will start with the
register() method. Append these lines of code to the user model file:

```
function registerUser(opts, callback) {
  let data = _.cloneDeep(opts);

  //hash the password
  passwordHelper.hash(opts.password, (err, hashedPassword, salt)
  => {
    if (err) {
      return callback(err);
    }

    data.password = hashedPassword;
    data.passwordSalt = salt;

    //create the user
    this.model('User').create(data, (err, user) => {
      if (err) {
        return callback(err, null);
      }

      // remove password and salt from the result
      user.password = undefined;
      user.passwordSalt = undefined;
      // return user if everything is ok
      callback(err, user);
    });
  });
}
```

This is a simple function that will save a user in MongoDB. Before saving the user,
we want to build a hash from the given password and save that hash with a salt in
the database, instead of a plain password string. Mongoose will also validate the
user data before saving it, based on the User schema.

For the `authenticate()` method, we will append the following lines of code:

```
function authenticateUser(email, password, callback) {
  this
  .findOne({ email: email })
  .select('+password +passwordSalt')
  .exec((err, user) => {
    if (err) {
      return callback(err, null);
    }

    // no user found just return the empty user
    if (!user) {
      return callback(err, user);
    }

    // verify the password with the existing hash from the user
    passwordHelper.verify(
      password,
      user.password,
      user.passwordSalt,
      (err, result) => {
        if (err) {
          return callback(err, null);
        }

        // if password does not match don't return user
        if (result === false) {
          return callback(err, null);
        }

        // remove password and salt from the result
        user.password = undefined;
        user.passwordSalt = undefined;
        // return user if everything is ok
        callback(err, user);
      }
    );
  });
}
```

The authentication method will find a user by e-mail. The `password` and `passwordSalt` fields are explicitly set to be read from the database only for this query. A password verification function will be called to match the existing password hash with the password sent to the authentication method.

Finally we will add a `changePassword()` method. This method will be available on user instances only. Mongoose gives us the ability to use the `methods` property on a schema to attach new functions. Append the following code:

```
function changeUserPassword(oldPassword, newPassword, callback) {
  this
  .model('User')
  .findById(this.id)
  .select('+password +passwordSalt')
  .exec((err, user) => {
    if (err) {
      return callback(err, null);
    }

    // no user found just return the empty user
    if (!user) {
      return callback(err, user);
    }

    passwordHelper.verify(
      oldPassword,
      user.password,
      user.passwordSalt,
      (err, result) => {
        if (err) {
          return callback(err, null);
        }

        // if password does not match don't return user
        if (result === false) {
          let PassNoMatchError = new Error('Old password does not
          match.');
          PassNoMatchError.type = 'old_password_does_not_match';
          return callback(PassNoMatchError, null);
        }

        // generate the new password and save the user
        passwordHelper.hash(newPassword, (err, hashedPassword,
        salt) => {
          this.password = hashedPassword;
          this.passwordSalt = salt;

          this.save((err, saved) => {
            if (err) {
```

```
            return callback(err, null);
          }

          if (callback) {
            return callback(null, {
              success: true,
              message: 'Password changed successfully.',
              type: 'password_change_success'
            });
          }
        });
      });
    }
  );
});
}
```

The change password functionality is built using three small steps. The first step is to get the user's password and salt from the database. The returned data is used to verify the existing password hash and salt with the old password entered by the user. If everything goes well, the new password is hashed using a generated salt and the user instance is saved into MongoDB.

Don't forget to move the following line of code to the end of the file, in order to compile the user model:

```
module.exports = mongoose.model('User', UserSchema);
```

Suppose we run our user model test with the following command:

```
mocha tests/integration/user.mode.test.js
```

We should see all of our tests passing:

```
User Model Integration
  #register()
    ✓ should create a new user (124ms)
    ✓ should not create a new user if email already exists (100ms)
  #authenticate()
    ✓ should return the user if the credentials are valid (63ms)
    ✓ should return nothing if the credential of the user are invalid
(62ms)
  #changePassword()
    ✓ should change the password of a user (223ms)
```

```
√ should not change password if old password does not match (146ms)


6 passing (1s)
```

Authenticating users

In the previous chapter, we used session-based authentication. For this chapter, we are going to explore a different solution—using access tokens to authenticate our users.

Access tokens are widely used for RESTful APIs. Because we are building our application with the premise that it could be used not only by our Angular app but also by many other client applications, we need to rely on something that can be used to identify users with something that they have.

An access token is a string that identifies a user, or even an app, and it can be used to make API calls to our system. Tokens can be issued via a number of methods. For example, tokens can be issued easily using OAuth 2.0.

For this chapter, we are going to build a custom module that is responsible for creating tokens. This will give us the ability to easily switch to any other available solution.

We are going to implement two strategies to authenticate our users. One of them will be an HTTP Basic authentication strategy, which will use a simple username (e-mail in our case) and password combo to authenticate a user and generate a token that will be used for further API calls. The second strategy is an HTTP Bearer authentication, which will use the access token issued by the Basic authentication to grant the user access to resources.

Describing the authentication strategies

Before implementing any code, we should create a test that will describe the desired behavior regarding user authentication. Create a file called `tests/integration/authentication.test.js` and describe the main test cases:

1. The first test case should consider a positive scenario, that is, when a user tries to authenticate with valid credentials. This would look like the following:

    ```
    it('should authenticate a user and return a new token',
    function(done) {
      request({
    ```

```
      method: 'POST',
      url: baseUrl + '/auth/basic',
      auth: {
        username: userFixture.email,
        password: 'P@ssw0rd!'
      },
      json:true
    }, function(err, res, body) {
      if (err) throw err;

      res.statusCode.should.equal(200);
      body.email.should.equal(userFixture.email);
      should.not.exist(body.password);
      should.not.exist(body.passwordSalt);
      should.exist(body.token);
      should.exist(body.token.hash);
      should.exist(body.token.expiresAt);
      done();
    });
  });
```

2. If a user tries to authenticate with invalid credentials, the system should return a bad request message:

```
it('should not authenticate a user with invalid
credentials', function(done) {
  request({
    method: 'POST',
    url: baseUrl + '/auth/basic',
    auth: {
      username: userFixture.email,
      password: 'incorrectpassword'
    },
    json:true
  }, function(err, res, body) {
    if (err) throw err;

    res.statusCode.should.equal(400);
    body.message.should.equal('Invalid email or
    password.');
    done();
  });
});
```

We described the basic strategy. We considered the fact that a user must send an e-mail as username and password via a POST call to the /api/auth endpoint and get back the user details and a valid token.

 The request library has a special property called auth that will encode the username-and-password tuple using base64 and set the appropriate headers for HTTP Basic authentication.

As you can see, our presumption is that a valid token will be generated when a user successfully authenticates into our system. For this reason, we are going to implement the token generation functionality before continuing further.

Implementing the token generation

Tokens can be generated in many ways. For this chapter, we are going to use the built-in crypto library from Node.js. We can use the randomBytes() method to generate a random string of a given length. One thing to note is that randomBytes() will throw an error if there is not enough accumulated entropy. This means that if there is not enough information in the entropy source to generate a random number, it will throw an error.

Let's create a new file called app/helpers/token.js and add the following lines of code:

```
'use strict';

const LEN = 16;
const crypto = require('crypto');

module.exports.generate = generateToken;

function generateToken(size, callback) {
  if (typeof size === 'function') {
    callback = size;
    size = LEN;
  }

  // we will return the token in `hex`
  size = size / 2;

  crypto.randomBytes(size, (err, buf) => {
    if (err) {
```

```
        return callback(err);
    }

    const token = buf.toString('hex');

    callback(null, token);
  });
}
```

We created a helper function that will generate a random token for us. The function takes two arguments: the number of random bytes, which is optional, and a callback function.

Persisting tokens in MongoDB

In order to check an access token sent by the user—that is, whether it's valid or not—we should store it somewhere. For this, we are going to use MongoDB as our storage engine for the tokens.

 Note that you should treat your tokens with the same responsibility as user passwords, because tokens will give access to the system's functionality. One option to consider for further security improvements is to store tokens encrypted in the database or even store them in a separate token storage.

Before anything, let's create a test for the token model. Create a file called `tests/integration/token.model.js` and add the following code:

```
process.env.NODE_ENV = 'test';

const chai = require('chai');
const should = chai.should();
const mongoose = require('../../config/mongoose').init();
const Token = require('../../app/models/token');

describe('Token Model Integration', function() {
  after(function(done) {
    mongoose.connection.db.dropDatabase(function(err) {
      if (err) throw err;

      setTimeout(done, 200);
    });
  });

  describe('#generate() - Token class method', function() {
```

```
    var _userId = new mongoose.Types.ObjectId();

    it('should generate a new token for a user', function(done) {
      Token.generate({
        user: _userId
      }, function(err, token) {
        if (err) throw err;

        should.exist(token);
        should.exist(token.id);
        token.hash.length.should.equal(32);
        token.user.toString().should.equal(_userId.toString());
        done();
      });
    });
  });

});
```

We are going to add a `generate()` method to the `Token` model, which will return a cryptographically strong token.

Create a file called `app/models/token.js`. It will hold the `Token` Mongoose schema and the preceding method:

```
'use strict';

const EXPIRATION = 30; // in days
const LEN = 32;

const mongoose = require('mongoose');
const tokenHelper = require('../helpers/token');
const Schema = mongoose.Schema;
const ObjectId = Schema.ObjectId;

const TokenSchema = new Schema({
  user: {
    type: ObjectId,
    ref: 'User',
    required: true
  },
  hash: {
    type: String,
  },
  expiresAt: {
```

```
          type: Date,
          default: function() {
            var now = new Date();
            now.setDate(now.getDate() + EXPIRATION);

            return now;
          }
        },
        createdAt: {
          type: Date,
          default: Date.now
        }
      });


      TokenSchema.statics.generate = generateToken

      function generateToken(opts, callback) {
        tokenHelper.generate(opts.tokenLength || LEN, (err, tokenString)
        => {
          if (err) {
            return callback(err);
          }

          opts.hash = tokenString;

          this.model('Token').create(opts, callback);
        });
      };

      // compile Token model
      module.exports = mongoose.model('Token', TokenSchema);
```

As you can see, we added an expiration date for our tokens. This could be used to automatically invalidate tokens after a given time. Usually, in an application, you don't want to have tokens without an expiration date. If there is a need for such tokens, another layer of authorization through API keys should be added to authorize the usage of the system for third-party clients.

Authentication using HTTP Basic

Before generating a token, we need to authenticate our users. One simple solution could be to use a simple username-and-password authentication and generate a token if the entered information is valid.

We can expose a route that will handle HTTP Basic authentication. This is the simplest technique for enforcing access control for a resource. In our case, the resource will be a token and it does not require cookies or identifying sessions. HTTP Basic authentication uses standard fields in the HTTP request header.

This method does not add any encryption or hashing in any way; just a simple base64 encoding is needed. For this reason, it is typically used over HTTPS. If the client wants to send the server the necessary credentials for authentication, it can use the `Authorization` header field.

We are going to use the `passport-http` module for the Basic authentication strategy. Let's create a file called `app/config/strategies/basic.js` and add the following lines of code:

```
'use strict';

const passport = require('passport');
const BasicStrategy = require('passport-http').BasicStrategy;
const mongoose = require('mongoose');
const User = mongoose.model('User');

module.exports.init = initBasicStrategy;

function initBasicStrategy() {
  passport.use('basic', new BasicStrategy((username, password,
  done) => {
    User.authenticate(username, password, (err, user) => {
      if (err) {
        return done(err);
      }

      if (!user) {
        return done(null, false);
      }

      return done(null, user);
    });
  }));
}
```

The strategy uses the `authenticate()` method to check whether the credentials are valid. As you can see, we are not adding any extra logic here.

Next, we are going to create a controller that will handle the basic authentication. Create a file called `app/controllers/authentication.js` and add the following content:

```
'use strict';

const _ = require('lodash');
const passport = require('passport');
const mongoose = require('mongoose');
const Token = mongoose.model('Token');

module.exports.basic = basicAuthentication;

function basicAuthentication(req, res, next) {
  passport.authenticate('basic', (err, user, info) => {
    if (err || !user) {
      return res.status(400).send({ message: 'Invalid email or
      password.' });
    }

    Token.generate({
      user: user.id
    }, (err, token) => {
      if (err || !token) {
        return res.status(400).send({ message: 'Invalid email or
        password.' });
      }

      var result = user.toJSON();
      result.token = _.pick(token, ['hash', 'expiresAt']);

      res.json(result);
    });

  })(req, res, next);
}
```

Passport has an `authenticate()` method that enables us to call a given strategy. We are using a custom callback in order to generate and persist a token in MongoDB. When returning the token to the client, we only need a few things from the stored data, such as the value and expiration date.

Adding authentication routes

Create a file called `app/routes/authentication.js` and add the following lines of code:

```
'use strict';

const express = require('express');
const router = express.Router();
const authCtrl = require('../controllers/authentication');

router.post('/basic, authCtrl.basic);

module.exports = router;
```

The `auth` route will allow users to make a post call and authenticate using the basic strategy. In order to create reusable routes, we do not mount the routes directly to the Express app instance. Instead, we use the `Router` class to instantiate a new router.

In order to be able to configure what routes we are mounting on our Express application, we can create a file called `config/routes.js` with the following lines of code:

```
'use strict';

module.exports.init = function(app) {
  var routesPath = app.get('root') + '/app/routes';

  app.use('/auth, require(routesPath + '/auth));
};
```

The preceding lines of code should be straightforward. We are defining the routes' base path and mounting them onto our application. One thing to note is that we are adding a prefix to the authentication routes.

Add the following highlighted code to the main `server.js` file in order to initialize the routes configuration file:

```
require('./config/express').init(app);
require('./config/routes').init(app);
```

Run our authentication test with the following command:

```
mocha tests/integration/authentication.test.js
```

This should have a similarly positive output:

```
Authentication
  Basic authentication
    √ should authenticate a user and return a new token
    √ should not authenticate a user with invalid credentials
2 passing
```

Verifying users using bearer authentication

For each request, tokens should be used to determine whether the requester has access to the system or not. We only used the basic strategy to issue a token if the user sent valid credentials. Passport has a `passport-http-bearer` module. Normally this is used to protect API endpoints, as in our case. The tokens are often issued using OAuth 2.0, but, in our case, we built a custom solution to issue tokens.

Also in our case, a token is a string representing an access authorization key issued to the client by the system. The client application, the Angular app, will use the access token to retrieve protected resources from the RESTful API.

Let's describe a simple use case to retrieve information using an access token. Append the following lines of code to `tests/integration/authentication.test.js`, after the basic authentication test suite:

```
describe('Bearer authentication', function() {
  var _token;

  before(function() {
    Token.generate({
      user: _user.id
    }, function(err, token) {
      if (err) throw err;

      _token = token;
      done();
    });
  });

  it('should authenticate a user using an access token',
  function(done) {
    request({
      method: 'GET',
```

```
        url: baseUrl + '/auth/info',
        auth: {
          bearer: _token.value
        },
        json:true
      }, function(err, res, body) {
        if (err) throw err;

        res.statusCode.should.equal(200);
        body.email.should.equal(userFixture.email);
        should.not.exist(body.password);
        should.not.exist(body.passwordSalt);
        done();
      });
    });

    it('should not authenticate a user with an invalid access
    token', function(done) {
      request({
        method: 'GET',
        url: baseUrl + '/auth/info',
        auth: {
          bearer: _token.value + 'a1e'
        },
        json:true
      }, function(err, res, body) {
        if (err) throw err;

        res.statusCode.should.equal(401);
        body.should.equal('Unauthorized');
        done();
      });
    });
  });
```

We assume the existence of an /auth/info route on which, if a GET call is made, it will return the token's owner credential. If the token is invalid, an unauthorized message is sent back, with the appropriate 401 HTTP status code.

Bearer strategy

Let's create a file called `config/strategies/bearer.js`. Add the following piece of code:

```
'use strict';

const passport = require('passport');
const BearerStrategy = require('passport-http-bearer').Strategy;
const mongoose = require('mongoose');
const Token = mongoose.model('Token');

module.exports.init = initBearerStrategy;

function initBearerStrategy() {
  passport.use('bearer', new BearerStrategy((token, done) => {
    Token
    .findOne({ hash: token })
    .populate('user')
    .exec((err, result) => {
      if (err) {
        return done(err);
      }

      if (!result) {
        return done(null, false, { message: 'Unauthorized.' });
      }

      if (!result.user) {
        return done(null, false, { message: 'Unauthorized.' });
      }

      done(null, result.user);
    });
  }));
}
```

The preceding code searches in the database for the given token. In order to retrieve the token owner, we can use the `populate()` method from Mongoose in combination with a normal query method, such as `findOne()`. This can be done because we explicitly added a reference to the User model in the Token model.

Protecting resources using tokens

In order to protect our resources, we need to add a layer that checks the presence of the access token. We did the first part of the Bearer strategy. Now we only need to use it; for this, we can create middleware that will validate the token.

Create a new file called `app/middlewares/authentication.js` and add the following code:

```
'use strict';

const passport = require('passport');

module.exports.bearer = function bearerAuthentication(req, res,
next) {
  return passport.authenticate('bearer', { session: false });
};
```

The preceding code is fairly simple. We just use passport's built-in `authenticate()` method to call the bearer strategy. We don't want to save any session on the server. This piece of middleware can be used on each route in combination with any other application logic.

Append the following lines of code to `app/controllers/authentication.js`. It will only check whether the user is present on the request object and return a JSON with the data:

```
module.exports.getAuthUser = getAuthUser;

function getAuthUser(req, res, next) {
  if (!req.user) {
    res.status(401).json({ message: 'Unauthorized.' });
  }

  res.json(req.user);
}
```

Now let's get back to our authentication route, `app/routes/authentication.js`, and add the following highlighted lines of code:

```
'use strict';

var express = require('express');
var router = express.Router();
var authCtrl = require('../controllers/authentication');
```

```
var auth = require('../middlewares/authentication');

router.post('/basic', authCtrl.basic);
router.get('/info', auth.bearer(), authCtrl.getAuthUser);

module.exports = router;
```

We added the authentication middleware before the execution of the logic from the controller in order to validate and retrieve the token's owner. Our bearer strategy will handle this and set the user on the request object; more precisely, it can be found on `req.user`.

If we run our authentication test:

```
mocha tests/integration/authentication.test.js
```

The following output should be printed:

```
Authentication
  Basic authentication
    √ should authenticate a user and return a new token
    √ should not authenticate a user with invalid credentials
  Bearer authentication
    √ should authenticate a user using an access token
    √ should not authenticate a user with an invalid access token


  4 passing
```

With this, we've finally added all the necessary authentication methods to grant users access to our system.

Tracking expenses

The main feature of our application is to track the user's expenses. A user should be able to insert expenses, be persisted in the system, and see the exact balance for his/her account.

There should always be a clear view of what is desired to be achieved. Let's take a high-level view of what we want to achieve:

- A user should be able to persist an expense in the system
- A user should be able to get all their expenses

- A user should be able to get the balance of their expenses
- A user should be able to define a category in which to save expenses, for example, groceries

Monetary values

In our case, an expense will store the exact value of money spent. In some cases, working with monetary data can get tricky. Often, applications that handle monetary data are required to work with fractional units of the currency.

We could store data in floating-point numbers. However, in JavaScript, floating-point arithmetic often does not conform to monetary arithmetic. In other words, values like one-third and one-tenth do not have an exact representation in binary floating-point numbers.

MongoDB, for example, stores numeric data as either IEEE 754 standard 64-bit floating-point numbers, 32-bit, or 64-bit signed integers. JavaScript treats numbers according to specs as double-precision 64-bit format IEEE 754 values. Because of this, we need to pay attention to such operations:

```
+ 0.2 = 0.30000000000000004
```

We won't be able to store values such as 9.99 USD, representing cents in decimal. Don't get me wrong; we can store them, but we are not going to get correct results if we use the built-in MongoDB aggregation framework or do server-side arithmetic (the same thing applies for the client side too in JavaScript).

Do not worry; there are a few solutions that we can use. There are two common approaches to storing monetary values in MongoDB:

- Exact precision is an approach that is used to multiply the monetary value by a power of 10.
- Arbitrary precision, on the other hand, uses two fields to represent the monetary value. One field stores the exact value as a non-numeric format, such as a string, and another field stores the floating-point approximation of the value.

For our implementation, we are going to use the exact precision model. We will discuss all the details as we progress with the code.

The category model

As we discussed earlier, we want to be able to add an expense to a specific category. A user should also be able to invite another user to add expenses to a category. We are not going to detail the test cases for this feature, but you should consider writing tests to make sure that everything works as expected.

Let's create a file called app/models/category.js and add the following lines of code:

```
'use strict';

const mongoose = require('mongoose');
const Schema = mongoose.Schema;
const ObjectId = Schema.ObjectId;

const CategorySchema = new Schema({
  name: {
    type: String,
    required: true
  },
  description: {
    type: String
  },
  owner: {
    type: ObjectId,
    ref: 'User',
    required: true
  },
  collaborators: {
    type: [
      {
        type: ObjectId,
        ref: 'User'
      }
    ]
  },
  createdAt: {
    type: Date,
    default: Date.now
  }
});

// compile Category model
module.exports = mongoose.model('Category', CategorySchema);
```

Two important things to note here: we define the owner of the category, which will always be the authenticated user that creates the category, and the collaborators field, which holds users that can insert expenses into the category.

Also, don't forget to change the model configuration file, `config/models.js`, by adding the following highlighted code:

```
['user', 'token', 'category', 'expense'].forEach(function(model) {
    require(modelsPath + model);
});
```

Categories routes

To expose a simple CRUD on the category collection, we have to define routes for those actions. For this, we are going to create a router file, called `app/routes/categories.js`, and add these lines of code:

```
'use strict';

const express = require('express');
const router = express.Router();
const categoryCtrl = require('../controllers/category');
const auth = require('../middlewares/authentication');

router.param('categoryId', expenseCtrl.findById);

router.get('/categories', auth.bearer(), categoryCtrl.getAll);
router.get('/categories/:categoryId', auth.bearer(),
categoryCtrl.getOne);
router.post('/categories', auth.bearer(), categoryCtrl.create);
router.put('/categories/:categoryId', auth.bearer(),
categoryCtrl.update);
router.delete('/categories/:categoryId', auth.bearer(),
categoryCtrl.delete);

module.exports = router;
```

Keep in mind that we actually have no implementation of the category controller at the moment. Let's create a category controller with the following name: `app/controllers/category.js`.

Getting the category by ID

Add the following lines of code to `app/controllers/category.js`:

```
'use strict';

const _ = require('lodash');
const mongoose = require('mongoose');
const Category = mongoose.model('Category');
const ObjectId = mongoose.Types.ObjectId;

module.exports.findById = findCategoryById;
module.exports.create = createCategory;
module.exports.getOne = getOneCategory;
module.exports.getAll = getAllCategories;
module.exports.update = updateCategory;
module.exports.delete = deleteCategory;

function findCategoryById(req, res, next, id) {
  if (!ObjectId.isValid(id)) {
    return res.status(404).json({ message: 'Not found.'});
  }

  Category.findById(id, (err, category) => {
    if (err) {
      return next(err);
    }

    if (!category) {
      return res.status(404).json({ message: 'Not found.'});
    }

    req.category = category;
    next();
  });
}
```

The preceding code will come in handy when the `categoryId` route `param` is present. It will automatically get a category, as we defined it in the route file.

Creating a category

To create a category, append the following lines of code to the controller file:

```
function createCategory(req, res, next) {
  const data = req.body;
  data.owner = req.user.id;

  Category.create(data, (err, category) => {
    if (err) {
      return next(err);
    }

    res.status(201).json(category);
  });
}
```

Before creating a category, we add the owner's ID, which is the current user's ID.

Getting one and all categories

We also want to get a single category and all categories. To get one category, we are going to use the results from getting a category by ID. To retrieve multiple categories, we are going to use the `find()` query method from Mongoose. We could easily add pagination or set limits, but we are going to presume that a user will not have so many categories. This could be a small improvement for our application later on.

Append the following lines of code to the controller:

```
function getOneCategory(req, res, next) {
  res.json(req.category);
}

function getAllCategories(req, res, next) {
  Category.find((err, categories) => {
    if (err) {
      return next(err);
    }

    res.json(categories);
  });
}
```

Updating and deleting a category

When we get a category by ID, we set the returned instance from Mongoose to the request object. Due to this, we can use that instance to change its properties and save it back to Mongo. Append this code:

```
function updateCategory(req, res, next) {
  const category = req.category;
  const data = _.pick(req.body, ['description', 'name']);
  _.assign(category, data);

  category.save((err, updatedCategory) => {
    if (err) {
      return next(err);
    }

    res.json(updatedCategory);
  });
}
```

The same thing can be used when deleting a category; also append the following lines of code:

```
function deleteCategory(req, res, next) {
  req.category.remove((err) => {
    if (err) {
      return next(err);
    }

    res.status(204).json();
  });
}
```

With the preceding lines of code, we have finished CRUD operations on categories.

Defining the expense model

Earlier, we discussed the fact that we cannot simply store monetary data as floating-point numbers in the database or use it for server-side arithmetic. The accepted solution for our scenario was to use exact precision to store monetary data. In other words, money values will be stored by multiplying the initial value with a number that is a power of 10.

We are going to assume that the required maximum precision will be a tenth of a cent. Going with this assumption, we will multiply the initial value by 1000. For example, if we have an initial value of 9.99 USD, the stored value in the database will be 9990.

For the current implementation of the application, we are going to use USD as our currency for monetary values. The scale factor will be 1000 to preserve precision up to one-tenth of a cent. Using the exact precision model, the scale factor needs to be consistent for the currency across the application and anytime given it should be determined from the currency.

Let's create our expense model, `app/models/expense.js`, and add the following lines of code:

```
'use strict';

const CURRENCY = 'USD';
const SCALE_FACTOR = 1000;

const mongoose = require('mongoose');
const Schema = mongoose.Schema;
const ObjectId = Schema.ObjectId;

const ExpenseSchema = new Schema({
  name: {
    type: String
  },
  amount: {
    type: Number,
    default: 0
  },
  currency: {
    type: String,
    default: CURRENCY
  },
  scaleFactor: {
    type: Number,
    default: SCALE_FACTOR
  },
  user: {
    type: ObjectId,
    ref: 'User',
    required: true
  },
```

```
      category: {
        type: ObjectId,
        ref: 'Category',
        required: true
      },
      createdAt: {
        type: Date,
        default: Date.now
      }
    }, {
      toObject: {
        virtuals: true
      },
      toJSON: {
        virtuals: true
      }
    });

    module.exports = mongoose.model('Expense', ExpenseSchema);
```

The following table will give a short description of the fields in the schema:

Field	Description
name	Name of the expense
amount	The scaled amount of money
currency	What currency is used to represent the money
scaleFactor	The scale factor used to obtain the amount
user	To whom the expense belongs
category	A category group that the expense belongs to
createdAt	The date when the expense object was created

Mongoose has an interesting feature, called `virtual attributes`. Such attributes are not persisted in the database but are really helpful in many scenarios. We are going to use a virtual attribute called `value`, which is going to represent the monetary value of the `amount` attribute.

Append the following lines of code before the model compilation:

```
    ExpenseSchema.virtual('value')
    .set(function(value) {
      if (value) {
```

```
      this.set('amount', value * this.scaleFactor);
    }
  })
  .get(function() {
    return this.amount / this.scaleFactor;
  });
```

Like all attributes, virtual attributes can have `getters` and `setters`. We are going to piggyback the setter and add our own logic, which will scale the value with a give factor and obtain the desired amount. Also, when getting the virtual `value` attribute, we are going to return the correct monetary representation, dividing the stored amount by the corresponding scale factor.

By default, when doing a query, Mongoose will not return `virtual attributes`, but we have overwritten the default options for the schema to return all `virtual attributes` when using the `.toJSON()` and `.toObject()` methods.

Describing the expense module functionality

Next, we are going to write some tests for the expense module in order to define the required behavior of the module.

 In order to go faster, we are only going to define a few test cases. The rest of the CRUD test cases are the same as in earlier implementations for different modules. For reference, you can check out the full code base for the test suite at the following link: https://www.packtpub.com/.

Let's create a file called `tests/integration/expense.test.js`. We are going to define the most important test cases:

1. When creating an expense, a value and a category must be present. The value should be a number that accepts decimal values too:

```
it('should save an expense', function(done) {
  request({
    method: 'POST',
    url: baseUrl + '/expenses',
    auth: {
      bearer: _token.value
    },
    form: {
      value: 14.99,
      category: _category.toString()
    },
```

```
          json:true
      }, function(err, res, body) {
        if (err) throw err;

        res.statusCode.should.equal(201);
        body.amount.should.equal(14990);
        body.scaleFactor.should.equal(1000);
        body.value.should.equal(14.99);
        body.category.should.equal(_category.toString());
        done();
      });
    });
```

2. We should be able to get all of the user's expenses from the database:

```
    it('should get balance for all expenses',
    function(done) {
      request({
        method: 'GET',
        url: baseUrl + '/expenses/balance',
        auth: {
          bearer: _token.value
        },
        json:true
      }, function(err, res, body) {
        if (err) throw err;

        res.statusCode.should.equal(200);
        should.exist(body);
        body.balance.should.equal(33.33);
        body.count.should.equal(3);
        done();
      });
    });
```

3. If necessary, we should get only the expenses for a given category. This will come in handy when we want to display expenses for a certain category:

```
    it('should get expenses balance only for a category',
    function(done) {
        request({
        method: 'GET',
        url: baseUrl + '/expenses/balance?category=' +
        _categoryOne.toString(),
        auth: {
          bearer: _token.value
```

```
            },
            json:true
        }, function(err, res, body) {
            if (err) throw err;

            res.statusCode.should.equal(200);
            should.exist(body);
            body.balance.should.equal(21.21);
            body.count.should.equal(2);
            done();
        });
    });
```

The preceding code tests the creation of an expense and that the virtual value attribute works correctly. It also checks whether an invalid token is sent and that the application will treat it accordingly. Now the fun part starts with the balance functionality, which should return an aggregated value of the expenses for different scenarios.

CRUD operations for expenses

Next, we are going to implement the CRUD operations for expenses one by one. Before going any further, we are going to create a new routes file called app/routes/expenses.js and add the following lines of code:

```
'use strict';

const express = require('express');
const router = express.Router();
const expenseCtrl = require('../controllers/expense');
const auth = require('../middlewares/authentication');

router.param('expenseId', expenseCtrl.findById);

router.get('/expenses', auth.bearer(), expenseCtrl.getAll);
router.get('/expenses/:expenseId', auth.bearer(), expenseCtrl.getOne);
router.post('/expenses', auth.bearer(), expenseCtrl.create);
router.put('/expenses/:expenseId', auth.bearer(), expenseCtrl.update);
router.delete('/expenses/:expenseId', auth.bearer(), expenseCtrl.
delete);

module.exports = router;
```

We added a bearer authentication for each route. You could have created a single route to catch all the resources that need authentication, but, in this way, you will have fine-grained control for each route.

Create expense

Let's create the controller that the routes file needs—`app/controllers/expense.js`—and add the create expense logic:

```
'use strict';

const _ = require('lodash');
const mongoose = require('mongoose');
const Expense = mongoose.model('Expense');
const ObjectId = mongoose.Types.ObjectId;

module.exports.create = createExpense;
module.exports.findById = findExpenseById
module.exports.getOne = getOneExpense;
module.exports.getAll = getAllExpenses;
module.exports.update = updateExpense;
module.exports.delete = deleteExpense;
module.exports.getBalance = getExpensesBalance;

function createExpense(req, res, next) {
  const data = _.pick(req.body, ['name', 'value', 'category',
'createdAt']);
  data.user = req.user.id;

  if (data.createdAt === null) {
    delete data.createdAt;
  }

  Expense.create(data, (err, expense) => {
    if (err) {
      return next(err);
    }

    res.status(201).json(expense);
  });
}
```

The expense that we want to create should be for the token owner. Hence, we explicitly set the user property to the authenticated user's ID.

Get expense by ID

The get one and update expense logic uses an expense instance to display or update it. Due to this, we are only going to add a single logic that retrieves an expense by ID. Append the following lines of code to the controller file:

```
function findExpenseById(req, res, next, id) {
  if (!ObjectId.isValid(id)) {
    return res.status(404).json({ message: 'Not found.'});
  }

  Expense.findById(id, (err, expense) => {
    if (err) {
      return next(err);
    }

    if (!expense) {
      return res.status(404).json({ message: 'Not found.'});
    }

    req.expense = expense;
    next();
  });
}
```

Because we are not going to do a final operation here, we only set the expense to be present on the request object and call the next handler in the route pipeline.

Get one expense

We are going to extend "get expense by ID" and just respond with a JSON representation of the resource. Getting an expense logic should be a few lines of code appended to the controller file:

```
function getOneExpense(req, res, next) {
  if (!req.expense) {
    return res.status(404).json({ message: 'Not found.'});
  }

  res.json(req.expense);
}
```

Get all expenses

When getting all expenses, we need to take a different approach—one that enables us to filter them by a specific query. Expenses should also be returned for a specific category. We don't need to implement different search logics for all these scenarios. Instead, we can create one that will wrap around our needs:

```javascript
function getAllExpenses(req, res, next) {
  const limit = +req.query.limit || 30;
  const skip = +req.query.skip || 0;
  const query = {};

  if (req.category) {
    query.category = req.category.id;
  } else {
    query.user = req.user.id;
  }

  if (req.query.startDate) {
    query.createdAt = query.createdAt || {};
    query.createdAt.$gte = new Date(req.query.startDate);
  }

  if (req.query.endDate) {
    query.createdAt = query.createdAt || {};
    query.createdAt.$lte = new Date(req.query.endDate);
  }

  if (req.query.category) {
    query.category = req.query.category;
  }

  Expense
  .find(query)
  .limit(limit)
  .skip(skip)
  .sort({ createdAt: 'desc' })
  .populate('category')
  .exec((err, expenses) => {
    if (err) {
      return next(err);
    }

    res.json(expenses);
  });
}
```

Before querying the database using Mongoose to retrieve the necessary data, we construct a query variable that will hold all our criteria. One nice thing to note here is that once again we used the query builder object provided by Mongoose. Expenses are going to be stored in a greater number in MongoDB. Hence, we add a `limit` and a `skip` to retrieve only a limited set of data.

Expenses can be queried using a date range. Due to this reason, the `createdAt` property will be progressively extended to match only a set of expenses in a period. Expenses should also be returned in a chronological order; newly added expenses should be returned first.

To have all the necessary information about each expense, we are going to populate the category property of an expense with the appropriate category object from the database.

Update expense

Append the following code for the update logic to the controller file:

```
function updateExpense(req, res, next) {
  const data = _.pick(req.body, ['name', 'value', 'category',
'createdAt']);
  const expense = req.expense;

  if (data.createdAt === null) {
    delete data.createdAt;
  }

  _.assign(expense, data);

  expense.save((err, updatedExpense) => {
    if (err) {
      return next(err);
    }

    res.json(updatedExpense);
  });
}
```

The update logic uses the expense instance set on the request object by the callback trigger for the expense ID parameter.

Delete expense

In order to delete an expense, we just remove the expense instance from the database, using the following code:

```
function deleteExpense(req, res, next) {
  req.expense.remove((err) => {
    if (err) {
      return next(err);
    }

    res.status(204).json();
  });
}
```

Getting the expense balance

Let's get back to the expense model and extend it with balance calculation. In order to get the balance in different scenarios, we are going to use the Aggregation framework from MongoDB. Aggregated data means computed results from operations on data from collections.

Mongo provides a complex set of operations to perform on datasets. Because we are using Mongoose, we have access to `Model.aggregate()`, which will help us create the aggregation pipelines.

Keep in mind that the data returned from aggregation is in the form of plain JavaScript objects, not Mongoose documents. This is due to the fact that any shape of document can be returned when using aggregations.

Append the following code before the expense model compilation:

```
ExpenseSchema.statics.getBalance = getExpensesBalance;

function getExpensesBalance(opts, callback) {
  const query = {};

  // set the current user
  query.user = opts.user;

  if (opts.category || opts.category === null) {
    query.category = new mongoose.Types.ObjectId(opts.category);
  }

  if (opts.startDate && opts.endDate) {
```

```
    query.createdAt = {
      $gte: new Date(opts.startDate),
      $lte: new Date(opts.endDate)
    };
  }

  this.model('Expense').aggregate([
    { $match: query },
    { $group: { _id: null, balance: { $sum: '$amount' }, count: {
    $sum: 1 } } }
  ], (err, result) => {

    // result is an array with a single item, we can just return
    that
    const final = result[0];
    final.balance = final.balance / SCALE_FACTOR;

    callback(err, final);
  });
}
```

The preceding static .getBalance() method will calculate the current balance in different scenarios, as described in the test case. The .aggregate() method goes through multiple stages. The first one is a match stage that will select all the documents for our defined query. The result from the match is sent to the group stage, where the documents are grouped by a specified identifier.

In addition, pipeline stages can use operators to perform different tasks, for example, calculating the balance in our scenario. We are using an accumulator operator called $sum that returns a numerical value for each group.

In the group stage, the _id field is mandatory, but you can specify a null value for it to calculate all the values for the input documents of the pipeline. The group operator has a limit of 100 megabytes of RAM, but you can set it to use the disk to write temporary files. To set this option, use Mongoose and take a look at the .allowDiskUse() method.

Add the missing controller function, app/controller/expense:

```
function getExpensesBalance(req, res, next) {
  Expense.getBalance({
    user: req.user._id,
    category: req.query.category,
    startDate: req.query.start,
    endDate: req.query.end
```

```
  }, (err, result) => {
    if (err) {
      return next(err);
    }

    res.json(result);
  });
}
```

Implementing the Angular client application

We have reached the point in our project at which we will start integrating the AngularJS application. This chapter will take a different approach at building the desired application. An ideal application should be structured in a modular way, each module addressing a specific functionality.

You are probably already familiar with the component-based approach when building Angular apps. What this means is that we will create small modules that encapsulate specific functionalities. This enables us to add functionality incrementally; imagine adding vertical blocks onto the application.

For this to work, we need to create a main block that glues everything together, pulling all features and modules together. Keep your main app module thin and move the rest of the logic to application modules.

One rule that I like to follow is to keep my folder structure as flat as possible. I always try to reduce the level of the folders so that I can locate code and functionality quickly. If your module grows too big, you can either split it up or add subfolders.

Bootstrapping the project

Let's get started and create a `public/package.json` file. We are going to use `npm` to install our dependencies for the frontend part of the project. The `package.json` file will have the following content:

```
{
  "private": true,
  "name": "mean-blueprints-expensetracker-client",
  "dependencies": {
    "systemjs": "^0.19.25",
    "es6-shim": "^0.35.0",
```

```
    "es6-promise": "^3.0.2",
    "rxjs": "^5.0.0-beta.2",
    "reflect-metadata": "^0.1.2",
    "zone.js": "^0.6.6",
    "angular2": "^2.0.0-beta.14"
  },
  "devDependencies": {
    "typings": "^0.7.12",
    "typescript": "^1.8.9"
  }
}
```

Run this command to install all the dependencies:

`npm install`

After a successful installation, create a folder called `public/src`. This folder will hold the main Angular application. Inside this folder, we will create our modules folder and application files.

Create your main app component file, called `public/src/app.component.ts`, and follow these steps to create the final version of the file:

1. Add the necessary dependencies:

    ```
    import { Component, OnInit } from 'angular2/core';
    import { RouteConfig, RouterOutlet, RouterLink } from 'angular2/
    router';
    import { Router } from 'angular2/router';
    import { AuthHttp, AuthService, SigninComponent, RegisterComponent
    } from './auth/index';
    import { ExpensesComponent } from './expense/index';
    import { CategoriesComponent } from './expense/index';
    ```

2. Configure your routes:

    ```
    @RouteConfig([
      { path: '/', redirectTo: ['/Expenses'], useAsDefault:
      true },
      { path: '/expenses', as: 'Expenses', component:
      ExpensesComponent },
      { path: '/categories', as: 'Categories', component:
      CategoriesComponent },
      { path: '/signin', as: 'Signin', component:
      SigninComponent },
      { path: '/register', as: 'Register', component:
      RegisterComponent }
    ])
    ```

We defined a default path that will redirect to the expenses view, displaying all the entries to the user. There is also a Signin and register route available.

3. Add the component annotation:

```
@Component({
    selector: 'expense-tracker',
    directives: [
      RouterOutlet,
      RouterLink
    ],
    template: `
      <div class="app-wrapper card whiteframe-z2">
        <div class="row">
          <div class="col">
            <a href="#">Expense tracker</a>
            <a href="#"
            [routerLink]="['Expenses']">Expenses</a>
          </div>
        </div>
        <div class="row">
          <router-outlet></router-outlet>
        </div>
      </div>
      `
})
```

4. Define the component's class:

```
export class AppComponent implements OnInit {
  public currentUser: any;
  private _authHttp: AuthHttp;
  private _authSerivce: AuthService;
  private _router: Router;

  constructor(authHttp: AuthHttp, authSerice: AuthService,
  router: Router) {
    this._router = router;
    this._authSerivce = authSerice;
    this._authHttp = authHttp;
  }

  ngOnInit() {
    this.currentUser = {};
    this._authHttp.unauthorized.subscribe((res) => {
      if (res) {
```

```
          this._router.navigate(['./Signin']);
        }
      });
      this._authSerivce.currentUser.subscribe((user) => {
        this.currentUser = user;
      });
    }
  }
```

If an unauthorized call is made, we redirect the user to the `Signin` route in order to authenticate itself with valid credentials.

Registering users

Our application should support user registration. We already have the backend logic for this functionality. Now, all we have to do is tie it up with our Angular application. To do this, we are going to create a generic module called `auth`, which will be used for both registering and authenticating users.

The auth service

We will continue with the `auth` service, which will hold all the communication logic with the Node.js backend application. Create a file called `public/src/auth/services/auth.service.ts` and implement the entire logic of the service by following these steps:

1. Import the dependencies:

```
import { Injectable } from 'angular2/core';
import { Http, Response, Headers } from 'angular2/http';
import { Subject } from 'rxjs/Subject';
import { BehaviorSubject } from
'rxjs/Subject/BehaviorSubject';
import { contentHeaders } from '../../common/index';
```

2. Define the service class:

```
@Injectable()
export class AuthService {
  public currentUser: Subject<any>;
  private _http: Http;

  constructor(http: Http) {
    this._http = http;
    this._initSession();
  }
}
```

3. Add the `signin()` method:

```
public signin(user: any) {
  let body = this._serialize(user);
  let basic = btoa(`${user.email}:${user.password}`);
  let headers = new Headers(contentHeaders);
  headers.append('Authorization', `Basic ${basic}`)

  return this._http
  .post('/auth/basic', '', { headers: headers })
  .map((res: Response) => res.json());
}
Append the register() method:
  public register(user: any) {
    let body = this._serialize(user);

    return this._http
    .post('/api/users', body, { headers: contentHeaders })
    .map((res: Response) => res.json());
  }
```

4. Set the current user:

```
public setCurrentUser(user: any) {
  this.currentUser.next(user);
}
```

We want to expose a simple function to set the next value of the `currentUser` Observable.

5. Initialize the session:

```
private _initSession() {
  let user =
  this._deserialize(localStorage.getItem('currentUser'));
  this.currentUser = new BehaviorSubject<Response>(user);
  // persist the user to the local storage
  this.currentUser.subscribe((user) => {
    localStorage.setItem('currentUser',
    this._serialize(user));
    localStorage.setItem('token', user.token.hash || '');
  });
}
```

When the application reloads, we want to retrieve the current user from the local storage in order to restore the session. One improvement you can add is to check whether the token has expired.

6. Append the helper methods:

```
private _serialize(data) {
  return JSON.stringify(data);
}

private _deserialize(str) {
  try {
    return JSON.parse(str);
  } catch(err) {
    console.error(err);
    return null;
  }
}
}
```

The preceding functions are simple abstractions for the `stringify` and `parse` JSON methods.

Register component

Create the appropriate component file, `public/src/auth/components/register.component.ts`, with the following lines of code in it:

```
import { Component } from 'angular2/core';
import { Router, RouterLink } from 'angular2/router';
import { AuthService } from '../services/auth.service';

export class RegisterComponent {
  private _authService: AuthService;
  private _router: Router;

  constructor(authService: AuthService, router: Router) {
    this._router = router;
    this._authService = authService;
  }

  register(event, name, email, password) {
    event.preventDefault();

    let data = { name, email, password };

    this._authService
    .register(data)
```

```
      .subscribe((user) => {
        this._router.navigateByUrl('/');
      }, err => console.error(err));
    }
  }
```

When the `register` method is called, we simply try to register our user using the `AuthService`. Error handling is not added in the preceding code. Only a simple log will be printed on the browser's console. Let's add the template:

```
@Component({
    selector: 'register',
    directives: [
      RouterLink
    ],
    template: `
      <div class="login jumbotron center-block">
        <h1>Register</h1>
        <form role="form" (submit)="register($event, name.value,
        email.value, password.value)">
          <div class="form-group">
            <label for="name">Full name</label>
            <input type="text" #name class="form-control"
            id="email" placeholder="please enter your name">
          </div>
          <div class="form-group">
            <label for="email">E-mail</label>
            <input type="text" #email class="form-control"
            id="email" placeholder="enter valid e-mail">
          </div>
          <div class="form-group">
            <label for="password">Password</label>
            <input type="password" #password class="form-control"
            id="password" placeholder="now your password">
          </div>
          <button type="submit" class="button">Submit</button>
        </form>
      </div>
      `
})
```

The register component is pretty straightforward. We are defining a simple register function that will use the auth service's `register` method. All the necessary fields also can be found in the `template` property.

Sign-in-user component

In order to authenticate users, we have added some extra functionality to the auth service to enable us to sign in a user. Because we are not persisting the state of a user on the backend — in other words, our backend is stateless — we have to store the current state of the user on the frontend.

Remember that we created an endpoint that will issue us a token for a valid username-and-password tuple. We are going to use that endpoint to retrieve a token that will grant us access to the rest of the API endpoints.

Our sign-in component is fairly simple and it's really reused from the previous chapter, but let's refresh our memory and take a look at it. `SigninComponent` is found under `public/src/auth/components/signin.component.ts`:

```
import { Component } from 'angular2/core';
import { Router, RouterLink } from 'angular2/router';
import { AuthService } from '../services/auth.service';

@Component({
    selector: 'signin',
    directives: [
      RouterLink
    ],
    template: `
      <div class="login jumbotron center-block">
        <h1>Login</h1>
        <form role="form" (submit)="signin($event, email.value,
        password.value)">
          <div class="form-group">
            <label for="email">E-mail</label>
            <input type="text" #email class="form-control"
            id="email" placeholder="enter your e-mail">
          </div>
          <div class="form-group">
            <label for="password">Password</label>
            <input type="password" #password class="form-control"
            id="password" placeholder="now your password">
          </div>
          <button type="submit" class="button">Submit</button>
        </form>
      </div>
    `
})
export class SigninComponent {
```

```
      private _authService: AuthService;
      private _router: Router;

      constructor(authService: AuthService, router: Router) {
        this._authService = authService;
        this._router = router;
      }

      signin(event, email, password) {
        event.preventDefault();

        let data = { email, password };

        this._authService
        .signin(data)
        .subscribe((user) => {
          this._authService.setCurrentUser(user);
          this._router.navigateByUrl('/');
        }, err => console.error(err));
      }
    }
```

Just as in `RegisterComponent`, we are using local variables for our fields. Using `AuthService`, we try to authenticate our user. We are not really focusing on handling errors, but, if the user successfully authenticates, we want to navigate to the `root` path and set the current user.

Common functionalities

There are a few functionalities that we used earlier and some extra functionality to consider before jumping further into development. For example, we used a common headers definition, found under `public/src/common/headers.ts`:

```
    import { Headers } from 'angular2/http';

    const HEADERS = {
      'Content-Type': 'application/json',
      'Accept': 'application/json'
    };

    export const contentHeaders = new Headers(HEADERS);
```

This is simply a way to define constants and use them across the application without repeating yourself. So, basically, we imported `Headers` from Angular 2 and created a new instance. You can easily add extra fields to this header instance using the `append()` method, like this for example:

```
contentHeaders.append('Authorization', 'Bearer <token_value>');
```

Now there a few other things to consider:

- When asking the server for resources through the API, we should send the required Bearer token
- If a user makes a call and the server responds with a status code that equals 401 — unauthorized — we should redirect the user to the sign-in page

Let's see what we can do about the preceding list.

Custom HTTP service

We did something similar in the previous chapter when we created a custom HTTP service to make calls to the Express backend application. But we need a few extra things, such as attaching the token to each call that is made through this service in order to identify the user.

Remember that we stored our user's token inside the browser's `LocalStorage`. This should be fairly simple to retrieve and I think we can even add it inside the service. Let's get started and create a new file called `public/src/auth/services/auth-http.ts`:

```
import { Injectable } from 'angular2/core';
import { Http, Response, Headers, BaseRequestOptions, Request,
RequestOptions, RequestOptionsArgs, RequestMethod } from 'angular2/
http';
import { Observable } from 'rxjs/Observable';
import { Subject } from 'rxjs/Subject';
import { BehaviorSubject } from 'rxjs/Subject/BehaviorSubject';

@Injectable()
export class AuthHttp {
  public unauthorized: Subject<Response>;
  private _http: Http;

  constructor(http: Http) {
    this._http = http;
```

```
    this.unauthorized = new BehaviorSubject<Response>(null);
  }

  public get(url: string, opts?: RequestOptionsArgs) {
    return this.request({ url: url, method: RequestMethod.Get},
    opts);
  }

  public post(url: string, body?: string, opts?:
  RequestOptionsArgs) {
    return this.request({ url: url, method: RequestMethod.Post,
    body: body}, opts);
  }

  public put(url: string, body?: string, opts?:
  RequestOptionsArgs) {
    return this.request({ url: url, method: RequestMethod.Put,
    body: body}, opts);
  }

  public delete(url: string, body?: string, opts?:
  RequestOptionsArgs) {
    return this.request({ url: url, method: RequestMethod.Delete,
    body: body}, opts);
  }

  // rest of the HTTP methods ...
}
```

So this is our custom `HttpAuth` service, which exposes a few public methods, the same as in the previous chapter. Now the changes occur in the private `request()` method:

```
private request(requestArgs: RequestOptionsArgs,
additionalArgs?: RequestOptionsArgs) {
  let opts = new RequestOptions(requestArgs);

  if (additionalArgs) {
    opts = opts.merge(additionalArgs);
  }

  let req:Request = new Request(opts);

  if (!req.headers) {
```

```
        req.headers = new Headers();
    }

    if (!req.headers.has('Authorization')) {
      req.headers.append('Authorization', `Bearer
      ${this.getToken()}`);
    }

    return this._http.request(req).catch((err: any) => {
      if (err.status === 401) {
        this.unauthorized.next(err);
      }

      return Observable.throw(err);
    });
}
```

Before we make a call, we attach the necessary token to the Authorization header. The token is stored in the browser's storage, so we use the getToken() method to retrieve it. If the request is unauthorized, we push it through our unauthorized data stream, which holds requests that failed authentication.

The getToken() method has a very simple implementation:

```
private getToken() {
  return localStorage.getItem('token');
}
```

Using a single export file

We can add an index.ts file in the root of each module folder in order to export all public members. In the auth module, we can have a file called public/src/auth/ index.ts with the following content:

```
export * from './components/register.component';
export * from './components/signin.component';
export * from './services/auth.service';
export * from './services/auth-http';
```

This technique will be used for each module and it's not going to be covered any further.

The categories module

The category module will hold all of the logic that is necessary to perform CRUD operations on categories and communicate with the backend through an Angular service.

Category service

The category service is going to be fairly simple, it's only going to manage the CRUD operations on categories. The following steps will describe the process to achieve this:

1. Create a file called `public/app/categories/category.service.js`.

2. Add the necessary business logic:

```
import { Injectable } from 'angular2/core';
import { Http, Response, Headers } from 'angular2/http';
import { Observable } from 'rxjs/Observable';
import { Subject } from 'rxjs/Subject';
import { BehaviorSubject } from 'rxjs/Subject/BehaviorSubject';
import { AuthHttp } from '../auth/index';
import { contentHeaders } from '../common/index';
import { Category } from './category.model';

@Injectable()
export class CategoryService {
  public category: Subject<Category>;
  public categories: Observable<Array<Category>>;

  private _authHttp: AuthHttp;
  private _categoriesObserver: any;

  constructor(authHttp: AuthHttp) {
    this._authHttp = authHttp;
    this.categories = new Observable(
      observer => {
        this._categoriesObserver = observer
      }
    ).share();
    this.category = new BehaviorSubject<Category>(null);
  }

  getAll() {
    return this._authHttp
```

```
    .get('/api/categories', { headers: contentHeaders })
    .map((res: Response) => res.json())
    .map((data) => {
      let categories = data.map((category) => {
        return new Category(
          category._id,
          category.name,
          category.description,
          category.owner,
          category.collaborators
        );
      });

      this._categoriesObserver.next(categories);

      return categories;
    });
}

findById(id) {
  return this._authHttp
  .get(`/api/categories/${id}`, { headers: contentHeaders })
  .map((res: Response) => res.json())
}

create(category) {
  let body = JSON.stringify(category);

  return this._authHttp
  .post('/api/categories', body, { headers:
  contentHeaders })
  .map((res: Response) => res.json())
}

update(category) {
  let body = JSON.stringify(category);

  return this._authHttp
  .put(`/api/categories/${category._id}`, body, {
  headers: contentHeaders })
  .map((res: Response) => res.json())
}

delete(category) {
```

```
        return this._authHttp
        .put(`/api/categories/${category._id}`, '', { headers:
        contentHeaders })
        .map((res: Response) => res.json())
      }
    }
```

As you can see, the service will expose all the methods needed for the CRUD operations. Each method will return an observable, which will emit a single response. We are also using our own `AuthHttp` in order to check whether a request is unauthorized and the user needs to sign in.

Note that, besides the returned observable, the `getAll()` method also updates the `categories` data stream in order to push the new values to each subscriber. This will come in handy when multiple subscribers use the same data source to display data in their own way.

The categories component

We are going to create a component that is used when we navigate to the `/categories` path, which we configured at the beginning of the chapter. The final version of `AppComponent` was used earlier in the chapter.

`CategoriesComponent` will use two other components to create a new category and list all the available entries from the system. Let's create a new file, `public/src/category/categories.component.ts`:

```
import { Component } from 'angular2/core';
import { CategoryListComponent } from './category-list.component';
import { CategoryCreateComponent } from './category-create.component';

@Component({
    selector: 'categories',
    directives: [
      CategoryCreateComponent,
      CategoryListComponent
    ],
    template: `
      <category-create></category-create>
      <category-list></category-list>
    `
})
export class CategoryComponent {
  constructor() {}
}
```

The previous component does not have much going on; we have no moving parts. We just import the two necessary components and include them in the template. Let's continue by implementing the other two components from this context.

Create a new category

A user must be able to interact with our application and add new categories, so we are going to create a separate component for this. Let's break it down into these steps:

1. First, create the view file, called `public/src/category/components/category-create.component.ts`.

2. Import the necessary dependencies:

```
import { Component, OnInit } from 'angular2/core';
import { CategoryService } from '../category.service';
import { Category } from '../category.model';
```

3. Define the component annotation, which includes the template:

```
@Component({
    selector: 'category-create',
    template: `
      <div>
        <form role="form" (submit)="onSubmit($event)">
          <div class="form-group">
            <label for="name">Name</label>
            <input type="text" [(ngModel)]="category.name"
            class="form-control" id="name">
          </div>
          <div class="form-group">
            <label for="description">Description</label>
            <textarea class="form-control" id="description"
              name="description"
              [(ngModel)]="category.description">
            </textarea>
          </div>
          <button type="submit" class="button">Add</button>
        </form>
      </div>
    `
})
```

4. Add the component's class:

```
export class CategoryCreateComponent implements OnInit {
  public category: Category;
  public categories: Array<Category>;
  private _categoryService: CategoryService;

  constructor(categoryService: CategoryService) {
    this._categoryService = categoryService;
  }

  ngOnInit() {
    this.category = new Category();
  }

  onSubmit(event) {
    event.preventDefault();

    this._categoryService
    .create(this.category)
    .subscribe((category) => {
      this._categoryService.category.next(category);
      this.category = new Category();
    }, err => console.error(err));
  }
}
```

Each time we add a new category, we want to broadcast the new item to all subscribers. For example, the categories list should have the new entry displayed. After we have successfully created the category, the form should be reset to its initial value.

List all categories

Now that we can create categories, we should be able to list them for the user. In order to list the categories, we are going to use two components, one component to iterate over the data from the server and another to display information about a category.

The latter component will also have encapsulated the update functionality. So anytime the user can change information about a category and persist the changes on the backend.

Let's create a new component file for the categories listing, called `public/src/category/components/category-list.component.ts`, and follow these steps:

1. Import the necessary modules:

```
import { Component, OnInit, OnDestroy } from 'angular2/core';
import { CategoryService } from '../category.service';
import { CategoryComponent } from './category.component';
import { Category } from '../category.model';
```

We imported a `CategoryComponent`, which doesn't exist at the moment, but we should already have an idea of how we are going to use our component.

2. Define the template and component annotation:

```
@Component({
    selector: 'category-list',
    directives: [CategoryComponent],
    template: `
      <div class="jumbotron center-block">
        <h2>List of all your categories</h2>
      </div>
      <div>
        <category *ngFor="#category of categories"
        [category]="category"></category>
      </div>
    `
})
```

We are using the `ngFor` directive to render the `category` template for each item from the list.

3. Declare the component's class:

```
export class CategoryListComponent implements OnInit,
OnDestroy {
  public categories: Array<Category>;
  private _categoryService: CategoryService;
  private _categorySubscription: any;

  constructor(categoryService: CategoryService) {
    this._categoryService = categoryService;
  }

  ngOnInit() {
    this._categorySubscription =
    this._categoryService.category
```

```
        .subscribe((category) => {
          if (category) {
            this.categories.push(category);
          }
        });
        this._categoryService.getAll()
        .subscribe((categories) => {
          this.categories = categories;
        });
      }

    ngOnDestroy() {
      this._categorySubscription.unsubscribe();
    }
  }
```

When the component is initialized, we are going to retrieve all the available categories from the backend using our `CategoryService`. Besides fetching all the necessary data, we also subscribe when a new category is created. Basically, we subscribe to a category data stream.

Each time a new category is added, it is going to be pushed to the `categories` list and displayed to the user. In order to render the information for the user, we are going to have a component for a single category.

When the component is destroyed, we want to unsubscribe from the data stream; otherwise, notifications will be pushed down the data stream.

The category component

To display information for a single category from our list, we are going to create a new component, called `public/src/category/components/category.component.ts`:

```
import { Component } from 'angular2/core';
import { CategoryService } from '../category.service';
import { Category } from '../category.model';

@Component({
    inputs: ['category'],
    selector: 'category',
    template: `
    <div>
      <form role="form" (submit)="onSubmit($event)">
```

```
          <div class="form-group">
            <label for="name">Name</label>
            <input type="text" [(ngModel)]="category.name"
            class="form-control" id="name">
          </div>
          <div class="form-group">
            <label for="description">Description</label>
            <textarea class="form-control" id="description"
              name="description" [(ngModel)]="category.description">
            </textarea>
          </div>
          <button type="submit" class="button">save</button>
        </form>
      </div>
      `
})
export class CategoryComponent {
  public category: Category;
  private _categoryService: CategoryService;

  constructor(categoryService: CategoryService) {
    this._categoryService = categoryService;
  }

  onSubmit(event) {
    event.preventDefault();
    this._categoryService.update(this.category)
    .subscribe((category) => {
      this.category = category;
    }, err => console.error(err));
  }
}
```

This category gets input data to display information about a category. It also triggers
an event when the **Save** button is clicked on and the form is submitted. We use our
service to communicate with the server and persist the changes in MongoDB.

The expenses module

In this module, we are going to treat functionality related to expenses. This is going to be the main module used by our users in the frontend application, because here they will add new expenses and store them in MongoDB through our backend API.

Expense service

The expense service will implement CRUD operations on expenses and one other important feature of it is getting the balance of expenses. In order to create the expense service, we will follow these steps:

1. Create a file called `public/src/expense/expense.service.js`.

2. Define the main logic of the service:

    ```
    import { Injectable } from 'angular2/core';
    import { Http, Response, Headers } from 'angular2/http';
    import { Observable } from 'rxjs/Observable';
    import { Subject } from 'rxjs/Subject';
    import { BehaviorSubject } from 'rxjs/Subject/BehaviorSubject';
    import { AuthHttp } from '../auth/index';
    import { contentHeaders, serializeQuery } from '../common/index';
    import { Expense } from './expense.model';

    @Injectable()
    export class ExpenseService {
      public expense: Subject<Expense>;
      public expenses: Observable<Array<Expense>>;
      public filter: Subject<any>;
      private _authHttp: AuthHttp;
      private _expensesObserver: any;

      constructor(authHttp: AuthHttp) {
        this._authHttp = authHttp;
        this.expenses = new Observable(
          observer => {
            this._expensesObserver = observer
          }
        );
        this.filter = new BehaviorSubject<any>(null);
        this.expense = new BehaviorSubject<Expense>(null);
      }
      create(expense) {
      }
    ```

```
        findById(id) {
        }
        getAll() {
        }
        update(expense) {
        }
        delete(expense) {
        }
    }
```

We just defined a list of exposed methods. We also exposed a few public properties, for the filter that can be updated externally, like the expense, and an Observable expenses data stream.

Now let's follow the methods one by one and append their actual implementation:

1. Creating an expense:

```
    create(expense) {
        let body = JSON.stringify(expense);

        return this._authHttp
        .post('/api/expenses', body, { headers: contentHeaders })
        .map((res: Response) => res.json())
        .map((expense) => {
            return new Expense(
                expense._id,
                expense.name,
                expense.currency,
                expense.amoun,
                expense.scaleFactor,
                expense.value,
                expense.user,
                expense.category,
                expense.createdAt
            );
        });
    }
Getting one expense by ID:
    findById(id) {
        return this._authHttp
        .get(`/api/expenses/${id}`, { headers: contentHeaders
        })
        .map((res: Response) => res.json())
        .map((expense) => {
```

```
        return new Expense(
          expense._id,
          expense.name,
          expense.currency,
          expense.amoun,
          expense.scaleFactor,
          expense.value,
          expense.user,
          expense.category,
          expense.createdAt
        );
      });
    }
```

2. Getting all expenses matching a given query criteria:

```
getAll(criteria?: any) {
  let query = '';

  if (criteria) {
    query = `?${serializeQuery(criteria)}`
  }

  this._authHttp
  .get(`/api/expenses${query}`, { headers: contentHeaders
  })
  .map((res: Response) => res.json())
  .map((data) => {
    return data.map((expense) => {
      return new Expense(
        expense._id,
        expense.name,
        expense.currency,
        expense.amoun,
        expense.scaleFactor,
        expense.value,
        expense.user,
        expense.category,
        expense.createdAt
      );
    });
  }).subscribe((expenses: Array<Expense>) => {
    this._expensesObserver.next(expenses);
  }, err => console.error(err));
}
```

The preceding method uses a `serializeQuery()` method, which will transform our criteria into `query string` parameters. We are doing this to filter our expenses by a given criteria. Also, rather than returning an Observable from the HTTP call, we update our `expenses` data stream to notify all subscribers of the newly available data.

3. Getting the balance of the expenses matching a query criteria:

```
getExpensesBalance(criteria?: any) {
   let query = '';

   if (criteria) {
      query = `?${serializeQuery(criteria)}`
   }

   return this._authHttp
   .get(`/api/expenses/balance${query}`, { headers:
   contentHeaders })
   .map((res: Response) => res.json())
}
```

We use the same `serializeQuery()` function to transform our criteria into a `query string`.

4. Updating an expense by ID with new data:

```
update(expense) {
   let body = JSON.stringify(expense);

   return this._authHttp
   .put(`/api/expenses/${expense._id}`, body, { headers:
   contentHeaders })
   .map((res: Response) => res.json())
}
Removing an existing expense by ID:
   delete(expense) {
      return this._authHttp
      .put(`/api/expenses/${expense._id}`, '', { headers:
      contentHeaders })
      .map((res: Response) => res.json())
   }
```

Filter expenses

As a start, we are going to implement expenses filtering. We just want to have all the necessary blocks in order to list the expenses properly. Basically, this component will be a simple form with three inputs: start date, end date, and category.

Using these simple criteria, we are going to filter our expenses on the backend. Remember, we need these in the `query` params so that the correct data is retrieved from the `expenses` collection.

This component will rely on the `CategoryService` and subscribe to the categories data stream. It will also push new values down the filter stream to notify each subscriber to filter the expenses.

Let's follow these steps to implement our component:

1. Import the modules:

```
import { Component, OnInit, OnDestroy } from 'angular2/core';
import { CategoryService, Category } from '../../category/index';
import { ExpenseService } from '../expense.service';
import { Expense } from '../expense.model';
```

2. Define our component's template:

```
@Component({
    selector: 'expense-filter',
    template: `
      <div>
        <form role="form">
          <div class="form-group">
            <label for="startDate">Start</label>
            <input type="date"
            [(ngModel)]="filter.startDate" class="form-
             control" id="startDate">
          </div>
          <div class="form-group">
            <label for="endDate">End</label>
            <input type="date" [(ngModel)]="filter.endDate"
             class="form-control" id="endDate">
          </div>
          <div class="form-group">
            <label for="category">Category</label>
            <select name="category"
            [(ngModel)]="filter.category">
              <option *ngFor="#category of categories"
              [value]="category._id">
```

```
          {{ category.name }}
        </option>
      </select>
    </div>
    <button type="submit" class="button"
    (click)="onFilter($event)">Filter</button>
    <button type="button" class="button"
    (click)="onReset($event)">Reset</button>
  </form>
</div>
```

```
})
```

3. Append the `ExpenseFilterComponent` class:

```
export class ExpenseFilterComponent implements OnInit, OnDestroy {
  public filter: any;
  public categories: Array<Category>;
  private _expenseService: ExpenseService;
  private _categoryService: CategoryService;

  constructor(
    expenseService: ExpenseService,
    categoryService: CategoryService
  ) {
    this._expenseService = expenseService;
    this._categoryService = categoryService;
  }
}
```

4. What will happen on initialization:

```
ngOnInit() {
  this.filter = {};
  this.categories = [];
  this._subscriptions = [];
  this._subscriptions.push(
    this._categoryService
    .categories
    .subscribe((categories) => {
      this.categories = categories;
    })
  );
}
```

5. When the component is destroyed:

```
ngOnDestroy() {
  this._subscriptions.forEach((subscription) => {
    subscription.unsubscribe();
  })
}
```

We have to unsubscribe from the data stream. We used a subscriptions list in order to hold all of them in one place and later on iterate over the subscriptions and dispose of them.

6. How we update the filter stream:

```
onFilter(event) {
  event.preventDefault();
  this._expenseService.filter.next(this.filter);
}
```

7. Resetting the filter:

```
onReset(event) {
  event.preventDefault();
  this.filter = {};
  this._expenseService.filter.next(this.filter);
}
```

When the component initializes, we subscribe to the `categories` data stream. If the user clicks on the `filter` button, we'll update the `filter` so that each subscriber can get the new filter criteria.

In order to reset everything, we can use the `reset` button and get back to the initial state. We can then notify all subscribers that we can retrieve all expenses once again.

Add a new expense

Because adding expenses will be a fairly well used feature, we are going to add the necessary logic into the same view and controller used to list expenses.

Remember that, in order to add a new expense, it must be included in a category. So we need a list of categories loaded into the component. This should be similar to what we did earlier in `ExpenseFilterComponent`.

Let's go through the following steps to implement the add expense functionality:

1. Create a new file, called `public/src/expense/components/expense-create.component.ts`.

2. Import the necessary modules:

```
import { Component, OnInit, OnDestroy } from 'angular2/core';
import { Router, RouterLink } from 'angular2/router';
import { CategoryService, Category } from '../../category/index';
import { ExpenseService } from '../expense.service';
import { Expense } from '../expense.model';
```

3. Append the annotation with the template:

```
@Component({
    selector: 'expense-create',
    directives: [
      RouterLink
    ],
    template: `
      <div>
        <form role="form" (submit)="onSubmit($event)">
          <div class="form-group">
            <label for="name">Name</label>
            <input type="text" [(ngModel)]="expense.name"
            class="form-control" id="name">
          </div>
          <div class="form-group">
            <label for="category">Category</label>
            <select name="category"
            [(ngModel)]="expense.category">
              <option *ngFor="#category of categories"
              [value]="category._id">
                {{ category.name }}
              </option>
            </select>
          </div>
          <div class="form-group">
            <label for="value">Amount</label>
            <input type="text" [(ngModel)]="expense.value"
            class="form-control" id="value">
          </div>
          <button type="submit" class="button">Add</button>
        </form>
      </div>
      `
})
```

4. Add the class:

```
export class ExpenseCreateComponent implements OnInit,
OnDestroy {
  public expense: Expense;
  public categories: Array<Category>;
  private _expenseService: ExpenseService;
  private _categoryService: CategoryService;
  private _subscriptions: Array<any>;

  constructor(
    expenseService: ExpenseService,
    categoryService: CategoryService
  ) {
    this._expenseService = expenseService;
    this._categoryService = categoryService;
  }
```

5. On initialization, we subscribe to the categories data stream and store the subscription so that we can dispose of it later on:

```
ngOnInit() {
  this.expense = new Expense();
  this.categories = [];
  this._subscriptions = [];
  this._subscriptions.push(
    this._categoryService
    .categories
    .subscribe((categories) => {
      this.categories = categories;
    })
  );
}
```

6. Unsubscribe when the component is destroyed:

```
ngOnDestroy() {
  this._subscriptions.forEach((subscription) => {
    subscription.unsubscribe();
  })
}
Create a new expense event:
  onSubmit(event) {
    event.preventDefault();

    this._expenseService
```

```
    .create(this.expense)
    .subscribe((expense) => {
      this._expenseService.expense.next(expense);
    }, err => console.error(err));
  }
```

List expenses

To display a list of expenses, we are going to query the server for the necessary information and create a table with the retrieved information. For this, we are going to go through the following steps:

1. Create the expenses controller file, called `public/src/expense/components/expense-list.component.ts`.

2. Import the service and other dependencies:

```
import { Component, OnInit, OnDestroy } from 'angular2/core';
import { ExpenseService } from '../expense.service';
import { Expense } from '../expense.model';
```

3. Define the expense table in the template:

```
@Component({
    selector: 'expense-list',
    directives: [],
    template: `
      <div class="jumbotron center-block">
        <h2>List of all your expenses</h2>
      </div>
      <div>
        <table>
          <thead>
            <tr>
              <th>Name</th>
              <th>Category</th>
              <th>Amount</th>
              <th>Date</th>
            </tr>
          </thead>
          <tbody>
            <tr *ngFor="#expense of expenses">
              <td>{{ expense.name }}</td>
              <td>{{ expense.category.name }}</td>
              <td>{{ expense.value }}</td>
              <td>{{ expense.createdAt | date }}</td>
```

```
        </tr>
      </tbody>
    </table>
  </div>
      `
})
```

4. Declare the `ExpenseListComponent` class:

```
export class ExpenseListComponent implements OnInit, OnDestroy {
  public expenses: Array<Expense>;
  private _expenseService: ExpenseService;
  private _subscriptions: Array<any>;

  constructor(expenseService: ExpenseService) {
    this._expenseService = expenseService;
  }
}
```

5. Subscribe to all data streams on initialization:

```
ngOnInit() {
  this.expenses = [];
  this._subscriptions = [];

  this._subscriptions.push(
    this._expenseService
    .expenses
    .subscribe((expenses) => {
      this.expenses = expenses;
    })
  );
  this._subscriptions.push(
    this._expenseService
    .expense
    .subscribe((expense) => {
      if (expense) {
        this.expenses.push(expense);
      }
    })
  );
  this._subscriptions.push(
    this._expenseService
    .filter
    .subscribe((filter) => {
      if (filter) {
```

```
                this._expenseService.getAll(filter);
            }
        })
    );
}
```

6. Dispose of subscriptions when the component is destroyed:

```
ngOnDestroy() {
    this._subscriptions.forEach(subscription => {
        subscription.unsubscribe();
    });
}
```

We mostly use streams of data to display information to the user. When a new expense is created, we just get notified and update the list of expenses. If a new set of expenses is loaded, the list is updated with the new values. We also subscribe to the change of filter so that we can fetch data from the backend using that filter.

Display balance

We want to display an accumulated value from the expenses amount. When we filter the expenses, the same filter should apply to the query for the balance. For example, we might want to display expenses from a specific category; in such a case, the balance should be displayed for expenses from that category.

Because we do all the heavy lifting on the backend and the result that we get through the API is nicely formatted, we only have to implement a few things to display the balance properly:

1. Create a new file for the component, called `public/src/expense/components/expense-balance.component.ts`.

2. Implement the base class:

```
import { Component, OnInit, OnDestroy } from 'angular2/core';
import { ExpenseService } from '../expense.service';

@Component({
    selector: 'expense-balance',
    directives: [],
    template: `
      <h2>
        Total balance: {{ info.balance }}
        <span>from {{ info.count }}</span>
      </h2>
      `
```

```
})
export class ExpenseBalanceComponent implements OnInit, OnDestroy
{
  public info: any;
  private _expenseService: ExpenseService;
  private _subscriptions: Array<any>;

  constructor(expenseService: ExpenseService) {
    this._expenseService = expenseService;
  }

  ngOnInit() {

  }

  ngOnDestroy() {

  }

}
Subscribe to the change of filter on init:
  ngOnInit() {
    this.info = {};
    this._subscriptions = [];

    this._subscriptions.push(
      this._expenseService
      .filter
      .subscribe((filter) => {
        if (filter) {
          this._getBalance(filter);
        }
      })
    );
  }
```

3. Retrieve the balance from the backend based on a criteria:

```
  ngOnDestroy() {
    this._subscriptions.forEach((subscription) => {
      subscription.unsubscribe();
    })
  }
```

4. Dispose of the subscriptions:

```
ngOnDestroy() {
  this._subscriptions.forEach((subscription) => {
    subscription.unsubscribe();
  })
}
```

Expenses component

Now that we have all the necessary components, we can implement our main expenses component, which will use all the previously implemented child components. We should create a new file, called `public/src/expense/components/expenses.component.ts`:

```
import { Component, OnInit } from 'angular2/core';
import { Router, RouterLink } from 'angular2/router';
import { ExpenseService } from '../expense.service';
import { CategoryService } from '../../category/index';
import { ExpenseCreateComponent } from './expense-create.component';
import { ExpenseListComponent } from './expense-list.component';
import { ExpenseBalanceComponent } from './expense-balance.component';
import { ExpenseFilterComponent } from './expense-filter.component';
@Component({
    selector: 'expenses',
    directives: [
      ExpenseCreateComponent,
      ExpenseListComponent,
      ExpenseBalanceComponent,
      ExpenseFilterComponent
    ],
    template: `
      <expense-balance></expense-balance>
      <expense-filter></expense-filter>
      <expense-create></expense-create>
      <expense-list></expense-list>
    `
})
export class ExpensesComponent implements OnInit {
  private _expenseService: ExpenseService;
  private _categoryService: CategoryService;

  constructor(
    expenseService: ExpenseService,
```

```
    categoryService: CategoryService
  ) {
    this._expenseService = expenseService;
    this._categoryService = categoryService;
  }

  ngOnInit() {
    this._categoryService.getAll().subscribe();
    this._expenseService.filter.next({});
  }
}
```

The component is fairly simple, but an interesting thing happens in the `ngOnInit()` method when we just get all the categories and set the filter to be an empty object. When this happens, all the rest of the components react to our actions and update accordingly.

With this, we have implemented the expenses module, which allows users to add expenses and see a list of all expenses. We left out some functionality, such as error handling, pagination, and other minor features, but you may improve this code as you desire.

Summary

This brings us to the end of a rather long chapter.

We learned to manipulate monetary data with JavaScript and Node.js and how to store it in MongoDB. We implemented a multiuser system in which users can easily register and sign in at any time.

We exposed most of our backend functionality through an API. We used a stateless authentication mechanism, granting access only by presenting a valid token.

In the next chapter, we are going to build a web page that is more public oriented, with different account types.

3
Job Board

In this chapter, we will build a job board application. Users will be able to create a profile and fill it with different types of information, such as job experience, projects they worked on, certifications, or even information related to education. Also, companies will be able to post job vacancies, for which users can apply.

Setting up the base application

In many cases, most developers will have already set up their own boilerplate code that they use for Node applications. One reason for this could be that there is more than one right way of doing things. Usually, your boilerplate will cover the initial functionalities of your application, such as user schema, sign-in, and registration.

Because we already have a solid base from the initial two chapters, we can reuse a lot of the code base. I've already put together a simple base application that we can start with. Just follow these steps to clone the project:

1. Clone the project from GitHub at `https://github.com/robert52/express-api-starter`.

2. Rename your boilerplate project to `jobboard`.

3. If you want, you can stop pointing to the initial Git repository by running the following command:

   ```
   git remote remove origin
   ```

4. Jump to your working directory:

   ```
   cd jobboard
   ```

5. Install all dependencies:

```
npm install
```

6. Create a development configuration file:

```
cp config/environments/example.js config/environments/development.
js
```

Your configuration file, `jobboard/config/environments/development.js`, should look similar to the following:

```
'use strict';

module.exports = {
  port: 3000,
  hostname: '127.0.0.1',
  baseUrl: 'http://localhost:3000',
  mongodb: {
    uri: 'mongodb://localhost/jobboard_dev_db'
  },
  app: {
    name: 'Job board'
  },
  serveStatic: true,
  session: {
    type: 'mongo',
    secret: 'someVeRyN1c3S#cr3tHer34U',
    resave: false,
    saveUninitialized: true
  }
};
```

Modifying the user backend

The user backend logic needs to change a little to fit our needs. For example, we need roles for our users. We will detail this when we talk about the user model. We must add authorization policies. We also need a profile for our users.

Modifying the user model

We need to make a few changes to the user model in order to support multiple account types and eventually assign roles to users. This will tell us whether the user is registered for a simple account, where they can define a profile with work experience, or to create a company that wants to post job opportunities.

The roles are going to define what actions the user can perform. For example, for a company we can have a company owner that has full control over the account, or we can have a user that is a member of that company and posts available job openings.

Let's modify the user schema from `jobboard/app/models/user.js` with the following:

```
var UserSchema = new Schema({
  email:  {
    type: String,
    required: true,
    unique: true
  },
  name: {
    type: String
  },
  password: {
    type: String,
    required: true,
    select: false
  },
  passwordSalt: {
    type: String,
    required: true,
    select: false
  },
  active: {
    type: Boolean,
    default: true
  },
  roles: {
    type: [
      {
        type: String,
        enum: ['user', 'member', 'owner']
      }
    ],
    default: ['user']
  },
  createdAt: {
    type: Date,
    default: Date.now
  }
});
```

We added an extra field to our user schema, more precisely `roles`, which holds what the user can do. You can add any type of role to the list of valid roles defined by the enum validation.

An authorization policy

In order to authorize our users to perform a requested action, we must check whether they can do it. For example, only a company owner can change the company information or add new members.

In the initial phase of a project, I like to keep my policies as simple and as separated as possible. In other words, I don't like to create something that manages everything, but instead use simple functions for my policies to check different scenarios.

Let's take a look at an authorization policy. Create a file called `jobboard/app/middlewares/authorization.js` and add the following:

```
module.exports.onlyMembers = authorizeOnlyToCompanyMembers;

function authorizeOnlyToCompanyMembers(req, res, next) {
  // check if user is member of company
  const isMember = req.resources.company.members.find((member) =>
{
    return member.toString() === req.user._id.toString();
  });

  if (!isMember) {
    return res.status(403).json({ message: 'Unauthorized' });
  }

  next();
}
```

This simple function will check whether the owner of a company is the authenticated user. The preceding policy can be used in the following way:

```
router.put(
  '/companies/:companyId',
  auth.ensured,
  companyCtrl.findById,
  authorize.onlyOwner,
  companyCtrl.update,
  response.toJSON('company')
);
```

The preceding code ensures that a user is authenticated, grabs a company by ID from MongoDB, and checks whether the policy that we implemented earlier authorizes the user to update the company or not.

The company backend module

We are going to implement our first backend module for our application. This module will handle everything that is related to a company.

The company model

We are going to add a simple but interesting functionality to the company model, which will create a so-called slug from the company name. A slug, in our context, is generated from the name of the company to be accepted as a valid URL. It will be used to reference the company in a meaningful way. For example, if we have a company named Your Awesome Company in the system, the resulting slug will be your-awesome-company.

To generate the slug, we'll implement a simple helper function so that we can reuse it later if necessary. Create a file called app/helpers/common.js and add the following lines of code:

```
'use strict';

module.exports.createSlug = createSlug;

function createSlug(value) {
    return value
    .toLowerCase()
    .replace(/[^\w\s]+/g,'')
    .trim()
    .replace(/[\s]+/g,'-');
}
```

Now that we have the helper function, we can define the company model and the necessary schema for it. Create a file called app/models/company.js and add the following code to it:

```
'use strict';

const mongoose = require('mongoose');
const commonHelper = require('../helpers/common');
const Schema = mongoose.Schema;
const ObjectId = Schema.ObjectId;
```

```
let CompanySchema = new Schema({
  name: {
    type: String,
    required: true
  },
  slug: {
    type: String
  },
  owner: {
    type: ObjectId,
    required: true,
    ref: 'User'
  },
  members: {
    type: Array,
    default: []
  },
  createdAt: {
    type: Date,
    default: Date.now
  }
});

CompanySchema.pre('save', (next) => {
  this.slug = commonHelper.createSlug(this.name);
  next();
});

// compile Company model
module.exports = mongoose.model('Company', CompanySchema);
```

We defined the company's mongoose schema and added a pre-save hook in order to generate the slug. In this pre-save hook, we are using the `createSlug()` method from the common helper. The middleware is running in series, so we need to call `next()` in order to signal the completion of the execution.

The company controller

Through the company controller, we are going to expose all of the business logic needed to manage companies. We are going to take the functionalities one by one and discuss them all.

Creating a company

After a user has successfully registered with a company type account, they can create a new company and become the owner. We'll implement a simple create functionality and mount it on an Express route. Let's create the controller file, called `jobboard/app/controllers/company.js`, with the following content:

```
'use strict';

const _ = require('lodash');
const mongoose = require('mongoose');
const Company = mongoose.model('Company');

module.exports.create = createCompany;

function createCompany(req, res, next) {
  let data = _.pick(req.body, ['name', 'country', 'address']);
  data.owner = req.user._id;
  data.members = [req.user._id];

  Company.create(data, (err, company) => {
    if (err) {
      return next(err);
    }

    res.status(201).json(company);
  });
}
```

Validation was added to the company model when we defined the schema. One thing we added is picking the necessary data for the create method. The owner of the company will by default be the user who creates it. Also, we add the user to the members list. After we have successfully created a new company, we return a JSON containing the information related to the freshly created company.

Getting a company by ID

Now that we can create a company, it's time to retrieve one by ID. We'll append the following code to the `app/controller/company.js` controller file:

```
module.exports.findById = findCompanyById;

function findCompanyById(req, res, next) {
  if (!ObjectId.isValid(id)) {
    res.status(404).send({ message: 'Not found.'});
```

```
    }

    Company.findById(req.params.companyId, (err, company) => {
      if (err) {
        return next(err);
      }

      req.resources.company = company;
      next();
    });
  }
```

In the preceding lines of code, we used the `findById` method provided by mongoose from the company model. Before we search for a company in MongoDB, we want to ensure that the ID is a valid `ObjectId`.

Another interesting thing we added here is a global `resource` object on the request. Instead of returning a JSON this time, we add it as a property to an object that we'll carry on the callback pipe of an Express route. This will come in handy when we want to reuse the same functionality in other situations.

Getting all companies

We also want to get all the companies stored in MongoDB. A simple query should be enough for this use case. We can add a simple filter by country and, by default, return up to 50 companies. The following code will implement this functionality:

```
module.exports.getAll = getAllCompanies;

function getAllCompanies(req, res, next) {
  const limit = +req.query.limit || 50;
  const skip = +req.query.skip || 0;
  let query = _.pick(req.query, ['country']);

  Company
  .find(query)
  .limit(limit)
  .skip(skip)
  .exec((err, companies) => {
    if (err) {
      return next(err);
    }

    req.resources.companies = companies;
    next();
  });
}
```

Updating a company

When updating a company, we only want some of the fields to be updated from the company model. We don't want to change the owner or add new members when updating a company. The change owner functionality will not be implemented; only add new member functionality will be, but it will be handled by a different module.

Append the following lines of code to `jobboard/app/controllers/company.js`:

```
module.exports.update = updateCompany;

function updateCompany(req, res, next) {
  let data = _.pick(req.body, ['name', 'country', 'address']);
  _.assign(req.resources.company, req.body);

  req.resources.company.save((err, updatedCompany) => {
    if (err) {
      return next(err);
    }

    req.resources.company = updatedCompany;
    next();
  });
}
```

Adding a company member

A company member will have limited access to the company. They can post vacant positions and screen profiles of users who applied for an available position. We are going to add this functionality to the same company controller, located at `jobboard/app/controllers/company.js`:

```
module.exports.addMember = addCompanyMember;

function addCompanyMember(req, res, next) {
  let includes = _.includes(req.resources.company.members, req.body.
member);

  if (includes) {
    return res.status(409).json({
      message: 'User is already a member of your company',
      type: 'already_member'
    });
  }
```

```
    req.resources.company.members.push(req.body.member);
    req.resources.company.save((err, updatedCompany) => {
      if (err) {
        return next(err);
      }

      req.resources.company = updatedCompany;
      next();
    });
}
```

Removing a company member

We also need to handle how we remove members from a company. We'll append this functionality after the add member logic:

```
module.exports.removeMember = removeCompanyMember;

function removeCompanyMember(req, res, next) {
  let includes = _.includes(req.resources.company.members, req.body.member);

  if (!includes) {
    return res.status(409).json({
      message: 'User is not a member of your company',
      type: 'not_member'
    });
  }

  _.pull(req.resources.company.members, req.body.member);
  req.resources.company.save((err, updatedCompany) => {
    if (err) {
      return next(err);
    }

    req.resources.company = updatedCompany;
    next();
  });
}
```

Company routes

Next, we are going to define all the necessary routes to access the previously implemented functionalities from the company controller. Let's create our router file, called `jobboard/app/routes/companies.js`, and add the following:

```
'use strict';

const express = require('express');
const router = express.Router();
const companyCtrl = require('../controllers/company');
const auth = require('../middlewares/authentication');
const authorize = require('../middlewares/authorization');
const response = require('../helpers/response');
```

Follow these steps to define the endpoints:

1. Create a company:

```
router.post(
  '/companies',
  auth.ensured,
  companyCtrl.checkUserCompany,
  companyCtrl.create
);
```

We make sure that the user has no company already in the system.

2. Get all companies:

```
router.get(
  '/companies',
  companyCtrl.getAll,
  response.toJSON('companies')
);
```

3. Get a company by ID:

```
router.get(
  '/companies/:companyId',
  companyCtrl.findById,
  response.toJSON('company')
);
```

4. Update a company:

```
router.put(
  '/companies/:companyId',
  auth.ensured,
```

```
    companyCtrl.findById,
    authorize.onlyOwner,
    companyCtrl.update,
    response.toJSON('company')
);
```

Updates to the company can only be made by the owner.

5. Add company members:

```
router.post(
    '/companies/:companyId/members',
    auth.ensured,
    companyCtrl.findById,
    authorize.onlyOwner,
    companyCtrl.addMember,
    response.toJSON('company')
);
```

Only the owner of the company can add a member.

6. Remove a company member:

```
router.delete(
    '/companies/:companyId/members',
    auth.ensured,
    companyCtrl.findById,
    authorize.onlyOwner,
    companyCtrl.removeMember,
    response.toJSON('company')
);
```

We are also restricting this action to only the company's owner.

7. Export the router:

```
module.exports = router;
```

The job backend module

This module will implement all of the backend logic related to jobs. We are going to define the necessary models and controllers. Only the most important parts of the module will be explained.

The job model

The job model will define a single entity from the `Jobs` collection and is going to handle the necessary validation when creating a new job. As for the company model, we are going to use a custom variable file for job industries and types. The two files will be located at `jobboard/config/variables/industries.js` and `jobboard/config/variables/jobtypes.js`, respectively. Both export a list of objects.

In order to implement the `job` model, we are going to follow these steps:

1. Create the model file, called `jobboard/app/models/job.js`.

2. Add the necessary dependencies:

```
const mongoose = require('mongoose');
const commonHelper = require('../helpers/common');
const Industries = require('../../config/variables/industries');
const Countries = require('../../config/variables/countries');
const Jobtypes = require('../../config/variables/jobtypes');
const Schema = mongoose.Schema;
const ObjectId = Schema.ObjectId;
```

3. Retrieve only a list of validation values from the variable files:

```
const indEnum = Industries.map(item => item.slug);
const cntEnum = Countries.map(item => item.code);
const jobEnum = Jobtypes.map(item => item.slug);
```

4. Define the Mongoose schema:

```
let JobSchema = new Schema({
  title: {
    type: String,
    required: true
  },
  slug: {
    type: String,
    required: true
  },
  summary: {
    type: String,
    maxlength: 250
  },
  description: {
    type: String
  },
  type: {
    type: String,
```

```
      required: true,
      enum: jobEnum
    },
    company: {
      type: ObjectId,
      required: true,
      ref: 'Company'
    },
    industry: {
      type: String,
      required: true,
      enum: indEnum
    },
    country: {
      type: String,
      required: true,
      enum: cntEnum
    },
    createdAt: {
      type: Date,
      default: Date.now
    }
  });
```

5. Add a pre-save hook:

```
JobSchema.pre('save', (next) => {
  this.slug = commonHelper.createSlug(this.name);
  next();
});
```

6. And finally compile the model:

```
module.exports = mongoose.model('Job', JobSchema);
```

Job controller

Our controller will integrate all the necessary business logic to handle all job CRUD operations. Afterwards, we can mount the exposed methods from the controller on specific routes, so that external clients can communicate with our backend.

Adding a new job for a company

When creating a new job, it should be created for a specific company, because a job represents a vacant position at a company. Because of this, we are going to need the company context when creating a job.

Create a controller file called `jobboard/app/controllers/job.js` and add the following create logic:

```
const MAX_LIMIT = 50;
const JOB_FIELDS = ['title', 'summary', 'description', 'type',
'industry', 'country'];

const _ = require('lodash');
const mongoose = require('mongoose');
const Job = mongoose.model('Job');
const ObjectId = mongoose.Types.ObjectId;

module.exports.create = createJob;

function createJob(req, res, next) {
  let data = _.pick(req.body, JOB_FIELDS);
  data.company = req.company._id;

  Job.create(data, (err, job) => {
    if (err) {
      return next(err);
    }

    res.status(201).json(job);
  });
}
```

As we said earlier, we need the company context to which we add the job. For that, we are going to add a get company by ID to our Express router request pipe. Don't worry; you 'll see this when we define our routes.

Finding a job by ID

We should also retrieve a job by ID from Mongo. A similar logic will be used here as was used in the company controller. Append the following code to the job controller:

```
module.exports.findById = findJobById;

function findJobById(req, res, next) {
  if (!ObjectId.isValid(id)) {
    res.status(404).send({ message: 'Not found.'});
  }

  Job.findById(req.params.jobId, (err, job) => {
    if (err) {
```

```
      return next(err);
    }

    res.resources.job = job;
    next();
  });
}
```

Getting all jobs

When retrieving all available jobs, there should be the possibility to apply some filters, such as type of job, to which industry it is assigned, or the country where the job is available. Beside these filters, we also need to get all available opening positions in a company. All of this logic will be implemented using the following code:

```
module.exports.getAll = getAllJobs;

function getAllJobs(req, res, next) {
  const limit = +req.query.limit || MAX_LIMIT;
  const skip = +req.query.skip || 0;
  let query = _.pick(req.query, ['type', 'country', 'industry']);

  if (req.params.companyId) {
    query.company = req.params.companyId;
  }

  Job
  .find(query)
  .limit(limit)
  .skip(skip)
  .exec((err, jobs) => {
    if (err) {
      return next(err);
    }

    req.resources.jobs = jobs;
    next();
  });
}
```

Updating a specific job

We also want to update a job posted by a company, but only by the company members. This restriction will be handled by middleware; for now, we are only going to implement the update functionality. Append the following code to `app/controllers/job.js`:

```
module.exports.update = updateJob;
function updateJob(req, res, next) {
  var data = _.pick(req.body, JOB_FIELDS);
  _.assign(req.resources.job, data);

  req.resources.job.save((err, updatedJob) => {
    if (err) {
      return next(err);
    }

    res.json(job);
  });
}
```

Job routes

For a start, we are going to create the route file, called `app/routes/jobs.js`, with the following code:

```
'use strict';

const express = require('express');
const router = express.Router();
const companyCtrl = require('../controllers/company');
const jobCtrl = require('../controllers/job');
const auth = require('../middlewares/authentication');
const authorize = require('../middlewares/authorization');
const response = require('../helpers/response');
```

Getting one and all jobs

Now that we have the base, we can start defining our routes. The first pair of routes will be available for public access, so no authentication is required to retrieve one or all jobs from the system. Append the following code:

```
router.get(
  '/jobs',
  jobCtrl.getAll,
```

```
      response.toJSON('jobs')
  );

  router.get(
    '/jobs/:jobId',
    jobCtrl.findById,
    response.toJSON('job')
  );
```

Bonus—getting the jobs of a certain company!

```
  router.get(
    '/companies/:companyId/jobs',
    jobCtrl.getAll,
    response.toJSON('jobs')
  );
```

Creating a route

Now, things get a little tricky when creating and updating a job. To create a job, append the following code:

```
  router.post(
    '/companies/:companyId/jobs',
    auth.ensured,
    companyCtrl.findById,
    authorize.onlyMembers,
    jobCtrl.create
  );
```

When creating a job, a user must be signed in and must be a member of the company under which he/she is posting the job. For this, we are retrieving a company from the database and using an authorization middleware. We compare and check whether the authenticated user is present in the members list. If everything goes well, the user can create a new job opening.

There are probably other ways to do all of this, but this solution can be beneficial because we request resources only when we need them. For example, we could have added the company object on the `req.user` object for each request if the user is authenticated, but that would have meant extra I/O for each request.

Updating a route

For the update functionality, append the following code:

```
router.put(
  '/companies/:companyId/jobs/:jobId',
  auth.ensured,
  companyCtrl.findById,
  authorize.onlyMembers,
  jobCtrl.findById,
  jobCtrl.update
);
```

As you can see, the same restriction principles are present here as for the create route. The only extra thing that we added is retrieving a job by ID, which is needed by the update functionality.

With this, we have finished implementing the backend logic for the `job` module.

Job applications

Each user can apply for a job, and a company would also like to know who has applied to their available job position. To handle such scenarios, we are going to store all applications for a job in a separate collection in MongoDB. We are going to describe the backend Node.js application logic.

The application model

The application model will be pretty simple and straightforward. We could have gone with an embedded data model. In other words, we could have saved all applications in the job entity. From my point of view, separate collections gives you more flexibility.

Let's create a file called `app/models/application.js` and add the following code to define the schema:

```
'use strict';

const mongoose = require('mongoose');
const Schema = mongoose.Schema;
const ObjectId = Schema.ObjectId;

let ApplicationSchema = new Schema({
  user: {
    type: ObjectId,
```

```
      required: true,
      ref: 'User'
    },
    status: {
      type: String,
      default: 'pending',
      enum: ['pending', 'accepted', 'processed']
    },
    job: {
      type: ObjectId,
      required: true,
      ref: 'Job'
    },
    createdAt: {
      type: Date,
      default: Date.now
    }
  });

  module.exports = mongoose.model('Application', ApplicationSchema);
```

Controller logic

The backend controller will handle all of the logic that is necessary to manage incoming requests on endpoints related to job applications. We will mount each exported method from the controller to a specific route.

Applying for a job

When a candidate applies for a job, we store a reference of that application in MongoDB. We defined the `Application` schema earlier. To persist an application, we are going to use the following backend logic in our `app/controllers/application.js` controller file:

```
  module.exports.create = createApplication;

  function createApplication(req, res, next) {
    Application.create({
      user: req.user._id,
      job: req.params.jobId
    }, (err, application) => {
      if (err) {
        return next(err);
```

```
    }

    res.status(201).json(application);
  });
}
```

Finding a given application by ID

We will need to find an application by its ID when updating and deleting it from the database. It's good to have a common logic to retrieve data; it can be reused in different scenarios. Append this code to the controller file:

```
module.exports.findById = findApplicationById;

function findApplicationById(req, res, next) {
  if (!ObjectId.isValid(id)) {
    res.status(404).send({ message: 'Not found.'});
  }

  Application.findById(req.params.applicationId, (err, application) =>
{
    if (err) {
      return next(err);
    }

    res.resources.application = application;
    next();
  });
}
```

Once again, we are using the `resource` property on the request object to populate it with the result from the query.

Getting all job applications

Each company will want to see all the applications for the jobs they listed. In order to provide that functionality, the job controller must return a list of applications, with the ability to filter them by status. The following code will implement this functionality:

```
module.exports.getAll = getAllApplications;

function getAllApplications(req, res, next) {
  const limit = +req.query.limit || 50;
  const skip = +req.query.skip || 0;
```

```
let query = {
  job: req.params.jobId
};

if (req.query.status) {
  query.status = req.query.status;
}

Application
.find(query)
.limit(limit)
.skip(offset)
.exec((err, applications) => {
  if (err) {
    return next(err);
  }

  req.resources.applications = applications;
  next();
});
}
```

Updating an application

In order to change the status of an application, we must update it with the specific status value. The `update` method from the controller will handle this use case. Append the update logic to the controller file:

```
module.exports.update = updateApplication;

function updateApplication(req, res, next) {
  req.resources.application.status = req.body.status;

  req.resources.application.save((err, updatedApplication) => {
    if (err) {
      return next(err);
    }

    res.json(updatedApplication);
  });
}
```

Removing an application from a job

A candidate should have the ability to remove an application for a vacant job. We will not let anybody else remove the application except the candidate. This restriction will be handled by middleware. The backend logic for deletion should look similar to this:

```
module.exports.remove = removeApplication;

function removeApplication(req, res, next) {
  req.resources.application.remove((err) => {
    if (err) {
      return next(err);
    }

    res.json(req.resources.application);
  });
}
```

Now, we are not going to talk about how to add the routes. You can find all the available routes in the final source code of the application.

Creating a new company

After a successful sign-up, a new company can be created by the user. We have already implemented the backend logic using Node.js, and we should be able to store the company in the companies collection in MongoDB.

The company service

Although we are discussing the create company functionality, we are going to add all the endpoints to the service:

1. Let's create the service file, called `jobboard/public/src/company/company.service.ts`.

2. Import the necessary dependencies:
   ```
   import { Injectable } from 'angular2/core';
   import { Http, Response, Headers } from 'angular2/http';
   import { AuthHttp } from '../auth/index';
   import { contentHeaders } from '../common/index';
   import { Company } from './company.model';
   ```

3. Create the `service` class:

```
@Injectable()
export class CompanyService {
  private _http: Http;
  private _authHttp: AuthHttp;
}
```

4. Add the `constructor`:

```
constructor(http: Http, authHttp: AuthHttp) {
  this._http = http;
  this._authHttp = authHttp;
}
```

5. Append the `create` method:

```
create(company) {
  let body = JSON.stringify(company);

  return this._authHttp
  .post('/api/companies', body, { headers: contentHeaders })
  .map((res: Response) => res.json())
}
```

6. Define the `findByid()` function:

```
findById(id) {
  return this._http
  .get(`/api/companies/${id}`, { headers: contentHeaders
  })
  .map((res: Response) => res.json())
}
```

7. Retrieve all companies from the backend:

```
getAll() {
  return this._http
  .get('/api/companies', { headers: contentHeaders })
  .map((res: Response) => res.json())
}
```

8. Update a company:

```
update(company) {
  let body = JSON.stringify(company);

  return this._authHttp
  .put(`/api/companies/${company._id}`, body, { headers:
  contentHeaders })
  .map((res: Response) => res.json())
}
```

Creating a company component

Now that we have a fully functioning service that communicates with the backend, we can start implementing our components. The create company component will be the first one.

Let's create a new file, called `public/src/company/components/company-create.component.ts`, and add the component's class and dependencies:

```
import { Component, OnInit } from 'angular2/core';
import { Router, RouterLink } from 'angular2/router';
import { CompanyService } from '../company.service';
import { Company } from '../company.model';
export class CompanyCreateComponent implements OnInit {
  public company: Company;
  private _router: Router;
  private _companyService: CompanyService;

  constructor(companyService: CompanyService, router: Router) {
    this._router = router;
    this._companyService = companyService;
  }

  ngOnInit() {
    this.company = new Company();
  }
}
```

The `Component` annotation should be similar to this:

```
@Component({
    selector: 'company-create',
    directives: [
      RouterLink
    ],
    template: `
      <div class="login jumbotron center-block">
        <h1>Register</h1>
      </div>
      <div>
        <form role="form" (submit)="onSubmit($event)">
          <div class="form-group">
            <label for="name">Company name</label>
            <input type="text" [(ngModel)]="company.name"
            class="form-control" id="name">
          </div>
```

```
        <div class="form-group">
          <label for="email">Country</label>
          <input type="text" [(ngModel)]="company.country"
          class="form-control" id="country">
        </div>
        <div class="form-group">
          <label for="email">Address</label>
          <input type="text" [(ngModel)]="company.address"
          class="form-control" id="address">
        </div>
        <div class="form-group">
          <label for="password">Summary</label>
          <textarea [(ngModel)]="company.summary" class="form-
          control" id="summary"></textarea>
        </div>
        <button type="submit" class="button">Submit</button>
      </form>
    </div>
`
  })
```

To bind the company data properties to each form input control, we used the ngModel two-way data binding. When submitting the form, the onSubmit() method is executed. Let's add the preceding method:

```
onSubmit(event) {
  event.preventDefault();

  this._companyService
  .create(this.company)
  .subscribe((company) => {
    if (company) {
      this.goToCompany(company._id, company.slug);
    }
  }, err => console.error(err));
}
```

This will try to create a new company through our service. If a company is successfully created, we navigate to the company details page. The goToCompany() method is described as follows:

```
goToCompany(id, slug) {
  this._router.navigate(['CompanyDetail', { id: id, slug:
  slug}]);
}
```

We use the router to navigate to the company's details. The router will construct the desired path needed for the navigation. Error handling is not covered. You can also add validation as an improvement.

Displaying companies

We have had a good start for the company module from earlier, when we implemented the "add new company" functionality. So, we can jump in and create and implement the rest of the files to display all companies.

In order to display a list of companies in our application, we create a new component file, called `public/src/company/components/company-list.component.ts`:

```
import { Component, OnInit } from 'angular2/core';
import { Router, RouterLink } from 'angular2/router';
import { CompanyService } from '../company.service';
import { Company } from '../company.model';

@Component({})
export class CompanyListComponent implements OnInit {
  public companies: Array<Company>;
  private _router: Router;
  private _companyService: CompanyService;

  constructor(companyService: CompanyService, router: Router) {
    this._router = router;
    this._companyService = companyService;
  }

  ngOnInit() {
    this._companyService
    .getAll()
    .subscribe((companies) => {
      this.companies = companies;
    });
  }
}
```

As you can see, we have a pretty basic component. On initialization, the companies are retrieved from the backend using `CompanyService`. We subscribed directly to the returned `Observable` to update the component's `companies` property.

Now all that is left is to add the `Component` annotation:

```
@Component({
    selector: 'company-list',
    directives: [
      RouterLink
    ],
    template: `
      <div class="jumbotron center-block">
        <h2>Companies list</h2>
        <p class="lead">Here you can find all the registered
        companies.</p>
      </div>
      <div>
      <div *ngFor="#company of companies" class="col col-25">
        <img src="http://placehold.it/208x140?
        text=product+image&txtsize=18"/>
        <h3>
          <a href="#"
            [routerLink]="['CompanyDetail', { id: company._id,
            slug: company.slug }]">
            {{ company.name }}
          </a>
          </h3>
      </div>
      </div>
      `
})
```

Using `ngFor`, we iterate over the companies data and display it accordingly. You can display additional data, but for now, the company name should be enough. Also, when clicking on the name, we use `RouterLink` to navigate to the desired company.

The job module

We are going to continue with the `job` module. The reason for this is that the `company` module uses a component from the `job` module in order to display a list of available jobs for a company.

The job service

The job service will handle communication with the backend, mostly for CRUD operations. We are going to create an Angular factory to accomplish this. Create a new file called `public/app/job/job.service.js` and follow these steps:

1. Define the base structure and exposed methods:

```
import { Injectable } from 'angular2/core';
import { Http, Response, Headers } from 'angular2/http';
import { AuthHttp } from '../auth/index';
import { contentHeaders, serializeQuery } from '../common/index';
import { Job } from './job.model';

@Injectable()
export class JobService {
  private _http: Http;
  private _authHttp: AuthHttp;

  constructor(http: Http, authHttp: AuthHttp) {
    this._http = http;
    this._authHttp = authHttp;
  }
}
```

2. Implement the `create` job method:

```
create(job) {
  let body = JSON.stringify(job);

  return this._authHttp
  .post('/api/jobs', body, { headers: contentHeaders })
  .map((res: Response) => res.json())
}
```

We are using the `AuthHttp` service because creating endpoints requires an authenticated user.

3. Add the code for finding a job by ID:

```
findById(id) {
  return this._http
  .get(`/api/jobs/${id}`, { headers: contentHeaders })
  .map((res: Response) => res.json())
}
```

4. Query all jobs from the backend:

```
getAll(criteria) {
  let query = '';
  let str = serializeQuery(criteria);

  if (str) {
    query = `?${str}`;
  }

  return this._http
    .get(`/api/jobs${query}`, { headers: contentHeaders })
    .map((res: Response) => res.json())
}
```

The `getAll()` method accepts a criteria as a parameter to filter the jobs. On some occasions, we only want to get a list of jobs for a given company. We construct our query strings using the `serializeQuery` function, which can be found under `public/src/common/query.ts` with the following content:

```
export function serializeQuery(query): string {
  var chunks = [];
  for(var key in query)
    if (query.hasOwnProperty(key)) {
      let k = encodeURIComponent(key);
      let v = encodeURIComponent(query[key]);
      chunks.push(`${k}=${v}`);
    }
  return chunks.join('&');
}
```

The job base component

We are going to build a base component for our `job` module. It will hold all the necessary `RouteConfig` to display the child components. Create a new file, called `public/src/job/components/job-base.component.ts`:

```
import { Component } from 'angular2/core';
import { RouterOutlet, RouteConfig } from 'angular2/router';
import { JobService } from '../job.service';
import { JobListComponent } from './job-list.component';
import { JobDetailComponent } from './job-detail.component';
import { JobCreateComponent } from './job-create.component';

@RouteConfig([
```

```
    { path: '/', as: 'JobList', component: JobListComponent,
    useAsDefault: true },
    { path: '/:id/:slug', as: 'JobDetail', component:
    JobDetailComponent },
    { path: '/create', as: 'JobCreate', component:
    JobCreateComponent }
])
@Component({
    selector: 'job-base',
    directives: [
      RouterOutlet
    ],
    template: `
      <router-outlet></router-outlet>
    `
})
export class JobBaseComponent {
  constructor() {}
}
```

We mounted each child component to a specific path. We are going to use the same
URL structure for `JobDetail` as for `CompanyDetail`. I think it has a nice, clean look
and feel with the use of the slug in the URL.

Next, we are going to define the components one by one.

The jobs component

The `jobs` component will be reused across the application. Its purpose will be to
display a list of jobs based on a few factors.

Create a file called `public/src/job/components/jobs.component.ts` with the
following content:

```
import { Component, OnInit } from 'angular2/core';
import { Router, RouterLink } from 'angular2/router';
import { JobService } from '../job.service';
import { Job } from '../job.model';

export class JobsComponent implements OnInit {
  public company: any;
  public jobs: Array<Job>;
  private _jobsService: JobService;
  private _router: Router;
```

```
    constructor(jobsService: JobService, router: Router) {
      this._router = router;
      this._jobsService = jobsService;
    }
  }
```

Add the ngOnInit method to retrieve the necessary data from the Express application, as follows:

```
  ngOnInit() {
    let query: any = {};

    if (this.company) {
      query.company = this.company;
    }

    this._jobsService
    .getAll(query)
    .subscribe((jobs) => {
      this.jobs = jobs;
    });
  }
```

Our component has a company property, which will be used when we want to query all jobs related to a company. Also, don't forget to add the following annotation:

```
@Component({
    selector: 'jobs',
    inputs: ['company'],
    directives: [RouterLink],
    template: `
      <div *ngFor="#job of jobs" class="col">
        <h3>
          <a href="#"
            [routerLink]="['/Jobs', 'JobDetail', { id: job._id,
            slug: job.slug }]">
            {{ job.title }}
          </a>
        </h3>
        <p>
          <a href="#"
            [routerLink]="['/Companies', 'CompanyDetail', { id:
            job.company._id, slug: job.company.slug }]">
            {{ job.company.name }}
          </a>
          <span>·</span>
```

```
      <span>{{ job.industry }}</span>
      <span>·</span>
      <span>{{ job.type }}</span>
      <span>·</span>
      <span>{{ job.createdAt }}</span>
    </p>
    <p>{{ job.summary }}</p>
  </div>
    `
})
```

Our component also has an input data bound property called company. This will reference a company's ID. Also create a link to the company's page.

The job list component

In this component, we can use the previously built jobs component in order to list all the available openings from the system. As all of the main logic can be found in the jobs component, we just need to include it.

Create a new file called public/src/job/componets/job-list.component.ts and add this code:

```
import { Component } from 'angular2/core';
import { JobService } from '../job.service';
import { Job } from '../job.model';
import { JobsComponent } from './jobs.component';

@Component({
    selector: 'job-list',
    directives: [JobsComponent],
    template: `
      <div class="login jumbotron center-block">
        <h2>Job openings</h2>
        <p class="lead">Take a look, maybe you will find something
        for you.</p>
      </div>
      <div>
        <jobs></jobs>
      </div>
    `
})
export class JobListComponent {
  public jobs: Array<Job>;
```

```
    private _jobsService: JobService;

    constructor(jobsService: JobService) {
      this._jobsService = jobsService;
    }
}
```

Job details

The job details page is going to display all the necessary information about the required job for the user. We are going to use the same user-friendly route as we did in the company details. Luckily, we already have a service to communicate with the backend API.

Create a file called public/src/job/components/job-detail.component.ts and add the following code:

```
import { Component, OnInit } from 'angular2/core';
import { RouteParams, RouterLink } from 'angular2/router';
import { JobService } from '../job.service';
import { Job } from '../job.model';

@Component({})
export class JobDetailComponent implements OnInit {
  public job: Job;
  private _routeParams: RouteParams;
  private _jobService: JobService;

  constructor(jobService: JobService, routerParams: RouteParams) {
    this._routeParams = routerParams;
    this._jobService = jobService;
  }

  ngOnInit() {
    const id: string = this._routeParams.get('id');
    this.job = new Job();
    this._jobService
    .findById(id)
    .subscribe((job) => {
      this.job = job;
    });
  }
}
```

The logic inside the component is pretty much the same as in
`CompanyDetailComponent`. Using the `id` router parameter, we fetch the
desired job from the backend.

The `Component` annotation should contain the necessary templates and
directives used:

```
@Component({
    selector: 'job-detail',
    directives: [
      RouterLink
    ],
    template: `
      <div class="job-header">
        <div class="col content">
          <p>Added on: {{ job.createdAt }}</p>
          <h2>{{ job.name }}</h2>
          <div class="job-description">
            <h4>Description</h4>
            <div>{{ job.description }}</div>
          </div>
        </div>
        <div class="sidebar">
          <h4>Country</h4>
          <p>{{ job.country }}</p>
          <h4>Industry</h4>
          <p>{{ job.industry }}</p>
          <h4>Job type</h4>
          <p>{{ job.type }}</p>
        </div>
      </div>
      `
})
```

Adding new jobs

Now that we can list all the available jobs, we can implement the add new
job functionality. This will be similar to the one that we implemented in the
company module.

It probably feels like you are doing the same thing over and over again, but the
purpose of the chapter is to create an application focused on CRUD operations.
Many enterprise-graded apps have tremendous modules implementing those
operations. So don't worry! We are going to have chapters in which we experiment
with different technologies and architectures.

Let's continue and create a file called `public/src/job/components/job-create.component.ts`:

```typescript
import { Component, OnInit } from 'angular2/core';
import { Router, RouterLink } from 'angular2/router';
import { JobService } from '../job.service';
import { Job } from '../job.model';

export class JobCreateComponent implements OnInit {
  public job: Job;
  private _router: Router;
  private _jobService: JobService;

  constructor(jobService: JobService, router: Router) {
    this._router = router;
    this._jobService = jobService;
  }

  ngOnInit() {
    this.job = new Job();
  }

  onSubmit(event) {
    event.preventDefault();

    this._jobService
    .create(this.job)
    .subscribe((job) => {
      if (job) {
        this.goToJob(job._id, job.slug);
      }
    });
  }

  goToJob(id, slug) {
    this._router.navigate(['JobDetail', { id: id, slug: slug}]);
  }
}
```

Prepend the following annotation to the `Component` class:

```typescript
@Component({
    selector: 'job-create',
    directives: [
      RouterLink
```

```
    ],
    template: `
      <div class="jumbotron center-block">
        <h1>Post a new job</h1>
        <p>We are happy to see that you are growing.</p>
      </div>
      <div>
        <form role="form" (submit)="onSubmit($event)">
          <div class="form-group">
            <label for="title">Job title</label>
            <input type="text" [(ngModel)]="job.title"
            class="form-control" id="title">
          </div>
          <div class="form-group">
            <label for="industry">Industry</label>
            <input type="text" [(ngModel)]="job.industry"
            class="form-control" id="industry">
          </div>
          <div class="form-group">
            <label for="country">Country</label>
            <input type="text" [(ngModel)]="job.country"
            class="form-control" id="country">
          </div>
          <div class="form-group">
            <label for="type">Job type</label>
            <input type="text" [(ngModel)]="job.type" class="form-
            control" id="type">
          </div>
          <div class="form-group">
            <label for="summary">Summary</label>
            <textarea [(ngModel)]="job.summary" class="form-
            control" id="summary"></textarea>
          </div>
          <div class="form-group">
            <label for="description">Description</label>
            <textarea [(ngModel)]="job.description" class="form-
            control" id="description"></textarea>
          </div>
          <button type="submit" class="button">Create a
          job</button>
        </form>
      </div>
    `

})
```

Company details

Probably, you have already observed that earlier, when we listed all the companies, we created some nice URLs. We are going to use that path to display all the details of a company together with the available jobs.

The URL also contains the company slug, which is a URL-friendly representation of the company name. It has no benefit for the user, it's just URL sugar we added to display the name of the company nicely. Only the company ID is used when querying the backend for data.

As we have all the necessary components and services, we can implement our details component by following these steps:

1. Create a new file, called `public/src/company/components/company-detail.component.ts`.

2. Add the necessary dependencies:

    ```
    import { Component, OnInit } from 'angular2/core';
    import { RouteParams, RouterLink } from 'angular2/router';
    import { CompanyService } from '../company.service';
    import { Company } from '../company.model';
    import { JobsComponent } from '../../job/index';
    ```

3. Append the `Component` annotation:

    ```
    @Component({
        selector: 'company-detail',
        directives: [
          JobsComponent,
          RouterLink
        ],
        template: `
          <div class="company-header">
            <h2>{{ company.name }}</h2>
            <p>
              <span>{{ company.country }}</span>
              <span>·</span>
              <span>{{ company.address }}</span>
            </p>
          </div>
          <div class="company-description">
            <h4>Description</h4>
          </div>
          <div class="company-job-list">
    ```

```
        <jobs [company]=company._id></jobs>
    </div>
    `
})
```

In the template, we are using the `jobs` component that we implemented earlier to list all the available jobs of a company, by sending the company's `id`.

4. Declare the `component` class:

```
export class CompanyDetailComponent implements OnInit {
  public company: Company;
  private _routeParams: RouteParams;
  private _companyService: CompanyService;

  constructor(companyService: CompanyService, routerParams:
  RouteParams) {
    this._routeParams = routerParams;
    this._companyService = companyService;
  }

  ngOnInit() {
    const id: string = this._routeParams.get('id');
    this.company = new Company();
    this._companyService
    .findById(id)
    .subscribe((company) => {
      this.company = company;
    });
  }
}
```

User profile

In our system, we have no account type. We only define roles for users, such as a company owner, a member of a company, or a candidate. So, any registered user can fill out their profile with different information.

Remember that we defined a `profile` property on the User schema. It will hold all the information regarding a user's work experience, education, or any other relevant data that the user wants to add.

The user's profile will be constructed using blocks. Each block will group a certain domain, such as experience, allowing the user to add new entries to each block.

Profile backend

The backend logic for managing profile data has not been implemented yet. I wanted to give a feeling that we are extending our existing backend with new functionalities. So, we are going to start by creating a new controller file, `app/controllers/profile.js`. Then add the following code:

```
'use strict';

const _ = require('lodash');
const mongoose = require('mongoose');
const User = mongoose.model('User');
const ProfileBlock = mongoose.model('ProfileBlock');
const ObjectId = mongoose.Types.ObjectId;

module.exports.getProfile = getUserProfile;
module.exports.createProfileBlock = createUserProfileBlock;
module.exports.updateProfile = updateUserProfile;
```

We'll export three functions to manage profile data. Let's define them by following these steps:

1. Get the current authenticated user and the whole profile data:

```
function getUserProfile(req, res, next) {
  User
  .findById(req.user._id)
  .select('+profile')
  .exec((err, user) => {
    if (err) {
      return next(err);
    }

    req.resources.user = user;
    next();
  });
}
```

2. Create a new profile block for the user:

```
function createUserProfileBlock(req, res, next) {
  if (!req.body.title) {
    return res.status(400).json({ message: 'Block title is
required' });
  }

  var block = new ProfileBlock(req.body);
```

```
    req.resources.user.profile.push(block);

    req.resources.user.save((err, updatedProfile) => {
      if (err) {
        return next(err);
      }

      req.resources.block = block;
      next();
    });
  }
```

We are using a custom schema for a `ProfileBlock` schema to create a new profile block and push it to the user's profile data. We are going to get back to our schema and define it.

3. Update an existing profile block:

```
function updateUserProfile(req, res, next) {
  // same as calling user.profile.id(blockId)
  // var block =
  req.resources.user.profile.find(function(b) {
  //    return b._id.toString() === req.params.blockId;
  // });

  let block =
  req.resources.user.profile.id(req.params.blockId);

  if (!block) {
    return res.status(404).json({ message: '404 not
    found.'});
  }

  if (!block.title) {
    return res.status(400).json({ message: 'Block title is
    required' });
  }

  let data = _.pick(req.body, ['title', 'data']);
  _.assign(block, data);

  req.resources.user.save((err, updatedProfile) => {
    if (err) {
      return next(err);
    }
```

```
        req.resources.block = block;
        next();
      });
    }
```

When updating a profile block, we need to search for that specific block and update it with the new data. After that, the changes will be saved and persisted in MongoDB.

Let's take a look at our `ProfileBlock` schema, which is found under app/models/ profile-block.js:

```
'use strict';

const mongoose = require('mongoose');
const commonHelper = require('../helpers/common');
const Schema = mongoose.Schema;

let ProfileBlock = new Schema({
  title: {
    type: String,
    required: true
  },
  slug: String,
  data: []
});

ProfileBlock.pre('save', function(next) {
  this.slug = commonHelper.createSlug(this.title);
  next();
});

module.exports = mongoose.model('ProfileBlock', ProfileBlock);
```

The preceding document schema will be embedded inside the user's document `profile` property. The `data` property will hold all the profile blocks, containing their own data.

In order to expose the functionalities we implemented earlier, let's create a profile routes file, called app/routes/profile.js:

```
'use strict';

const express = require('express');
const router = express.Router();
const profileCtrl = require('../controllers/profile');
```

```
const auth = require('../middlewares/authentication');
const response = require('../helpers/response');

router.get(
  '/profile',
  auth.ensured,
  profileCtrl.getProfile,
  response.toJSON('user')
);

router.post(
  '/profile/blocks',
  auth.ensured,
  profileCtrl.getProfile,
  profileCtrl.createProfileBlock,
  response.toJSON('block')
);

router.put(
  '/profile/blocks/:blockId',
  auth.ensured,
  profileCtrl.getProfile,
  profileCtrl.updateProfile,
  response.toJSON('block')
);

module.exports = router;
```

Synchronizing profile data

In order to store and retrieve profile data related to a user, we are going to create an Angular service that will handle the communication with the backend.

The frontend `profile` module will be inside the `user` module, as they are related, and we can group them by their domain context. Create a file called `public/src/user/profile/profile.service.ts` and add the following baseline code:

```
import { Injectable } from 'angular2/core';
import { Http, Response, Headers } from 'angular2/http';
import { Subject } from 'rxjs/Subject';
import { BehaviorSubject } from 'rxjs/Subject/BehaviorSubject';
import { Observable } from 'rxjs/Observable';
import { contentHeaders } from '../../common/index';
import { AuthHttp } from '../../auth/index';
```

```
import { Block } from './block.model';

@Injectable()
export class ProfileService {
  public user: Subject<any> = new BehaviorSubject<any>({});
  public profile: Subject<Array<any>> = new BehaviorSubject<Array<a
ny>>([]);
  private _http: Http;
  private _authHttp: AuthHttp;
  private _dataStore: { profile: Array<Block> };
}
```

This time, we are going to use `Observables` and `Subject` for the data flow. They are more suitable in this case because there are many moving parts. The profile data can be updated from many different sources, and the changes need to travel to all subscribers.

To have a local copy of the data, we are going to use a data store in the service. Now let's implement each method one by one:

1. Add a class constructor:

   ```
   constructor(http: Http, authHttp: AuthHttp) {
     this._http = http;
     this._authHttp = authHttp;
     this._dataStore = { profile: [] };
     this.profile.subscribe((profile) => {
       this._dataStore.profile = profile;
     });
   }
   ```

2. Get the profile information about the user:

   ```
   public getProfile() {
     this._authHttp
     .get('/api/profile', { headers: contentHeaders })
     .map((res: Response) => res.json())
     .subscribe((user: any) => {
       this.user.next(user);
       this.profile.next(user.profile);
     });
   }
   ```

3. Create a new profile block:

   ```
   public createProfileBlock(block) {
     let body = JSON.stringify(block);
   ```

```
      this._authHttp
      .post('/api/profile/blocks', body, { headers:
      contentHeaders })
      .map((res: Response) => res.json())
      .subscribe((block: any) => {
        this._dataStore.profile.push(block);
        this.profile.next(this._dataStore.profile);
      }, err => console.error(err));
    }
```

4. Update an existing profile block:

```
    public updateProfileBlock(block) {
      if (!block._id) {
        this.createProfileBlock(block);
      } else {
        let body = JSON.stringify(block);

        this._authHttp
        .put(`/api/profile/blocks/${block._id}`, body, {
        headers: contentHeaders })
        .map((res: Response) => res.json())
        .subscribe((block: any) => {
          this.updateLocalBlock(block);
        }, err => console.error(err));
      }
    }
```

When updating a profile block, we check whether an ID exists for that block. If not, it means that we want to create a new block and so we'll use createProfileBlock().

5. Update a block from the local store:

```
    private updateLocalBlock(data) {
      this._dataStore.profile.forEach((block) => {
        if (block._id === data._id) {
          block = data;
        }
      });

      this.profile.next(this._dataStore.profile);
    }
```

Editing profile data

To edit the user's profile, we are going to create a separate component. The user profile is built using blocks. For this reason, we should create another component just for the profile block.

Follow these steps to implement `ProfileEditComponent`:

1. Add the necessary dependencies:

```
import { Component, OnInit } from 'angular2/core';
import { ProfileBlockComponent } from './profile-block.component';
import { ProfileService } from '../profile.service';
import { Block } from '../block.model';
```

2. Place the `Component` annotation:

```
@Component({
    selector: 'profile-edit',
    directives: [ProfileBlockComponent],
    template: `
    <section>

      <div class="jumbotron">
        <h2>Hi! {{user.name}}</h2>
        <p class="lead">Your public e-mail is
        <span>{{user.email}}</span> <br> and this is your
        profile</p>
      </div>

      <div class="row">
        <div class="col-md-12">
          <div class="profile-block" *ngFor="#block of
          profile">
            <profile-block [block]="block"></profile-block>
          </div>
        </div>
      </div>

      <form class="form-horizontal col-md-12">
        <div class="form-group">
          <div class="col-md-12">
            <input [(ngModel)]="newBlock.title"
            type="text" class="form-control"
            placeholder="Block title">
          </div>
        </div>
        <div class="form-group">
```

```
                <div class="col-md-12">
                    <button (click)="onClick($event)"
                    class="button">New block</button>
                </div>
            </div>
        </form>
    </div>

    </section>
                `
})
```

3. Add the properties and constructor:

```
export class ProfileEditComponent implements OnInit {
    public user: any;
    public profile: any;
    public newBlock: Block;
    private _profileService: ProfileService;

    constructor(profileService: ProfileService) {
        this._profileService = profileService;
    }
}
```

4. Append the ngOnInit() method:

```
ngOnInit() {
    this.user = {};
    this.newBlock = new Block();
    this._profileService.user.subscribe((user) => {
        this.user = user;
    });
    this._profileService.profile.subscribe((profile) => {
        this.profile = profile;
    });
    this._profileService.getProfile();
}
```

5. Define how the user can add new blocks:

```
onClick(event) {
    event.preventDefault();
    let profile = this.profile.slice(0);   // clone the
    profile
    let block = Object.assign({}, this.newBlock); // clone
    the new block
```

```
        profile.push(block);
        this._profileService.profile.next(profile);
        this.newBlock = new Block();
    }
```

We'll subscribe to the profile data stream and display all the blocks. To display the profile blocks, we use a separate component. This component gets the block as a data input.

When the user adds a new block, we push the freshly created block to the profile. This is fairly easy to do because we are using a `Subject` from RxJS. In this way, we can synchronize our profile data with all our components.

The profile block component

Because the profile is made out of blocks, we can create a separate component that is reusable and encapsulates all of the block's functionality. Let's create our component, as follows:

1. Create a new file, called `public/src/user/profile/components/profile-block.component.ts`.

2. Add the necessary dependencies:

   ```
   import { Component, OnInit } from 'angular2/core';
   import { ProfileService } from '../profile.service';
   import { Block } from '../block.model';
   import { Entry } from '../entry.model';
   ```

3. Configure the `Component` annotation:

   ```
   @Component({
       selector: 'profile-block',
       inputs: ['block'],
       template: `
         <div class="panel panel-default">
           <div class="panel-heading">
             <h3 class="panel-title">{{block.title}}</h3>
           </div>
           <div class="panel-body">
             <div class="profile-block-entries">
               <div *ngFor="#entry of block.data">
                 <div class="form-group">
                   <label>Title</label>
                   <input class="form-control" type="text"
                     (keydown.enter)="onEnter($event)"
                     [(ngModel)]="entry.title">
   ```

```
      </div>
      <div class="form-group">
        <label>Sub title</label>
        <input class="form-control" type="text"
          (keydown.enter)="onEnter($event)"
          [(ngModel)]="entry.subTitle">
      </div>
      <div class="form-group">
        <label>Description</label>
        <textarea class="form-control"
          (keydown.enter)="onEnter($event)"
          [(ngModel)]="entry.description">
        </textarea>
      </div>
      <hr>
    </div>
  </div>
  <button class="btn btn-default btn-xs btn-block"
  (click)="addEntry($event)">
    <i class="glyphicon glyphicon-plus"></i> Add
    new entry
  </button>
    </div>
  </div>
  `
})
```

4. Define the `ProfileBlockComponent` class:

```
export class ProfileBlockComponent implements OnInit {
  public block: any;
  private _profileService: ProfileService;

  constructor(profileService: ProfileService) {
    this._profileService = profileService;
  }

  ngOnInit() {
    console.log(this.block);
  }

  addEntry(event) {
    event.preventDefault();
    this.block.data.push(new Entry());
  }
```

```
    onEnter(event) {
      event.preventDefault();
      this._profileService.updateProfileBlock(this.block);
    }
  }
```

Using the `addEntry()` method, we can add more entries to our block. It's a simple operation that pushes a new entry to the block's data. In order to save the changes, we bind to the keydown event, which matches the *Enter* key to call the `onEnter()` method. This method will update the profile block using the service implemented earlier.

If a block was freshly added and has no `id`, `ProfileService` will handle this situation, so we don't need to add different method calls in our component.

Extra models

We used a few extra models—ones that are not found on the backend—in order to help us with the Angular part. They come in handy when creating initial values or when having default values for properties.

The `Entry` model described a single entry from a profile block. The model can be found under `public/src/user/profile/entry.model.ts`:

```
export class Entry {
  title: string;
  subTitle: string;
  description: string;

  constructor(
    title?: string,
    subTitle?: string,
    description?: string
  ) {
    this.title = title || '';
    this.subTitle = subTitle || '';
    this.description = description || '';
  }
}
```

We also used a second helper model in our module—`public/src/user/profile/block.model.ts`:

```
import { Entry } from './entry.model';

export class Block {
```

```
  _id: string;
  title: string;
  slug: string;
  data: Array<any>;

  constructor(
    _id?: string,
    title?: string,
    slug?: string,
    data?: Array<any>
  ) {
    this._id = _id;
    this.title = title;
    this.slug = slug;
    this.data = data || [new Entry()];
  }
}
```

The preceding model used the `Entry` model to initialize the `data` property with an initial value in case no data was present. You can also add validation to your models. This depends on the complexity of the application.

The remaining functionalities can be found in the final project repository found at the following link: `https://github.com/robert52/mean-blueprints-jobboard`

Summary

Finally, we have reached the end of this chapter.

In this chapter, we started building an application from a boilerplate, extended some of its functionalities, and added our own new functionalities. We created a system with multiple user types and added authorization policies. Also, in the final steps, we extended our backend API with new functionalities and added an extra module to our Angular 2 application.

In the next chapter, we will use real-time communication and see how users can interact with each other in an application.

4
Chat Application

In this chapter, we will build a chat application. The application that we are going to build will serve perfectly as an in-house communication tool for a company. Teams could create channels to discuss certain things related to their projects, even send auto-deleting messages with sensitive data, such as login credentials for servers and so on.

Setting up the base application

We are going to start by setting up the base application using the same boilerplate code used in the previous chapter. Follow these simple steps to achieve this:

1. Clone the project from GitHub: `https://github.com/robert52/express-api-starter`.

2. Rename your boilerplate project `mean-blueprints-chatapp`.

3. If you want, you can stop pointing to the initial Git repository by running the following command:

    ```
    git remote remove origin
    ```

4. Jump to your working directory:

    ```
    cd mean-blueprints-chatapp
    ```

5. Install all dependencies:

    ```
    npm install
    ```

6. Create a development configuration file:

    ```
    cp config/environments/example.js config/environments/development.js
    ```

Your configuration file, `config/environments/development.js`, should look similar to the following:

```
module.exports = {
  port: 3000,
  hostname: '127.0.0.1',
  baseUrl: 'http://localhost:3000',
  mongodb: {
    uri: 'mongodb://localhost/chatapp_dev_db'
  },
  app: {
    name: 'MEAN Blueprints - chat application'
  },
  serveStatic: true,
  session: {
    type: 'mongo',
    secret: 'someVeRyN1c3S#cr3tHer34U',
    resave: false,
    saveUninitialized: true
  },
  proxy: {
    trust: true
  },
  logRequests: false
};
```

Modifying the user model

We don't need much information about a user, so we can reduce the `User` schema to only the strictly necessary information. Also, we can add a `profile` field, which can hold any extra info about the user, such as social media profile info or other accounts data.

Let's modify the `User` schema from `app/models/user.js` with the following:

```
const UserSchema = new Schema({
  email: {
    type: String,
    required: true,
    unique: true
  },
  name: {
    type: String
  },
```

```
  password: {
    type: String,
    required: true,
    select: false
  },
  passwordSalt: {
    type: String,
    required: true,
    select: false
  },
  profile: {
    type: Mixed
  },
  createdAt: {
    type: Date,
    default: Date.now
  }
});
```

The message history data model

The message history will be a collection of user-submitted messages through the chat application. We can choose from a number of approaches when storing such data in MongoDB. The good thing is that there is no correct implementation, although we have a number of common approaches and considerations for each implementation.

Our starting point will be that messages sent by users are part of a conversation thread. When two or more users chat with each other, initially a conversation thread is created for them. The messages become private for that conversation. This means that the messages have a parent-child relationship with another entity, a thread entity in our case.

Keeping in mind our application's requirements, we can explore the following implementations to store our messages:

- **Store each message in a separate document**: This is the easiest to implement and it's the most flexible one, but it comes with some application-level complexity.

- **Embed all messages in the thread document**: Because of MongoDB's limit on document size, this is not an acceptable solution.

- **Implement a hybrid solution**: Messages are stored separately from the thread document but are held in a bucket-like manner, each bucket storing a limited number of documents. So, instead of storing all messages for a thread in one bucket, we are going to spread them out.

For our application, we can go with the one-document-per-message implementation. It will provide us with the greatest flexibility and ease of implementation. Also, we can easily retrieve messages in a chronological and threaded order.

The thread schema

Each message is going to be part of a conversation thread. Information such as who is participating in the conversation will be stored in a document in the threads collection.

We are going to start with a simple schema with only the necessary fields, in which we'll store simple information about a thread. Create a new file called /app/models/ thread.js with the following schema design:

```
'use strict';

const mongoose = require('mongoose');
const Schema = mongoose.Schema;
const ObjectId = Schema.ObjectId;

const ThreadSchema = new Schema({
  participants: {
    type: [
      {
        type: ObjectId,
        ref: 'User'
      }
    ]
  },
  createdAt: {
    type: Date,
    default: Date.now
  }
});

module.exports = mongoose.model('Thread', ThreadSchema);
```

The most important part for us at the moment is the `participants` field, which describes who is participating in the current conversation. By design, our application will support multiple users participating in the same conversation thread. Imagine it to be a channel, where your team can discuss a specific project.

The message schema

As we said earlier, we are going to use the one-document-per-message approach. For now, we are going to have a fairly simple schema for our messages. This can change based on the application's complexity.

We are going to define our schema in `app/models/message.js`:

```js
'use strict';

const mongoose = require('mongoose');
const Schema = mongoose.Schema;
const ObjectId = Schema.ObjectId;

const MessageSchema = new Schema({
  sender: {
    type: ObjectId,
    required: true,
    ref: 'User'
  },
  thread: {
    type: ObjectId,
    required: true,
    ref: 'Thread'
  },
  body: {
    type: String,
    required: true
  },
  createdAt: {
    type: Date,
    default: Date.now
  }
});

module.exports = mongoose.model('Message', MessageSchema);
```

The schema is fairly simple. We have a sender that has a reference to a user and to a thread. In the thread entity, we are going to store additional data regarding the conversation.

Thread backend

In the Node.js backend application, we are going make available endpoints, defined in our Express application routes, related to managing conversation threads. Also, there should be a way to get the message history from a specific thread.

Thread controller

We are going to add the necessary business logic to manage our threads in a new controller file, called `app/controllers/thread.js`, by following these steps:

1. Add the required modules:

   ```
   'use strict';

   const mongoose = require('mongoose');
   const Thread = mongoose.model('Thread');
   ```

2. Export the module's methods:

   ```
   module.exports.allByUser = allThreadsByUser;
   module.exports.find = findThread;
   module.exports.open = openThread;
   module.exports.findById = findThreadById;
   ```

3. Find all the threads for a specific user:

   ```
   function allThreadsByUser(req, res, next) {
     Thread
     .find({
       participants: req.user._id
     })
     .populate('participants')
     .exec((err, threads) => {
       if (err) {
         return next(err);
       }

       req.resources.threads = threads;
       next();
     });
   }
   ```

4. Find a thread by different criteria, for example, by the currently logged-in user and the ID of another user who participates in the conversation:

   ```
   function findThread(req, res, next) {
     let query = {};
     if (req.body.userId) {
   ```

```
        query.$and = [
          { participants: req.body.userId },
          { participants: req.user._id.toString() }
        ];
      }

      if (req.body.participants) {
        query.$and = req.body.participants.map(participant => {
          return { participants: participant };
        });
      }

      Thread
      .findOne(query)
      .populate('participants')
      .exec((err, thread) => {
        if (err) {
          return next(err);
        }

        req.resources.thread = thread;
        next();
      });
    }
```

5. Open a new conversation:

```
function openThread(req, res, next) {
  var data = {};

  //  If we have already found the thread
  //  we don't need to create a new one
  if (req.resources.thread) {
    return next();
  }

  data.participants = req.body.participants || [req.user._id, req.
body.user];

  Thread
  .create(data, (err, thread) => {
    if (err) {
      return next(err);
    }
```

```
thread.populate('participants', (err, popThread) => {
  if (err) {
    return next(err);
  }

  req.resources.thread = popThread;
  next();
});
});
}
```

6. And finally, finding a thread by its ID:

```
function findThreadById(req, res, next) {
  Thread
  .findById(req.params.threadId, (err, thread) => {
    if (err) {
      return next(err);
    }

    req.resources.thread = thread;
    next();
  });
}
```

Defining routes

All of the necessary business logic is implemented in the controller file. We just need to mount the methods from the controller to the routes so that they can be called externally. Create a new file called `app/routes/thread.js`. Add the following code:

```
const express = require('express');
const router = express.Router();
const threadCtrl = require('../controllers/thread');
const messageCtrl = require('../controllers/message');
const auth = require('../middlewares/authentication');
const authorize = require('../middlewares/authorization');
const response = require('../helpers/response');

module.exports = router;
```

After we have added the necessary module dependencies, we can implement each route one by one:

1. Get all the user's threads:

```
router.get(
   '/threads',
   auth.ensured,
   threadCtrl.allByUser,
   response.toJSON('threads')
);
```

2. Open a new thread. If a thread already exists for the participants, it will be returned:

```
router.post(
   '/thread/open',
   auth.ensured,
   threadCtrl.find,
   threadCtrl.open,
   response.toJSON('thread')
);
```

3. Get a thread by ID:

```
router.get(
   '/threads/:threadId',
   auth.ensured,
   threadCtrl.findById,
   authorize.onlyParticipants('thread'),
   response.toJSON('thread')
)
```

4. Get all messages for a thread:

```
router.get(
   '/threads/:threadId/messages',
   auth.ensured,
   threadCtrl.findById,
   authorize.onlyParticipants('thread'),
   messageCtrl.findByThread,
   response.toJSON('messages')
);
```

We jump a few steps and already used a method from the message controller; don't worry, we are going to implement it in the next step.

Message controller

Our API should return the message history for a specific conversation. We are going to keep things simple and just retrieve all the data from the `Message` collection from MongoDB. Create a new controller file, `app/controllers/message.js`, and add the following logic to find all message documents for a thread:

```
'use strict';

const mongoose = require('mongoose');
const Thread = mongoose.model('Thread');
const Message = mongoose.model('Message');
const ObjectId = mongoose.Types.ObjectId;

module.exports.findByThread = findMessagesByThread;

function findMessagesByThread(req, res, next) {
  let query = {
    thread: req.resources.thread._id
  };

  if (req.query.beforeId) {
    query._id = { $lt: new ObjectId(req.query.sinceId) };
  }

  Message
  .find(query)
  .populate('sender')
  .exec(function(err, messages) {
    if (err) {
      return next(err);
    }

    req.resources.messages = messages;
    next();
  });
}
```

Because we have a lot of ground to cover, we are not going to treat pagination for the message history, neither on the backend nor on the frontend. But I've added a little bit of help in the preceding code. If the `beforeId` query string is sent, then messages can be easily paginated by the last known ID. Also remember that the `_id` field can be used to sort by, if it stores an `ObjectId` value, is almost equivalent as sorting by creation time.

Let's dive a little bit deeper into this _id field. Most MongoDB clients will generate the ObjectId value to the _id field by themselves. If no _id field is sent with the document, mongod (the primary daemon process for MongoDB) will add the field.

One problem we could encounter is if the message documents are generated by multiple processes or systems within a single second. In such a case, the insertion order will not be strictly preserved.

Backend chat service

So far, we've only scratched the surface of our backend application. We are going to add a service layer to our server. This abstraction layer will implement all the business logic, such as instant messaging. The service layer will handle interaction with other application modules and layers.

As for the WebSockets part of the application, we are going to use socketIO, which is a real-time communication engine. They have a really neat chat application example. If you haven't heard of it, you can take a look at the following link:

https://socket.io/get-started/chat/

Chat service implementation

Now that we are familiar with socketIO, we can continue and implement our chat service. We are going to start by creating a new file called app/services/chat/index.js. This will be the main file for our chat service. Add the following code:

```
'use strict';

const socketIO = require('socket.io');
const InstantMessagingModule = require('./instant-messaging.module');

module.exports = build;

class ChatService {
}

function build(app, server) {
  return new ChatService(app, server);
}
```

Don't worry about the `InstantMessagingModule`. We just added it as a reference so that we'll not forget about it. We'll come back later to reveal the mystery. Our class should have a constructor. Let's add that now:

```
constructor(app, server) {
  this.connectedClients = {};
  this.io = socketIO(server);
  this.sessionMiddleware = app.get('sessionMiddleware');
  this.initMiddlewares();
  this.bindHandlers();
}
```

In the constructor, we initialize `socketIO`, get the session middleware, and finally bind all the handlers to our `socketIO` instance. More information about the session middleware can be found in our Express configuration file, `config/express.js`. Look for something similar:

```
var sessionOpts = {
  secret: config.session.secret,
  key: 'skey.sid',
  resave: config.session.resave,
  saveUninitialized: config.session.saveUninitialized
};

if (config.session.type === 'mongodb') {
  sessionOpts.store = new MongoStore({
    url: config.mongodb.uri
  });
}

var sessionMiddleware = session(sessionOpts);
app.set('sessionMiddleware', sessionMiddleware);
```

The nice thing is that we can share this session logic with `socketIO` and mount it with the `.use()` method. This will be done in the `.initMiddlewares()` method:

```
initMiddlewares() {
  this.io.use((socket, next) => {
    this.sessionMiddleware(socket.request, socket.request.res,
    next);
  });

  this.io.use((socket, next) => {
    let user = socket.request.session.passport.user;

    // authorize user
```

```
    if (!user) {
      let err = new Error('Unauthorized');
      err.type = 'unauthorized';
      return next(err);
    }

    // attach user to the socket, like req.user
    socket.user = {
      _id: socket.request.session.passport.user
    };
    next();
  });
}
```

First, we mount the session middleware to our instance, which will do something similar to mounting it on our Express app. Second, we check whether the user is present on the socket's session, in other words, whether the user is authenticated or not.

Being able to add middleware is a pretty neat feature and enables us to do interesting things for each connected socket. We should also add the last method from the constructor:

```
bindHandlers() {
  this.io.on('connection', socket => {
    // add client to the socket list to get the session later
    this.connectedClients[socket.request.session.passport.user]
    = socket;
    InstantMessagingModule.init(socket, this.connectedClients,
    this.io);
  });
}
```

For each successfully connected client, we are going to initialize the instant messaging module and store the connected clients in a map, for later reference.

Instant messaging module

To be a little bit modular, we'll split functionalities that represent connected clients into separate modules. For now there will be only one module, but in the future, you can easily add new ones. The InstantMessagingModule will be found in the same folder with the main chat file, more precisely, app/services/chat/instant-messaging.module.js. You can safely add the following code to it:

```
'use strict';

const mongoose = require('mongoose');
```

```
const Message = mongoose.model('Message');
const Thread = mongoose.model('Thread');

module.exports.init = initInstantMessagingModule;

class InstantMessagingModule {
}

function initInstantMessagingModule(socket, clients) {
  return new InstantMessagingModule(socket, clients);
}
```

The service will use the Message and Thread models to validate and persist data. We are exporting an initialization function instead of the entire class. You could easily add extra initialization logic to the exported function.

The class constructor will be fairly simple, and it will look something similar to this:

```
constructor(socket, clients) {
  this.socket = socket;
  this.clients = clients;
  this.threads = {};
  this.bindHandlers();
}
```

We just assign the necessary dependencies to each property, and bind all the handlers to the connected socket. Let's continue with the .bindHandlers() method:

```
bindHandlers() {
  this.socket.on('send:im', data => {
    data.sender = this.socket.user._id;

    if (!data.thread) {
      let err = new Error('You must be participating in a
      conversation.')
      err.type = 'no_active_thread';
      return this.handleError(err);
    }

    this.storeIM(data, (err, message, thread) => {
      if (err) {
        return this.handleError(err);
      }

      this.socket.emit('send:im:success', message);
```

```
            this.deliverIM(message, thread);
        });
    });
}
```

When sending a new message through WebSockets, it will be stored using the
`.storeIM()` method and delivered to each participant by the `.deliverIM()` method.

We slightly abstracted the logic to send instant messages, so let's define our first
method, which stores the messages:

```
storeIM(data, callback) {
    this.findThreadById(data.thread, (err, thread) => {
        if (err) {
            return callback(err);
        }

        let user = thread.participants.find((participant) => {
            return participant.toString() === data.sender.toString();
        });

        if (!user) {
            let err = new Error('Not a participant.')
            err.type = 'unauthorized_thread';
            return callback(err);
        }

        this.createMessage(data, (err, message) => {
            if (err) {
                return callback(err);
            }

            callback(err, message, thread);
        });
    });
}
```

So basically, the `.storeIM()` method finds the conversation thread and creates a new
message. We have also added a simple authorization when storing a message. The
sender must be a participant in the given conversation. You could move that piece
of logic into a more suitable module. I'll leave it to you as practice.

Let's add the next two methods that we used before:

```
findThreadById(id, callback) {
    if (this.threads[id]) {
```

```
      return callback(null, this.threads[id]);
    }

  Thread.findById(id, (err, thread) => {
    if (err) {
      return callback(err);
    }

    this.threads[id] = thread;
    callback(null, thread);
  });
}

createMessage(data, callback) {
  Message.create(data, (err, newMessage) => {
    if (err) {
      return callback(err);
    }

    newMessage.populate('sender', callback);
  });
}
```

Finally, we can deliver our message to the rest of the participants. The implementation can be found in the following class method:

```
deliverIM(message, thread) {
  for (let i = 0; i < thread.participants.length; i++) {
    if (thread.participants[i].toString() ===
    message.sender.toString()) {
      continue;
    }

    if (this.clients[thread.participants[i]]) {
      this.clients[thread.participants[i]].emit('receive:im',
      message);
    }
  }
}
```

We have reached the end with our backend application. It should have all the necessary features implemented to start working on the client Angular application.

Bootstrapping the Angular app

It's time to start building our client application using Angular 2. We are going to integrate SocketIO with the client to communicate with our backend application. We are going to showcase only the most important parts of the application, but you can look at the final version anytime.

The boot file

We are going to boot our application from a specific file, and — probably you have already guessed it — it will be called `public/src/boot.ts`. For better transparency and to foresee what we are going to build, the following code snippet from the `boot.ts` file will be the final version, with all the necessary data added to it:

```
import { bootstrap } from 'angular2/platform/browser';
import { provide } from 'angular2/core';
import { HTTP_PROVIDERS } from 'angular2/http';
import { ROUTER_PROVIDERS, LocationStrategy, HashLocationStrategy }
from 'angular2/router';
import { AppComponent } from './app.component';
import { ChatService }  from './services/chat.service';
import { ThreadService }  from './services/thread.service';
import { MessageService }  from './services/message.service';
import { UserService } from './services/user.service';

import 'rxjs/add/operator/map';
import 'rxjs/add/operator/share';
import 'rxjs/add/operator/combineLatest';
import 'rxjs/add/operator/distinctUntilChanged';
import 'rxjs/add/operator/debounceTime';

bootstrap(AppComponent, [
  HTTP_PROVIDERS, ROUTER_PROVIDERS,
  ChatService,
  ThreadService,
  MessageService,
  UserService,
  provide(LocationStrategy, {useClass: HashLocationStrategy})
]);
```

We are going to implement four services for this particular application, and we'll start with an app component. For the sake of simplicity, we are going to use a hash-based location strategy.

App component

The main component of our application is the app component. We are going to keep it simple for now, only adding a router outlet to it, and configure the routes of our application.

Create a new file called public/src/app.component.ts with the following code:

```
import { Component } from 'angular2/core';
import { RouteConfig, RouterOutlet } from 'angular2/router';
import { Router } from 'angular2/router';
import { ChatComponent } from './chat/chat.component';

@RouteConfig([
  { path: '/messages/...', as: 'Chat', component: ChatComponent,
  useAsDefault: true }
])
@Component({
    selector: 'chat-app',
    directives: [
      RouterOutlet
    ],
    template: `
      <div class="chat-wrapper row card whiteframe-z2">
        <div class="chat-header col">
          <h3>Chat application</h3>
        </div>
        <router-outlet></router-outlet>
      </div>
    `
})
export class AppComponent {
  constructor() {
  }
}
```

We created the main application component and configured a route that will have child routes. By default, the ChatComponent will be mounted. So, this was very basic. Before we continue with our application's components, let's take a break and define custom data types.

Custom data types

In order to group similar functionalities and have custom type checking, we are going to define classes for each entity used in our application. This will give us access to custom initialization and default values when creating entities.

User type

Our first custom data type used in the frontend Angular application will be a user. You can use an interface to define a custom type or a regular class. If you need default values or custom validation, go with a regular class definition.

Create a new file called `public/src/datatypes/user.ts` and add the following class:

```
export class User {
  _id: string;
  email: string;
  name: string;
  avatar: string;
  createdAt: string;

  constructor(_id?: string, email?: string, name?: string,
  createdAt?: string) {
    this._id = _id;
    this.email = email;
    this.name = name;
    this.avatar =
    'http://www.gravatar.com/avatar/{{hash}}?s=50&r=g&d=retro'
    .replace('{{hash}}', _id);
    this.createdAt = createdAt;
  }
}
```

When instantiating a new user, the `user` instance will have the `avatar` property prepopulated, with a specific link for the avatar picture. I've used a `gravatar` for this and added the user's ID as a hash to generate the image. Normally, you have to use the user's e-mail as an `md5` hash. Obviously, the avatar image can be provided by any service. You can even try adding file upload and profile management to this application.

Thread type

Next, we are going to define a thread class, with some custom initialization logic. Create a new file, called `public/src/datatypes/thread.ts`:

```
import { User } from './user';

export class Thread {
  _id: string;
  name: string;
  participants: Array<User>;
  createdAt: string;

  constructor(_id?: string, name?: string, participants?: Array<User>,
  createdAt?: string) {
    this._id = _id;
    this.name = name || '';
    this.participants = participants || [];
    this.createdAt = createdAt;
  }

  generateName(omittedUser) {
    let names = [];
    this.participants.map(participant => {
      if (omittedUser._id !== participant._id) {
        names.push(participant.name);
      }
    });

    return (names[1]) ? names.join(', ') : names[0];
  }
}
```

As you can see, the user data type was imported and used to signal that the participants for a given thread must be an array of users. Also, a class method was defined to generate a custom name for a specific thread-based on the participating users in the conversation thread.

Message type

At last, we are going to define what structure a message will have in our application. For that, we are going to create a new file called `public/src/datatypes/message.ts` with the following logic:

```
export class Message {
  _id: string;
```

```
  sender: any;
  thread: string;
  body: string;
  createdAt: string;
  time: string;
  fulltime: string;

  constructor(_id?: string, sender?: any, thread?: string, body?:
  string, createdAt?: string) {
    this._id = _id;
    this.sender = sender;
    this.body = body;
    this.createdAt = createdAt;
    this.time = this._generateTime(new Date(createdAt));
    this.fulltime = this._generateDateTime(new Date(createdAt));
  }

  private _generateTime(date) {
    return  date.getHours() + ":"
          + date.getMinutes() + ":"
          + date.getSeconds();
  }

  private _generateDateTime(date) {
    return date.getDate() + "/"
          + (date.getMonth()+1)  + "/"
          + date.getFullYear() + " @ "
          + this._generateTime(date);
  }
}
```

You may already be thinking, "Why not include the User data type and mark the sender as a user?" To be honest, this is not a must have. You can have *any* type you like and the code would be still valid. It's up to you how much granularity you want to add to your code.

Getting back to our code, we have added two extra methods to the Message class in order to generate two timestamps, one that displays the time when the message was created and one that displays a full timestamp with date and time.

Application services

In the initial chapters, we grouped our files by their domain context. We did things a bit differently this time to highlight the fact that you can also start with a more flat approach. And, if necessary, you can start grouping your files based on their domain context instead of their type.

Still, we are going to group our components based on their context in order to locate them faster. Also imagine that you can load the whole application into a different application, and having a flatter folder structure will reduce the unnecessary navigation hassle.

User service

We are going to start with a simple service that will handle all of the user application logic. Create a new file called `public/src/services/user.service.ts` with the following code:

```
import { Injectable } from 'angular2/core';
import { Http, Response, Headers } from 'angular2/http';
import { Observable } from 'rxjs/Observable';
import { contentHeaders } from '../common/headers';
import { User } from '../datatypes/user';

type ObservableUsers = Observable<Array<User>>;

@Injectable()
export class UserService {
  public users: ObservableUsers;
  public user: User;
  private _http: Http;
  private _userObservers: any;
  private _dataStore: { users: Array<User> };

  constructor(http: Http) {
    this._http = http;
    this.users = new Observable(observer => this._userObservers =
    observer).share();
    this._dataStore = { users: [] };
    this.getAll();
  }
}
```

We exposed a `users` property, which is an observable, and transformed it to a `hot` observable. We defined an internal data storage for the service, which is a simple object. Almost forgot to mention! Remember to import your dependencies. As a closing line for our constructor, we retrieve all users from the backend. We are doing this in the service so that we don't have to call it explicitly from a component.

Actually, the `.getAll()` method is not implemented, so let's append the following method to the class:

```
getAll() {
  return this._http
  .get('/api/users', { headers: contentHeaders })
  .map((res: Response) => res.json())
  .subscribe(users => this.storeUsers(users));
}
```

We have also moved the data persistence to another method, just in case we want to use it somewhere else. Add the following method to the `UserService` class:

```
storeUsers(users: Array<User>) {
  this._dataStore.users = users;
  this._userObservers.next(this._dataStore.users);
}
```

For now, our application has all the necessary functionalities from `UserService`, and we can move on to implementing other application components.

The thread service

The thread service will handle and share across our application data related to threads. We are going to store the retrieved threads from the backend. Also, the currently active thread will be stored in this service.

Let's start by creating the service file, called `public/src/services/thread.service.ts`. After that, follow a few steps to implement the core logic of the service:

1. Load the necessary dependencies:

```
import { Injectable } from 'angular2/core';
import { Http, Response, Headers } from 'angular2/http';
import { Subject } from 'rxjs/Subject';
import { BehaviorSubject } from 'rxjs/Subject/BehaviorSubject';
import { Observable } from 'rxjs/Observable';
import { contentHeaders } from '../common/headers';
import { Thread } from '../datatypes/thread';
import { User } from '../datatypes/user';
```

2. Define a few custom data types:

```
type ObservableThreads = Observable<Array<Thread>>;
type SubjectThread = Subject<Thread>;
```

3. Define the base class:

```
@Injectable()
export class ThreadService {
  public threads: ObservableThreads;
  public currentThread: SubjectThread = new
  BehaviorSubject<Thread>(new Thread());
  private _http: Http;
  private _threadObservers: any;
  private _dataStore: { threads: Array<Thread> };
  private _currentUser: any;
}
```

4. Add the constructor:

```
constructor(http: Http) {
  this._http = http;
  this._dataStore = { threads: [] };
  this.threads = new Observable(
    observer => this._threadObservers = observer
  ).share();
}
```

5. Append the necessary method to get all threads from the server:

```
getAll() {
  return this._http
  .get('/api/threads', { headers: contentHeaders })
  .map((res: Response) => res.json())
  .map(data => {
    return data.map(thread => {
      return new Thread(thread._id, thread._id,
      thread.participants, thread.createdAt)
    });
  })
  .subscribe(threads => {
    this._dataStore.threads = threads;
    this._threadObservers.next(this._dataStore.threads);
  });
```

This method will retrieve all the threads from the backend service. It will store them inside the service's data store and push the latest values to the thread observers so that all subscribers can get the latest values.

6. Define how to open a new thread:

```
open(data: any) {
  return this._http
  .post('/api/thread/open', JSON.stringify(data),
  { headers: contentHeaders })
  .map((res: Response) => res.json())
  .map(data => {
    return new Thread(data._id, data.name,
    data.participants, data.createdAt);
  });
}
```

The `open()` method will return an observable instead of handling data inside the service.

7. We also need to be able to set the current thread:

```
setCurrentThread(newThread: Thread) {
  this.currentThread.next(newThread);
}
```

`currentThread` is a `BehaviorSubject` that will hold only the last value and share it with any new subscriber. This comes in handy when storing the current thread. Remember that you need to initialize the subject with an initial value.

8. Expose a method to store threads from an external data source:

```
storeThread(thread: Thread) {
  var found = this._dataStore.threads.find(t => {
    return t._id === thread._id;
  });

  if (!found) {
    this._dataStore.threads.push(thread);
    this._threadObservers.next(this._dataStore.threads);
  }
}
```

We don't want to store the same thread twice. One thing we can improve is updating the thread if it has changed, but we don't need this in our application at this point. It is something you should remember when you are improving this application.

With the last implemented logic, we should have the minimal functionality required for the conversation threads.

The message service

The message service is going to be a little bit different, because we are going to use socket.io to send and receive data through `WebSockets` from the socket server, which was set up earlier in this chapter. No worries! The difference will not be reflected in the rest of the application. A service should always abstract the underlining logic.

We are going to start by creating the service file, called `public/src/services/message.service.ts`, and import the necessary dependencies:

```
import { Injectable } from 'angular2/core';
import { Http, Response, Headers } from 'angular2/http';
import { Observable } from 'rxjs/Observable';
import { ThreadService } from './thread.service';
import { contentHeaders } from '../common/headers';
import { Message } from '../datatypes/message';
import { User } from '../datatypes/user';
import * as io from 'socket.io-client';
```

You can see that we imported everything from the `socket.io-client` library as `io`. Next, we are going to append the class definition:

```
type ObservableMessages = Observable<Array<Message>>;

@Injectable()
export class MessageService {
  public messages: ObservableMessages;

  private _http: Http;
  private _threadService: ThreadService;
  private _io: any;
  private _messagesObservers: any;
  private _dataStore: { messages: Array<Message> };

  constructor(http: Http, threadService: ThreadService) {
    this._io = io.connect();
    this._http = http;
    this._threadService = threadService;
    this.messages = new Observable(observer =>
    this._messagesObservers = observer).share();
    this._dataStore = { messages: [] };
    this._socketOn();
  }
}
```

In the constructor, we are going to initialize and connect to the socket server. Because we are using the default configuration both on the server side and the client side, we can just call the `.connect()` method. The `_socketOn()` private method will define all event bindings for the socket; let's append this method:

```
private _socketOn() {
  this._io.on('receive:im', message =>
  this._storeMessage(message));
  this._io.on('send:im:success', message =>
  this._storeMessage(message));
}
```

We just defined two events to listen for and call the `_storeMessage()` method. For each event, a new message will arrive through the socket. Following this, we should add the method to our `MessageSerivce` class:

```
private _storeMessage(message: Message) {
  let sender = new User(
    message.sender._id,
    message.sender.email,
    message.sender.name,
    message.sender.createdAt
  );
  let m = new Message(
    message._id,
    new User(sender._id, sender.email, sender.name,
    sender.createdAt),
    message.thread,
    message.body,
    message.createdAt
  );
  this._dataStore.messages.push(m);
  this._messagesObservers.next(this._dataStore.messages);
}
```

When storing a new message, we are going to create a new `User` instance in order to have all the necessary data regarding the message sender. This method will only be used internally within the service, but we need to expose a method to send messages, and it will be accessed by other components:

```
sendMessage(message: Message) {
  this._io.emit('send:im', message);
}
```

Sending a message was not so hard. We had to emit the `send:im` event and attach the message itself. Besides sending and receiving messages, we also need to get the message history for a given thread and store the messages in the service's data store. Let's do that right now:

```
getByThread(threadId) {
  this._http
  .get('/api/threads/'+threadId+'/messages', { headers:
  contentHeaders })
  .map((res: Response) => res.json())
  .map(res => {
    return res.map(data => {
      let sender = new User(
        data.sender._id,
        data.sender.email,
        data.sender.name,
        data.sender.createdAt
      );
      return new Message(
        data._id,
        sender,
        data.thread,
        data.body,
        data.createdAt
      );
    });
  })
  .subscribe(messages => {
    this._dataStore.messages = messages;
    this._messagesObservers.next(this._dataStore.messages);
  });
}
```

The preceding method should retrieve for us the necessary data from the Express application. We are doing the same thing for each message as before when we stored an incoming message. More precisely, we are instantiating a new user with the sender's information. This should be all for the message service.

The chat component

Now that we have all the necessary data types and services, we can get back to our application's components. Looking back at the `app` component, a good thing would be to start with the `chat` component. Create a new file called `public/src/chat/chat.component.ts` and add the following imports:

```
import { Component } from 'angular2/core';
import { RouteConfig, RouterOutlet } from 'angular2/router';
import { ChatService } from '../services/chat.service';
```

```
import { ThreadListComponent } from '../thread/thread-
list.component';
import { MessageListComponent } from '../message/message-
list.component';
import { MessageFormComponent } from '../message/message-
form.component';
import { UserListComponent } from '../user/user-list.component';
import { ChatHelpComponent } from './chat-help.component';
```

After we have imported all our required modules, we can actually implement our component:

```
@RouteConfig([
  { path: '/',              as: 'ThreadMessagesDefault', component:
  ChatHelpComponent, useAsDefault: true },
  { path: '/:identifier', as: 'ThreadMessages', component:
  MessageListComponent }
])
@Component({
  selector: 'chat',
  directives: [
    ThreadListComponent,
    MessageFormComponent,
    UserListComponent,
    RouterOutlet
  ],
  template: `
    <div class="threads-container col sidebar">
      <user-list></user-list>
      <thread-list></thread-list>
    </div>

    <div class="messages-container col content">
      <router-outlet></router-outlet>

      <div class="message-form-container">
        <message-form></message-form>
      </div>
    </div>
  `
})
export class ChatComponent {
  private _chatService: ChatService;

  constructor(chatService: ChatService) {
    this._chatService = chatService;
  }
}
```

In the component's template are included components that we'll implement later on, for example, the thread list component, which will display all the current conversations with other users. The chat component will be the container for our smaller components, but we are also adding a RouterOutlet to dynamically load components matched to the current route.

The default route will load a helper component in case no thread ID is added as a parameter in the route. We can associate this with a home page for our component. You can make the default view as complex as you want; for example, you can add a link for the last opened thread. We are going to keep it simple for now. Create a new file called public/src/chat-help.component.ts and add the following code:

```
import { Component } from 'angular2/core';

@Component({
  selector: 'chat-help',
  template: `
    <h2>Start a new conversation with someone</h2>
  `
})
export class ChatHelpComponent {
  constructor() {
  }
}
```

Noting fancy here! Just a simple component with an inline template that has a nice message displayed for the user. Now that we have covered this, we can move on and implement the rest of our components.

The user list component

The user list component will give us the ability to search for users and start a new conversation with them. We will need to display a list of users and filter them by a search criterion. Also, by clicking on a user from the list, a new conversation thread should open. All this should be fairly simple to implement. Let's start by creating the component file. Create a new file called public/src/user/user.component.ts, with the following base structure:

```
import { Component } from 'angular2/core';
import { Router } from 'angular2/router'
import { Subject } from 'rxjs/Subject';
import { ReplaySubject } from 'rxjs/Subject/ReplaySubject';
```

```
import { UserService } from '../services/user.service';
import { ThreadService } from '../services/thread.service';
import { User } from '../datatypes/user';

@Component({
    selector: 'user-list',
    template: ``
})
export class UserListComponent {
  public users: Array<User>;
  public filteredUsers: Array<User>;
  public selected: boolean = false;
  public search: Subject<String> = new ReplaySubject(1);
  public searchValue: string = '';
  private _threadService: ThreadService;
  private _userService: UserService;
  private _router: Router;

  constructor(userService: UserService, threadService:
  ThreadService, router: Router) {
    this._userService = userService;
    this._threadService = threadService;
    this._router = router;
  }
}
```

We imported the necessary dependencies and defined the base for our component. The component will have two major parts, a list of users and an input field, which will be used to search for a given user from the list. Let's define the template for our component:

```
<div class="user-search-container">
  <input
    type="text"
    class="form-control block"
    placeholder="start a conversation"
    [(ngModel)]="searchValue"
    (focus)="onFocus($event)"
    (input)="onInput($event)"
    (keydown.esc)="onEsc($event)"
  />
</div>
<div class="user-list-container">
  <div class="users-container" [ngClass]="{active: selected
  }">
```

```
<div class="user-list-toobar">
  <a href="#" (click)="onClose($event)" class="close-
  button">
    <span>x</span>
    <span class="close-text">esc</span>
  </a>
</div>
<div *ngFor="#user of filteredUsers">
  <a href="javascript:void(0);"
  (click)="openThread($event, user)">{{user.name}}</a>
</div>
</div>
</div>
```

In order to show a list of users, we are going to subscribe to the users observable from the user service. Append the following code to the constructor:

```
this._userService.users.subscribe(users => {
  this.filteredUsers = this.users = users;
});
```

To display a list of filtered users, we are going to use the following logic. Append this code to the constructor:

```
this.search
  .debounceTime(200)
  .distinctUntilChanged()
  .subscribe((value: string) => {
    this.filteredUsers = this.users.filter(user => {
      return user.name.toLowerCase().startsWith(value);
    });
  });
```

To feed data from the input, we can use something like this method, which will execute only when the user starts typing:

```
onInput(event) {
  this.search.next(event.target.value);
}
```

In order to open a new thread, we bound a click event for each user displayed in the list. Let's add the required method for this:

```
openThread(event, user: User) {
  this._threadService.open({ userId: user._id
  }).subscribe(thread => {
    this._threadService.storeThread(thread);
```

```
      this._router.navigate(['./ThreadMessages', { identifier:
      thread._id}]);
      this.cleanUp();
    });
}
```

The preceding code will just call the `.open()` method from the thread service, and upon success, it will navigate to the returned thread. We are also calling the `cleanUp()` method from this component, which will reset our component to the initial state.

Finally, let's add all the missing logic from our component. Just append the methods to the component:

```
onFocus() {
  this.selected = true;
}

onClose(event) {
  this.cleanUp();
  event.preventDefault();
}

onEsc(event) {
  this.cleanUp();
  let target: HTMLElement = <HTMLElement>event.target;
  target.blur();
  event.preventDefault();
}
cleanUp() {
  this.searchValue = '';
  this.selected = false;
  this.search.next('');
}
```

As a quick recap, we created a user list component that displays all users in a list when focusing on the search input; by default, the list is hidden. We added some special events; for example, by pressing the *Esc* key, the list should be hidden.

Displaying threads

A user must know in which conversation he/she is participating, so we need to display this information to the user. To do so, we are going to implement a thread listing component.

Thread component

In order to display a list of threads, we are going to use a component for each thread to encapsulate all the information displayed to the user and functionalities. To create the desired component, follow these steps:

1. Create the component file, called `public/src/thread/thread.component.ts`.

2. Import the necessary dependencies:

```
import { Component, OnInit } from 'angular2/core';
import { RouterLink } from 'angular2/router';
import { ThreadService } from '../services/thread.service';
import { Thread } from '../datatypes/thread';
```

3. Add the component annotation:

```
@Component({
    inputs: ['thread'],
    selector: 'thread',
    directives: [ RouterLink ],
    template: `
      <div class="thread-item">
        <a href="#" [routerLink]="['./ThreadMessages', {
        identifier: thread._id }]" data-
        id="{{thread._id}}">
          {{thread.name}}
          <span *ngIf="selected"> &bull; </span>
        </a>
      </div>
    `
})
```

4. Define the component's class:

```
export class ThreadComponent implements OnInit {
  public thread: Thread;
  public selected: boolean = false;
  private _threadService: ThreadService;

  constructor(threadService: ThreadService) {
    this._threadService = threadService;
  }

  ngOnInit() {
    this._threadService.currentThread.subscribe( (thread:
    Thread) => {
```

```
        this.selected = thread && this.thread && (thread._id
        === this.thread._id);
      });
    }
  }
}
```

We created a single thread component to be used to display information in a list. We are using `routerLink` to navigate to the desired conversation thread. On initialization, we check which is the current thread so that we can mark the selected thread.

Thread list component

Now that we have our thread component, we can display them in a list. For this, a new component will be used. Let's do something similar to what was done before:

1. Create the component file, called `public/src/thread/thread-list.component.ts`.

2. Import the necessary dependencies, together with the `thread` component:

```
import { Component, ChangeDetectionStrategy } from 'angular2/
core';
import { Observable } from 'rxjs/Observable';
import { ThreadService } from '../services/thread.service';
import { Thread } from '../datatypes/thread';
import { ThreadComponent } from './thread.component';
```

3. Build the component annotation:

```
@Component({
    selector: 'thread-list',
    directives: [ThreadComponent],
    // changeDetection:
    ChangeDetectionStrategy.OnPushObserve,
    // changeDetection: ChangeDetectionStrategy.OnPush,
    template: `
      <h4>Recent <span
      class="muted">({{threads.length}})</span></h4>
      <thread
        *ngFor="#thread of threads"
        [thread]="thread">
      </thread>
    `
})
```

4. Define the `ThreadListComponent` class:

```
export class ThreadListComponent {
  public threads: Array<Thread> = [];
  private _threadService: ThreadService;

  constructor(threadService: ThreadService) {
    this._threadService = threadService;
    this._threadService.threads.subscribe(threads => {
      this.threads = threads;
    });
    this._threadService.getAll();
  }
}
```

This should display a nice list of opened conversation threads for the user. We are using the `thread` service to get the necessary data for the component. If the `threads` collection from the service changes, the update strategy will handle the necessary updates for us.

Messaging

Now that we can initiate and resume a conversation, we need to be able to send messages in that conversation to the participants. We are going to focus on achieving this functionality.

The flow for sending messages is pretty simple. First, we send the desired message to the backend application, storing the message for history purposes, and we notify the recipient of a new message. Both the sender and the recipient have the message displayed on their devices.

Sending messages

Earlier, in the `chat` component, we used a `message form` component. This component will permit us to input messages and send them to the Node.js backend service. Let's keep it simple and add only the necessary functionalities. Create a new component file called `public/src/message/message-form.component.ts`.

We are going to import two services in our component. We append the following code for our dependencies:

```
import { Component, OnInit } from 'angular2/core';
import { ThreadService } from '../services/thread.service';
import { MessageService } from '../services/message.service';
```

```
import { Message } from '../datatypes/message';
import { User } from '../datatypes/user';
import { Thread } from '../datatypes/thread';
```

Now we are going to add the component annotation and define the component's class:

```
@Component({
    selector: 'message-form',
    // changeDetection: ChangeDetectionStrategy.OnPush,
    template: `
      <input
        class="message-form form-control"
        autocorrect="off" autocomplete="off" spellcheck="true"
        (keydown.enter)="onEnter($event)"
        [(ngModel)]="draftMessage.body"
      >
      `
})
export class MessageFormComponent implements OnInit {

  constructor() {
  }

  ngOnInit() {
  }
}
```

To define the rest of the necessary logic, we are going to follow these steps:

1. Add the following properties to the class:
    ```
    public draftMessage: Message;
    private _messageService: MessageService;
    private _threadService: ThreadService;
    private _thread: Thread;
    ```

2. Change the constructor to something similar to the following:
    ```
    constructor(messageService: MessageService,
    threadService: ThreadService) {
      this._messageService = messageService;
      this._threadService = threadService;
      this._threadService.currentThread.subscribe(thread =>
      this._thread = thread);
    }
    ```

3. Modify the component's initialization to reset the `draft message` value:

```
ngOnInit() {
  this.draftMessage = new Message();
}
```

4. Add the send message logic:

```
sendMessage() {
  let message: Message = this.draftMessage;
  message.thread = this._thread._id;
  this._messageService.sendMessage(message);
  this.draftMessage = new Message();
}
```

This will simply call the `.sendMessage()` method from the `thread` service.

5. Define what happens when the user hits the *Enter* key:

```
onEnter(event: any) {
  this.sendMessage();
  event.preventDefault();
}
```

Technically, we can now send messages to the backend and persist them in MongoDB to construct the message history.

The message component

To display all the messages, we are going to start small and create the message component. This component will be a single entry from the list of messages. We should already have the necessary data and logic to display a single message.

To implement the `message` component, create a new file called `public/src/message/message.component.ts` and append the following code:

```
import { Component, AfterViewInit } from 'angular2/core';

@Component({
    inputs: ['message'],
    selector: 'message',
    template: `
      <div class="message-item">
        <div class="message-identifier">
          <img src="{{message.sender.avatar}}" width="36"
          height="36"/>
        </div>
        <div class="message-content">
```

```
          <div class="message-sender">
            <span class="user-name">{{message.sender.name}}</span>
            <span class="message-timestamp"
            title={{message.fulltime}}>{{message.time}}</span>
          </div>
          <div class="message-body">
            {{message.body}}
          </div>
        </div>
      </div>
    `
})
export class MessageComponent implements AfterViewInit {
  constructor() {
  }

  ngAfterViewInit() {
    var ml = document.querySelector('message-list .message-list');
    ml.scrollTop = ml.scrollHeight;
  }
}
```

The component is fairly simple. It just displays data about a single message, and after the view has initialized, it will scroll the message list to the bottom. With the last functionality, if there are more messages than can actually fit in the view, it will simply scroll to the latest message.

The message list component

Before we implemented a single message component, this was necessary for our message list component, which will display all messages to the user. We are going to use a similar pattern to implement this component as for the thread list.

Follow these steps to implement the message list component:

1. Import the necessary dependencies:

```
import { Component } from 'angular2/core';
import { RouteParams } from 'angular2/router';
import { MessageService } from '../services/message.service';
import { ThreadService } from '../services/thread.service';
import { Thread } from '../datatypes/thread';
import { Message } from '../datatypes/message';
import { MessageComponent } from './message.component';
```

2. Append the Angular component annotation:

```
@Component({
    selector: 'message-list',
    directives: [MessageComponent],
    template: `
      <div class="message-list">
        <div *ngIf="messages.length === 0" class="empty-
        message-list">
          <h3>No messages so far :)</h3>
        </div>
        <message
          *ngFor="#message of messages"
          [message]="message"
        ></message>
      </div>
      `
})
```

3. Define the component's class:

```
export class MessageListComponent {
  public messages: Array<Message> = [];
  private _messageService: MessageService;
  private _threadService: ThreadService;
  private _routeParams:RouteParams;
}
Add the constructor:
  constructor(
    messageService: MessageService,
    threadService: ThreadService,
    routeParams: RouteParams
  ) {
    this._routeParams = routeParams;
    this._messageService = messageService;
    this._threadService = threadService;
    this._messageService.messages.subscribe(messages =>
    this.messages = messages);
    let threadId: string =
    this._routeParams.get('identifier');
    this._threadService.setCurrentThread(new
    Thread(threadId));
    this._messageService.getByThread(threadId);
  }
```

Because we are reloading the component each time we navigate to the matched route, we can get the current `identifier` parameter and load messages by the current thread ID. We are also setting the current thread ID so that other subscribers can take actions accordingly. For example, in the `thread` component, we check whether the current thread matches the component's thread.

Summary

We have reached the end of this chapter. The chapter was about building a real-time chat application. We used `WebSockets` for the real-time communication, stored the message history in MongoDB, and created threaded conversations. We also left some room for improvements, or to add new functionalities.

In the next chapter, we'll try to build an e-commerce application.

E-commerce Application

5

This chapter will focus on building an e-commerce like application. We are going to experiment with a different application architecture by building a core that will hold all the business logic and consume it with smaller apps. Also one more interesting thing to note is that the front store of our e-commerce application will be built using server-side rendering.

This new architecture will enable us to build micro apps; for example, one app could be the admin application that is going to manage the product catalog. The benefit is that each micro app can be built using different approaches.

As a demonstration, we are not going to build our front store in Angular. Sounds crazy I know, but for educational purposes, it's going to be great. Also, we want to highlight how easy it is to build hybrid applications.

The admin part of the application is going to be built using Angular 2. Because of this, we are going to build a headless core backend service. This core application will be consumed by our micro apps.

Setting up the base application

In previous chapters, we used our own boilerplate to bootstrap the application's development. This chapter is going to have a fresh folder structure, but don't worry; we are still going to use a lot of code from the existing boilerplate.

A new folder structure will give us more flexibility, as at the moment we have outgrown our initial architecture. One benefit, which we are not going to cover in this chapter, is that you can move each module to a separate package and install them as dependencies.

Before jumping into things, let's see a high-level view of our architecture:

```
apps/
-- admin/
-- api/
-- auth/
-- frontstore/
-- shared/
core/
---- helpers/
---- middlewares
---- models
---- services
config/
---- environments/
---- strategies
tests/
```

The explanation for the folder structure is as follows:

- `apps`: This folder will contain several micro apps, such as `frontstore`, which will serve as the client application for users visiting our e-commerce store.

- `core`: This is going to be the heart of our application, containing all the necessary business logic:
    - `middlewares`: In this folder, we'll store all our pieces of functions that will manipulate the request and response object. A good example would be authentication middleware.
    - `models`: This folder will store all the backend models.
    - `services`: This will group all common sets of application logic available for different clients and will coordinate the consumption of business logic.

- `config`: All application configuration files go here.
    - `environments`: This folder contains files loaded according to the current environment

- `tests`: This folder contains all the tests necessary to test the application backend logic.

Data modeling

Now that we have a high-level view of our architecture, let's define our models and see how they interact. This will give you a high-level view of how you are going to store your data in the database. Also, it will reflect the connections between different entities and you can decide, in the case of MongoDB, what documents will be embedded and which ones will be referenced.

Custom money data type

In the earlier Expense Tracker application, we concluded that there is a way to work with monetary data in JavaScript and MongoDB. It only needs extra application logic to handle the Exact Precision solution.

Because we are working with Mongoose as our ODM for Mongo, we can define a custom model for monetary data. I know it sounds strange, but it will give us the upper hand by defining virtual properties and reusing the money data type in our application.

Let's create a file called `core/models/money.js` and add the following Mongoose schema:

```
'use strict';

const DEF_CURRENCY = 'USD';
const DEF_SCALE_FACTOR = 100;

const mongoose = require('mongoose');
const Schema = mongoose.Schema;
const ObjectId = Schema.ObjectId;

const MoneySchema = new Schema({
  amount:   { type: Number, default: 0 },
  currency: { type: String, default: DEF_CURRENCY },
  factor:   { type: Number, default: DEF_SCALE_FACTOR }
}, {
  _id:      false,
  toObject: { virtuals: true },
  toJSON:   { virtuals: true }
});

MoneySchema
.virtual('display')
.set(function(value) {
  if (value) {
    this.set('amount', value * this.factor);
```

```
  }
})
.get(function() {
  return this.amount / this.factor;
});

module.exports = mongoose.model('Money', MoneySchema);
```

For easier readability, I did the following:

1. Defined a default currency with a default scale factor. To achieve better customization, you can add these into a configuration file.

2. Added a virtual named `display`, which will be the display value of the money model, for example, 18.99.

Now, having that out of the way, let's see what is going on with the preceding code. We created a custom Money model, which will serve us as a Money data type. As you can see, we disabled the autogeneration of the `_id` property. This way, if we use the model as an embedded document, Mongoose will not generate an `_id` property.

Let's see an example:

```
var price = new Money();
price.display = 18.99;
console.log(price.toObject());
// { amount: 1899, currency: 'USD', factor: 100, display: 18.99 }
```

When transforming the price to an object, the output will contain all of the necessary information and we don't need to do any calculations using floats. Remember that we are storing the scale factor and the currency within the price model because this needs to be consistent across the application with the currency.

The product model

When creating an e-commerce application, you have to think about storing many different product types in your catalog. The MongoDB data model will come in handy in this situation due to the fact that we can represent data in any structure.

Structuring data in an RDBMS would be a little bit harder; for example, one approach would be to represent each product type in a separate table. Each would have a different table structure. An alternative and popular approach would be **EAV**, which stands for **Entity Attribute Values**. In this case, you maintain a table with at least three columns: `entity_id`, `attribute_id`, and `value`. The EAV solution is very flexible, but it comes with a downside. Complex queries require a large number of JOIN operations, which can degrade performance.

Luckily for us, as pointed out earlier, MongoDB has a dynamic schema solution, and we can store all of the product data in one collection. We could have generic information of a product and product-specific information for different product types. Let's get down to business and define our product schema. Create a file called `core/models/product.js`, and add the following code:

```
'use strict';

const mongoose = require('mongoose');
const Money = require('./money').schema;
const commonHelper = require('../helpers/common');
const Schema = mongoose.Schema;
const ObjectId = Schema.ObjectId;
const Mixed = Schema.Types.Mixed;

const ProductSchema = new Schema({
  sku:          { type: String, required: true },
  category:     { type: String },
  title:        { type: String, required: true },
  summary:      { type: String },
  description:  { type: String },
  slug:         { type: String },
  images:       { type: [
    {
      caption:  { type: String },
      filename: { type: String }
    }
  ] },
  price:        { type: Money },
  details:      { type: Mixed },
  active:       { type: Boolean, default: false }
});

module.exports = mongoose.model('Product', ProductSchema);
```

As you can see, we have a few fields that all types of products are going to have, and we have a mixed property called `details` that will hold all the necessary details about a specific product. Also we used our custom data type for the `price` property. A product, by default, will be flagged as inactive in the product catalog so that it will be shown only when all the necessary information is added.

Earlier in the book—more precisely in *Chapter 3, Job Board*—we used the `slug` definition for URL-friendly titles for our job openings. This time, we are going to use it for our product titles. To simplify things, we are going to automatically generate them when a new entry is created.

Prepend the following code in your product model file, before the `module.exports` line:

```
ProductSchema.pre('save', function(next) {
  this.slug = commonHelper.createSlug(this.title);
  next();
});
```

To freshen up your memory, we used the same technique in *Chapter 3, Job Board* to create a slug from a title. So, this basically generates a URL-friendly string from the product title before saving in the database.

This pretty much sums up our product schema and should give us a solid start for storing products in MongoDB.

The order model

Due to the fact that we are trying to build an e-commerce application, we somehow need to be able to store what users have purchased from our store. We are going to store all of this information in an `orders` collection in MongoDB. An `order` entry should contain information about what products were bought, shipping details, and who made the purchase.

When you analyze this, the first thing that you think about is that we would also need to have a cart before placing an order. But if we reduce everything to a simple use case, we can consider that a cart is a special kind of an order. What I mean is that a cart holds product items that will be purchased and an order will be created for that purchase.

So, in simple terms, only the perspective changes how we see an order. We could have a `type` property for an order to determine its state. So we have a few key points to define our order schema. Now we can create a new file called `core/models/order.js`, and add the following schema:

```
'use strict';

const mongoose = require('mongoose');
const Money = require('./money').schema;
const Schema = mongoose.Schema;
const ObjectId = Schema.ObjectId;
const Mixed = Schema.Types.Mixed;

const OrderSchema = new Schema({
  identifier:   { type: String },
  user:         { type: ObjectId, ref: 'User' },
```

```
type:           { type: String, default: 'cart' },
status:         { type: String, default 'active' },
total:          { type: Money },
details:        { type: Mixed },
shipping:       { type: Mixed },
items:          { type: [
  {
    sku:        { type: String },
    qty:        { type: Number, default: 1},
    title:      { type: String },
    price:      { type: Money },
    product:    { type: ObjectId, ref: 'Product' }
  }
]},
expiresAt:      { type: Date, default: null },
updatedAt:      { type: Date, default: Date.now },
createdAt:      { type: Date, default: Date.now }
}, {
  toObject:     { virtuals: true },
  toJSON:       { virtuals: true }
});

module.exports = mongoose.model('Order', OrderSchema);
```

As you can see, an order will store all selected products in the items property, together with simple information, such as the sku, quantity, and price of the product. We store some non-trivial data in the items list as the product's title so that we don't have to retrieve it for non-trivial operations.

When we are dealing with a cart entry, we want it to eventually expire if it is not finalized as an order. This is because we want to release items from the cart to be available.

Probably, we are going to store extra details about the order and shipping details that could vary from order to order. That's why we marked them as mixed data types.

The inventory model

Until now, we have defined the product schema and the order schema. Neither mentioned anything about the inventory status. In the order schema, we store for each product item, what quantity was placed in the order, but this won't reflect the initial stock or the current stock.

There are a few approaches when working with inventory data, each with its own benefits and downsides. For example, we can store a single record for each physical product; so if we have 100 stock units of a product, we store 100 records in the inventory.

In a large product catalog, this would not be a good solution, as the `inventory` collection would grow very quickly. Storing separate entries for each unit can be beneficial when you have physical products and a low volume of stock units. An example is a wood shop that builds furniture and wants to track more details for each physical unit.

An alternative would be to store a single entry for each product, with the quantity of the product in stock. Now that we have a good hint about what needs to be done, let's create the inventory model, called `core/models/inventory.js`, with the following code:

```
'use strict';

const mongoose = require('mongoose');
const Schema = mongoose.Schema;
const ObjectId = Schema.ObjectId;
const Mixed = Schema.Types.Mixed;

const InventorySchema = new Schema({
  sku:          { type: String },
  status:       { type: String, default: 'available' },
  qty:          { type: Number, default: 0 },
  carted:       { type: [
    { type: {
        sku:     { type: String },
        qty:     { type: Number, default: 1 },
        order:   { type: ObjectId, ref: 'Order' },
        product: { type: ObjectId, ref: 'Product' }
      }
    }
  ]},
  createdAt:    { type: Date, default: Date.now }
});

module.exports = mongoose.model('Inventory', InventorySchema);
```

We pushed things a little bit further and added a `carted` property. This will hold all the items that are active in a cart to help us track the progress of each reserved item in the inventory.

This way, you can have a clean history of the level of the inventory. You can omit the `carted` property and only rely on information from the `orders` collection.

The core Service Layer

Because our application will have different clients consuming business logic, we are going to add a Service Layer; it will coordinate operations for different use cases. So, we are going to move most of our business logic from controllers to services. Probably, it's too early to see the benefits of this, but as we progress with this chapter, it will make more sense.

One benefit would be that you can simply expose your Service Layer as a RESTful API, or add another client that will render on the server-side templates and display all the necessary information to the user. Regardless of the application's client implementation, you can test the business logic of your application.

The product catalog

The product catalog will contain all the products you want to be shown or simply exist in the system. Each item in the catalog will be stored in MongoDB, in the `products` collection. We are going to create a `ProductCatalog` service, which will hold all the business logic for managing the products in our e-commerce application.

Let's follow a few steps in order to create the product catalog service:

1. Create the service file, called `core/services/product-catalog.js`.
2. Add the following code:

```
'use strict';

const MAX_PRODUCT_SHOWN = 50;
const _ = require('lodash');
const Product = require('../models/product');

class ProductCatalog {
  constructor() {
  }
}

module.exports = ProductCatalog;
```

3. Declare the class constructor:

    ```
    constructor(opts, ProductModel) {
      opts = opts || {};
      this.maxProductsShown = opts.maxProductsShown ||
      MAX_PRODUCT_SHOWN;
      this.Product = ProductModel || Product;
    }
    ```

4. Adding a product to the catalog:

    ```
    add(data, callback) {
      this.Product.create(data, callback);
    }
    ```

5. We'll add each class method one by one.

6. Edit an existing product:

    ```
    edit(sku, data, callback) {
      //  remove sku; this should not change,
      //  add a new product if it needs to change
      delete data.sku;

      this.Product.findBySKU(sku, (err, product) => {
        if (err) {
          return callback(err);
        }

        _.assign(product, data);
        //  tell mongoose to increment the doc version `__v`
        product.increment();
        product.save(callback);
      });
    }
    ```

7. List all products:

    ```
    list(query, limit, skip, callback) {
      if (typeof query === 'funciton') {
        callback = limit;
        limit = this.maxProductsShown;
        skip = 0;
      }

      // make sure we only allow retriving `50` products from
      the catalog
      if (+limit > this.maxProductsShown) {
        limit = this.maxProductsShown;
    ```

```
        }

        this.Product.find(query).limit(limit).skip(skip)
    .exec(callback);
        }
```

8. Get more details using the `sku` identifier:

```
details(sku, callback) {
    this.Product.findBySKU(sku, callback);
}
```

9. Get a product by `slug`:

```
detailsBySlug(slug, callback) {
    this.Product.findBySlug(slug, callback);
}
Remove a product:
remove(sku, callback) {
    this.Product.findBySKU(sku, (err, product) => {
      if (err) {
        return callback(err);
      }

      product.remove(callback);
    });
}
```

We managed to put down a base for our product catalog service. As you can see, it only masks certain functionalities from the end module, which should not know of the underlining layer or how data is stored. It can be a database, as MongoDB is in our case, or simply a filesystem.

The first benefit that we get is testability, as we can test our application's business logic and run an integration test before even implementing a higher-level layer. For example, we can have the following piece of code, extracted from `tests/integration/product-catalog.test.js`:

```
const ProductCatalog = require('../../core/services/product-
catalog');

// … rest of the required modules

describe('Product catalog', () => {
  let mongoose;
  let Product;
  let productCatalog;
```

```
let productData = { ... };  // will hold the product related
data

before(done => {
  mongoose = require('../../config/mongoose').init();
  productCatalog = new ProductCatalog();
  // … more code
  done();
});

it('should add a new product to the catalog', done => {
  productCatalog.add(productData, (err, product) => {
    if (err) { throw err; }

    should.exist(prod);
    prod.title.should.equal('M.E.A.N. Blueprints');
    done();
  });
});
});
});
```

The preceding test case will simply check whether all the operations done by the service are correct. We did a lot of test-driven development in the earlier chapters, and in the later chapters, we focused more on functionality, but this does not mean that we skipped writing tests. The tests are available in the full source code for you to check out and follow while developing the application.

The inventory manager

Lots of e-commerce solutions out in the wild come with an inventory manager, which will help you keep track of a product's stock level, replenish your product's stock level, or adjust it as desired.

We didn't want to embed inventory information in the product document, so we are going to store it separately for each product. There are many ways you can track your inventory; we have chosen a solution that fits most of the use cases, and it's easy to implement.

Before we begin coding, I would like to go through the test cases to give you a hint about what we are going to implement:

1. We should be able to track the inventory for a product:

   ```
   it('should create an inventory item for a product', done
   => {
     inventoryManager.create({
       sku: 'MEANB',
   ```

```
        qty: 1
    }, (err, inventoryItem) => {
        if (err) throw err;

        should.exist(inventoryItem);
        inventoryItem.sku.should.equal('MEANB');
        inventoryItem.qty.should.equal(1);
        done();
    });
});
```

2. A desired quantity of a given product should be reserved from the inventory on demand:

```
it('should reserve an item if there is enough on stock',
done => {
    inventoryManager.reserve('MEANB', new
    mongoose.Types.ObjectId(), 2, (err, result) => {
        if (err) throw err;

        should.exist(result);
        result.sku.should.equal('MEANB');
        done();
    });
});
```

3. If there is not adequate inventory, the service should not satisfy the request:

```
it('should not reserve an item if there is not enough on
stock', done => {
    inventoryManager.reserve('MEANB', new
    mongoose.Types.ObjectId(), 2, (err, result) => {
        should.not.exist(result);
        should.exist(err);
        err.message.should.equal('Stock lever is lower then
        the desired quantity.');
        err.status.should.equal(409);
        err.type.should.equal('not_enough_stock_units')
        done();
    });
});
```

4. Increase the available quantity:

```
it('should increase the quantity for an inventory unit',
done => {
    inventoryManager.increase('MEANB', 5, (err, inventory)
    => {
```

```
      if (err) throw err;

      inventory.qty.should.equal(6);
      done();
    });
  });
```

5. Or you can decrease the available quantity to make adjustments:

```
it('should decrease the quantity for an inventory unit',
done => {
  inventoryManager.decrease('MEANB', 2, (err, inventory)
  => {
    if (err) throw err;

    inventory.qty.should.equal(4);
    done();
  });
});
```

Now that we have taken a glance at what needs to be done, let's follow a few steps to create our inventory manager service:

1. Create a new file, `core/services/inventory-manager.js`.

2. Define a starting point:

```
'use strict';

const Inventory = require('../models/inventory');

class InventoryManager {
  constructor() {}
}

module.exports = InventoryManager;
```

3. Complete the class constructor:

```
constructor(opts, InventoryModel) {
  this.opts = opts || {};
  this.Inventory = InventoryModel || Inventory;
}
```

Remember that we can inject a custom `InventoryModel` inside our service as long as it has at least the necessary properties and methods.

4. Create a new inventory item method:

```
create(data, callback) {
  data.carted = [];
  this.Inventory.create(data, callback);
}
```

5. Modify the quantity private method:

```
_modifyQuantity(sku, qty, reduce, callback) {
  qty = (reduce) ? qty * -1 : qty;

  this.Inventory.update({
    sku: sku
  }, {
    $inc: { qty: qty }
  }, (err, result) => {
    if (err) {
      return callback(err);
    }

    if (result.nModified === 0) {
      let err = new Error('Nothing modified.');
      err.type = 'nothing_modified';
      err.status = 400;
      return callback(err);
    }

    this.Inventory.findOne({ sku: sku }, callback);
  });
}
```

We created a private method, prefixed with an underscore for semantics. This will serve as the main entry point when manipulating stock levels. If nothing has changed, we return an error. After a successful operation, we return the current state of the inventory entry.

6. Increase and decrease the quantity:

```
increase(sku, quantity, callback) {
  this._modifyQuantity(sku, quantity, false, callback);
}

decrease(sku, quantity, callback) {
  this._modifyQuantity(sku, quantity, true, callback);
}
Reserve the quantity in the inventory:
```

```
reserve(sku, orderId, quantity, callback) {
  let query = {
    sku: sku,
    qty: { $gte: quantity }
  };

  let update = {
    $inc: { qty: -quantity },
    $push: {
      carted: {
        qty: quantity,
        order: orderId
      }
    }
  };

  this.Inventory.update(query, update, (err, result) => {
    if (err) {
      return callback(err);
    }

    if (result.nModified === 0) {
      let err = new Error('Stock lever is lower then the
      desired quantity.');
      err.type = 'not_enough_stock_units';
      err.status = 409;
      return callback(err);
    }

    callback(null, {
      sku: sku,
      order: orderId,
      qty: quantity
    });
  });
}
```

The preceding code will reserve the available quantity of a product in the inventory. In some cases, the system cannot satisfy the requested quantity, so we check to make sure that we have the desired availability before decrementing the quantity. If we cannot fulfill the request, we return a specific error.

Also you might notice that we have progressively added our own custom Error object, which also contains a suggestion for the status code itself. At this time, errors returned from the service have no standard format, due to the fact that the underlining ODM could return different Error objects.

We won't be able to satisfy all use cases in this book, so sometimes you have to put the pieces together.

Shopping cart

By this time, we should have all the necessary services used by the shopping cart service. Now this service will be quite interesting, if you permit me to say so. Regularly, e-commerce solutions have a shopping cart in which customers can easily add or remove items, change quantities, and even abandon them.

One important thing to note is that we have to make sure that a customer cannot add items that are unavailable. In other words, if a product stock doesn't match the requested quantity, the add action should not succeed.

Basically, our shopping cart service will handle all the business logic described previously. Also, when a customer adds an item to the cart, the inventory should be properly updated. Remember that our orders collection will hold the carts as well.

Things are pretty clear about what needs to be done. If not, go and take a quick look at the test cases. Let's create our shopping cart service, `core/services/shopping-cart.js`, and add the following class:

```
'use strict';

const EXPIRATION_TIME = 15*60; // 15 minutes
const commonHelper = require('../helpers/common');
const Order = require('../models/order');
const InventoryManager = require('./inventory-manager');
const ProductCatalog = require('./product-catalog');

class ShoppingCart {
}

module.exports = ShoppingCart;
```

Noting fancy here. We can move on by adding our constructor:

```
constructor(opts, OrderModel, ProductService, InventoryService)
{
  InventoryService = InventoryService || InventoryManager;
  ProductService = ProductService || ProductCatalog;
  this.opts = opts || {};
  this.opts.expirationTime = this.opts.expirationTime ||
  EXPIRATION_TIME;
```

```
    this.Order = OrderModel || Order;
    this.inventoryManager = new InventoryService();
    this.productCatalog = new ProductService();
}
```

Before I forget, we are going to use the other two services we implemented earlier to manage the inventory and retrieve products from our catalog. Moreover, before adding a new item into the cart, we need to create it. So let's add the createCart() method:

```
createCart(userId, data, callback) {
  data.user = userId;
  data.expiresAt =
  commonHelper.generateExpirationTime(this.opts.expirationTime);
  this.Order.create(data, callback);
}
```

When adding a new item into the shopping cart, we have to take care of a few things, and we must verify that the inventory meets the request's requirements. Let's sketch out the addProduct() method of the cart service:

```
addProduct(cartId, sku, qty, callback) {
  this.productCatalog.findBySKU(sku, (err, product) => {
    if (err) {
      return callback(err);
    }

    let prod = {
      sku: product.sku,
      qty: qty
      title: product.title,
      price: product.price,
      product: product._id
    };

    // push carted items into the order
    this._pushItems(cartId, prod, (err, result) => {
      if (err) {
        return callback(err);
      }

      // reserve inventory
      this.inventoryManager.reserve(product.sku, cartId, qty,
      (err, result) => {
        // roll back our cart updates
        if (err && err.type === 'not_enough_stock_units') {
```

```
            return this._pullItems(cartId, sku, () =>
            callback(err));
        }

        // retrive current cart state
        this.findById(cartId, callback);
      });
    });
  });
}
```

When adding a product into the cart, we want to store some additional information, so we first need to retrieve the product from the catalog using the SKU. The product needs to be added with the desired quantity to the cart's items. After successfully populating the cart with the new item, we need to decrease the number of units available in the inventory.

If there are not enough items in the inventory, we must roll back the cart update and raise an error in the application. Finally, we get a fresh copy of the persisted cart.

Beside the methods used from the other two services, we have a few left to implement for the ShoppingCart class, such as the _pushItems() method:

```
_pushItems(cartId, prod, callback) {
  let exdate =
  commonHelper.generateExpirationTime(this.opts.expirationTime);
  let now = new Date();
  //  make sure the cart is still active and add items
  this.Order.update({
    { _id: cartId, status: 'active' },
    {
      $set: { expiresAt: exdate, updatedAt: now },
      $push: { items: prod }
    }
  }, (err, result) => {
    if (err) {
      return callback(err);
    }

    if (result.nModified === 0) {
      let err = new Error('Cart expired.');
      err.type = 'cart_expired';
      err.status = 400;
      return callback(err);
```

```
      }

    //  TODO: proper response
    callback(null, result);
  });
}
```

The cart must be active in order to add items to it. Also, we have to update the expiration date. Remember that we are doing atomic operations on our documents, so only the raw responses of the operations are returned.

If we want to roll back our cart, we need to pull out the added items; the _pullItems() method does exactly this:

```
_pullItems(cartId, sku, callback) {
  this.Order.update({
    { _id: cartId },
    { $pull: { items: { sku: sku } } }
  }, (err, result) => {
    if (err) {
      return callback(err);
    }

    if (result.nModified === 0) {
      let err = new Error('Nothing modified.');
      err.type = 'nothing_modified';
      err.status = 400;
      return callback(err);
    }

    //  TODO: proper response
    callback(null, result);
  });
}
```

By this time, we should be able to manage our cart easily with the implemented functionalities. The ShoppingCart service has used both the InventoryManager and ProductCatalog services, exposing the exact business logic we need to handle operations on a cart.

The Auth micro app

The Auth micro app will handle authentications in different scenarios. It's going to be our main entry point to authenticate users, using stateful and stateless approaches.

Our core module already exposes middleware to check whether a user is authenticated or not, and authorization-related middleware. This functionality can be used in any module or micro app.

Defining the class

This is going to be our first micro app, so let's go through a few steps:

1. Create a new micro app called `apps/auth/index.js`.

2. Add the following base content:

    ```
    'use strict'

    const express = require('express');
    const router = express.Router();
    const Controller = require('./controller');

    class Auth {
    }
    ```

3. Define the constructor:

    ```
    constructor(config, core, app) {
      this.core = core;
      this.controller = new Controller(core);
      this.app = app;
      this.router = router;
      this.rootUrl = '/auth';
      this.regiterRoutes();
      this.app.use(this.rootUrl, this.router);
    }
    ```

    We defined a base URL for our micro app and mounted the router on the main Express application. We also created a new instance of the Controller used in the `Auth` micro app.

4. Register all necessary routes:

    ```
    regiterRoutes() {
      this.router.post('/register',
      this.controller.register);

      /**
       * Stateful authentication
       */
      this.router.post('/signin', this.controller.signin);
    ```

```
this.router.get('/signout', this.controller.signout);

/**
 *  Stateless authentication
 */
this.router.post('/basic', this.controller.basic);
}
```

In order to save development time, we borrowed code from previous chapters, so the preceding lines of code are probably already familiar to you.

5. Initialize your micro app in the main `server.js` file:

```
const Auth = require('./apps/auth');
let auth = new Auth(config, core, app);
```

In the main `server.js` file, we are going to initialize each app. You can take a look at the final version of the `server.js` file to see exactly where to put things.

The controller

Earlier, I stated that we are reusing code from previous chapters. We also did this for the controller. We turned our controller into a class called `AuthController` and exposed the following methods:

1. To sign in users using a stateful authentication strategy:

```
signin(req, res, next) {
  passport.authenticate('local', (err, user, info) => {
    if (err || !user) {
      return res.status(400).json(info);
    }

    req.logIn(user, function(err) {
      if (err) {
        return next(err);
      }

      res.status(200).json(user);
    });
  })(req, res, next);
}
```

2. Authenticate using a stateless strategy:

```
basic(req, res, next) {
  passport.authenticate('basic', (err, user, info) => {
    if (err) {
```

```
        return next(err);
      }

      if (!user) {
        return res.status(400).json({ message: 'Invalid
        email or password.' });
      }

      Token.generate({ user: user.id }, (err, token) => {
        if (err) {
          return next(err);
        }

        if (!token) {
          return res.status(400).json({ message: 'Invalid
          email or password.' });
        }

        const result = user.toJSON();
        result.token = _.pick(token, ['hash',
        'expiresAt']);

        res.json(result);
      });

    })(req, res, next);
  }
```

In some cases, we don't need to persist the user's session. Instead, we create a token that will be used at each request to see who tries to access our endpoints.

3. Register a user in our system:

```
register(req, res, next) {
  const userData = _.pick(req.body, 'name', 'email',
  'password');

  User.register(userData, (err, user) => {
    if (err && (11000 === err.code || 11001 ===
    err.code)) {
      return res.status(400).json({ message: 'E-mail is
      already in use.' });
    }

    if (err) {
```

```
        return next(err);
      }

      // just in case :)
      delete user.password;
      delete user.passwordSalt;

      res.json(user);
    });
  }
```

Exposing an API

Our core business logic needs to be accessed in some way, and I think a RESTful API would serve us in a good way. In order to get a better understanding and move through the whole app, we are only going to showcase a few parts from our API.

We are more interested in the whole app from an architectural point of view, instead of having detailed and fully integrated functionalities.

The Api class

For this micro app, we are going to group our files by type context. First, we are going to create our micro app class, `apps/api/index.js`, and add the following content:

```
'use strict';

const ProductsRoutes = require('./routes/products');
const ProductController = require('./controllers/product');

class Api {
  constructor(config, core, app) {
    let productController = new ProductController(core);
    let productRoutes = new ProductsRoutes(core,
    productController);

    this.config = config;
    this.core = core;
    this.app = app;
    this.root = app.get('root');
    this.rootUrl = '/api';

    this.app.get('/api/status', (req, res, next) => {
      res.json({ message: 'API is running.' });
```

```
    });

    this.app.use(this.rootUrl, productRoutes.router);
  }
}

module.exports = Api;
```

This portion of the app mounts the routes exposed by `ProductRoutes` on the main Express app. The preceding `ProductRoutes` class takes a `ProductController` as a required parameter.

Now we are not going to discuss each controller and route in particular, and are only going to focus on the product part. We are going to use the `ProductCatalog` core service and call the required business logic.

Product controller

This controller is going to handle the requests to manage products. We are going to follow these steps to implement it:

1. Create a new file called `apps/api/controller/product.js`.

2. Define the controller:

   ```
   'use strict';

   const _ = require('lodash');

   let productCatalog;

   class ProductsController {
     constructor(core) {
       this.core = core;
       productCatalog = new core.services.ProductCatalog();
     }
   Add the create product method:
     create(req, res, next) {
       productCatalog.add(req.body, (err, product) => {
         if (err && err.name === 'ValidationError') {
           return res.status(400).json(err);
         }

         if (err) {
           return next(err);
   ```

```
    }

      res.status(201).json(product);
    });
  }
```

3. Attach the `getAll` products method:

```
getAll(req, res, next) {
  const limit = +req.query.limit || 10;
  const skip = +req.query.skip || 0;
  const query = {} // you cloud filter products

  productCatalog.list(query, limit, skip, (err, products)
  => {
    if (err) {
      return next(err);
    }

    res.json(products);
  });
}
Implement a method that retrieves a single product:
getOne(req, res, next) {
  productCatalog.details(req.params.sku, (err, product)
  => {
    if (err) {
      return next(err);
    }

    res.json(product);
  });
}
```

Product router

Defining the routes is similar to what we did earlier in the `Auth` micro app, but we moved our routes into a separate file, called `apps/api/routes/products.js`. The content of the file is fairly simple:

```
'use strict';

const express = require('express');
const router = express.Router();
```

```
class ProductsRoutes {
  constructor(core, controller) {
    this.core = core;
    this.controller = controller;
    this.router = router;
    this.authBearer = this.core.authentication.bearer;
    this.regiterRoutes();
  }

  regiterRoutes() {
    this.router.post(
      '/products',
      this.authBearer(),
      this.controller.create
    );

    this.router.get(
      '/products',
      this.authBearer(),
      this.controller.getAll
    );

    this.router.get(
      '/products/:sku',
      this.authBearer(),
      this.controller.getOne
    );
  }
}

module.exports = ProductsRoutes;
```

As you can see, the bearer authentication middleware was used from the core module to check whether a user has a valid token or not. This function has the following body:

```
function bearerAuthentication(req, res, next) {
  return passport.authenticate('bearer', { session: false });
}
```

I think we have the big picture of how our Api micro app works and what needs to be done. You can follow the rest of the code in the project's repository.

Shared resources

Many of our micro apps will use the same static assets in order not to replicate these resources across apps. We can create a micro app that will serve all the shared resources.

Instead of having a main `public` folder, each micro app that wants to serve static files can have a separate `public` folder. This means that we can move all of our shared static resources, and move them to the inner `public` folder.

We will have the following folder structure:

```
apps/
-- shared/
---- public
------ assets/
---- index.js
```

The `index.js` file will have the following content:

```javascript
'use strict';

const path = require('path');
const serveStatic = require('serve-static');

class Shared {
  constructor(config, core, app) {
    this.app = app;
    this.root = app.get('root');
    this.rootUrl = '/';
    this.serverStaticFiles();
  }

  serverStaticFiles() {
    let folderPath = path.resolve(this.root, __dirname, './public');
    this.app.use(this.rootUrl, serveStatic(folderPath));
  }
}

module.exports = Shared;
```

We define a class and serve all the static resources from the `public` folder. The `resolve` method was used from the `path` module to resolve the path to the `public` folder.

As you can see, it's fairly simple to make changes to our previous architecture from earlier chapters. Also, the preceding technique will be used in our `admin` micro app.

The admin section

Usually, e-commerce solutions come with an admin section, where you can manage your products and inventory. The admin section for our application is going to be built with Angular 2. Nothing fancy; we have already built a few apps with Angular, right?

We are not going to go through all the details but only the most important parts of the application. Don't worry! Full source code is available for the project.

The admin micro app

We made a few architectural changes right from the beginning. Each of our micro apps will serve a specific purpose. The admin micro app will host the administration application built using Angular 2.

In the preceding chapters, we used server-static to expose our public folder's content. This app will have its own public folder and will contain only the files related to our admin Angular application.

This micro app is going to be fairly simple. Create a file called apps/admin/index.js with the following content:

```
'use strict';

const path = require('path');
const serveStatic = require('serve-static');

class Admin {
  constructor(config, core, app) {
    this.app = app;
    this.root = app.get('root');
    this.rootUrl = '/admin';
    this.serverStaticFiles();
  }

  serverStaticFiles() {
    let folderPath = path.resolve(this.root, __dirname, './public');
    this.app.use(this.rootUrl, serveStatic(folderPath));
  }
}

module.exports = Admin;
```

The `Admin` class will define our micro app and use the `serverStaticFiles()` method to expose the public folder's content for external use. The file serving for the admin app is mounted on the `/admin` URL path.

Don't forget to take a look at the main `server.js` file to initialize your `admin` micro app correctly.

Changing the auth module

The `admin` app uses a token to grant access to the API's endpoints. So we need to make a few changes to our `AuthHttp` service, from `apps/admin/public/src/auth/auth-http.ts`.

The changes affect the `request` method, which will look like this:

```
private request(requestArgs: RequestOptionsArgs,
additionalArgs?: RequestOptionsArgs) {
  let opts = new RequestOptions(requestArgs);

  if (additionalArgs) {
    opts = opts.merge(additionalArgs);
  }

  let req:Request = new Request(opts);

  if (!req.headers) {
    req.headers = new Headers();
  }

  if (!req.headers.has('Authorization')) {
    req.headers.append('Authorization', `Bearer
    ${this.getToken()}`);
  }

  return this._http.request(req).catch((err: any) => {
    if (err.status === 401) {
      this.unauthorized.next(err);
    }

    return Observable.throw(err);
  });
}
```

For each request, we add the `Authorization` header with the necessary token. Also, we need to retrieve the token from `localStorage` using the following method:

```
private getToken() {
  return localStorage.getItem('token');
}
```

The token will be persisted to the `localStorage` on a successful sign-in. In `AuthService`, we are going to store the current user and its token and persist to `localStorage`:

```
public setCurrentUser(user: any) {
  this.currentUser.next(user);
}

private _initSession() {
  let user =
  this._deserialize(localStorage.getItem('currentUser'));
  this.currentUser = new BehaviorSubject<Response>(user);
  // persist the user to the local storage
  this.currentUser.subscribe((user) => {
    localStorage.setItem('currentUser', this._serialize(user));
    localStorage.setItem('token', user.token.hash || '');
  });
}
```

When the user successfully signs in, we store the current user in a subject and notify all subscribers of that change.

Remember that we can expose all the members from a context simply by using a single `index.ts` file, located in the root of the bounded context. For the `auth` module, we can have the following structure:

```
auth/
-- components/
-- services/
-- index.ts
```

For instance, our `AuthHttp` service can be exported with `index.ts` using the following:

```
export * from './services/auth-http';
```

And we can import it into another component using this line:

```
import { AuthHttp } from './auth/index';
```

Instead of the following approach:

```
import { AuthHttp } from './auth/services/auth-http';
```

Products administration

On the backend part, we created a service and exposed an API to manage products. Now on the client side, we need to create a module that will consume the API and let us do different operations.

The product service

We are going to talk about only a few methods from our product service, because basically we are going to do only simple CRUD operations in the admin section. Let's create a file called `apps/admin/public/src/services/product.service.ts`, with the following base content:

```
import { Injectable } from 'angular2/core';
import { Http, Response, Headers } from 'angular2/http';
import { Observable } from 'rxjs/Observable';
import { ProductService } from './product.service';
import { contentHeaders } from '../common/headers';
import { Product } from './product.model';

type ObservableProducts = Observable<Array<Product>>;

@Injectable()
export class ProductService {
  public products: ObservableProducts;

  private _authHttp: AuthHttp;
  private _productsObservers: any;
  private _dataStore: { products: Array<Product> };

  constructor(authHttp: Http) {
    this._authHttp = authHttp;
    this.products = new Observable(observer =>
    this._productsObservers = observer).share();
    this._dataStore = { products: [] };
  }
}
```

Following this, we'll add the `getAll` products method. We are going to use this when we want to show a list of products. Append the following code to the `ProductService`:

```
getAll() {
  this._authHttp
  .get('/api/products', { headers: contentHeaders })
  .map((res: Response) => res.json())
  .subscribe(products => {
    this._dataStore.products = products;
    this._productsObservers.next(this._dataStore.products);
  });
}
```

The rest of the methods are in the full source code of the project.

List products

In the main product administration section, we are going to list all the available products from the catalog. For this, we create another component found under `apps/admin/public/product/components/product-list.component.ts`:

```
import { Component, OnInit } from 'angular2/core';
import { ProductService } from '../product.service';
import { Router, RouterLink } from 'angular2/router';
import { Product } from '../product.model';

@Component({
    selector: 'product-list',
    directives: [RouterLink],
    template: `
      <div class="product-list row">
        <h2 class="col">Products list</h2>
        <div *ngIf="products.length === 0" class="empty-product-
        list col">
          <h3>Add your first product to you catalog</h3>
        </div>
        <div class="col col-25">
          <a href="#" [routerLink]="['ProductCreate']" class="add-
          product-sign">+</a>
        </div>
        <div *ngFor="#product of products" class="col col-25">
          <img src="http://placehold.it/208x140?text
          =product+image&txtsize=18" />
          <h3>
```

```
          <a href="#"
             [routerLink]="['ProductEdit', { sku: product.sku
             }]">
             {{ product.title }}
          </a>
          </h3>
      </div>
     </div>
       `
  })
  export class ProductListComponent implements OnInit {
    public products: Array<Product> = [];
    private _productService: ProductService;

    constructor(productService: ProductService) {
      this._productService = productService;
    }

    ngOnInit() {
      this._productService.products.subscribe((products) => {
        this.products = products
      });
      this._productService.getAll();
    }
  }
```

The preceding code will just list all the products retrieved from the service and have a route link to edit a specific product. You can easily list extra details of a product; you just need to modify the template.

The main product component

To manage our routes, we have to create a main entry point and create a component for this. To have a final picture, I'm going to show you the final version of ProductComponent, found under apps/admin/public/src/product/product.component.ts:

```
import { Component } from 'angular2/core';
import { RouteConfig, RouterOutlet } from 'angular2/router';
import { ProductListComponent } from './product-list.component';
import { ProductEditComponent } from './product-edit.component';
import { ProductCreateComponent } from './product-create.component';
```

```
@RouteConfig([
  { path: '/', as: 'ProductList', component: ProductListComponent,
  useAsDefault: true },
  { path: '/:sku', as: 'ProductEdit', component:
  ProductEditComponent },
  { path: '/create', as: 'ProductCreate', component:
  ProductCreateComponent }
])
@Component({
    selector: 'product-component',
    directives: [
      ProductListComponent,
      RouterOutlet
    ],
    template: `
      <div class="col">
        <router-outlet></router-outlet>
      </div>
    `
})
export class ProductComponent {
  constructor() {}
}
```

We are using this component to configure our routes for the products listing, for creating a new product, and for editing an existing product by a specific SKU. This way, we can easily mount it on a higher level component.

Add and edit a product

Basically, what we did is used the same template to edit and add a product. In this application, when viewing the product details, you are actually editing the product. In this way, we don't have to implement or mask the edit functionality separately from the detailed view.

Due to the fact that the application is in an early stage and there is no difference between creating a new product and updating an existing one, we can reduce the workload and implement both at the same time.

The edit product source code can be found in `apps/admin/public/src/product/components/product-edit.component.ts`.

Order handling

The system should handle orders, which means that someone needs to handle the status of the orders. Usually, orders can have a few states. I will try to explain some of these in the following table:

Name	Status	Description
Pending	pending	The order is received (usually unpaid).
Failed	failed	Something went wrong; that is, the payment failed or was declined.
Processing	processing	The order is awaiting fulfillment.
Completed	completed	The order is fulfilled and completed. Usually, no further action is required.
On-hold	on_hold	The stock is reduced but waiting further confirmation, that is, payment.
Cancelled	cancelled	The order was cancelled by the customer or admin.

We are not going to handle all the scenarios we just described. The full version of the application supports only a few of them: pending, processing, cancelled, and completed. As we won't implement a payment method, there is no need to handle all the scenarios.

After so much code, I think we can take a break and only discuss this part. You can check out the working version from the GitHub repository.

Retrieving orders

To manage all the incoming orders, we need to list all of them to the admin. We are not going to get into the details of the code because it is very similar to what we have done so far.

The service found at `public/src/order/order.service.ts` will handle all operations on the order entity. A nice touch that can be added in this application is getting a stream of orders from the backend. This is something similar to what we did in *Chapter 4, Chat Application*, when we worked with WebSockets.

In other words, we can notify all clients of the new orders available as soon as they are added into the system. This will give a boost when you have a high volume of incoming orders and would like to be notified as soon as possible so as to handle them as quickly as you can.

View and update orders

Normally, before handling an order, you would like to see more information about it, such as the shipping address, or any other information the client provided to you. But at the same time, the actions required to handle an order should be kept at a minimum.

Keeping all this in mind, we went with a solution in which one can view and edit the order in the same context. So, `OrderDetailsComponent` does exactly that; it can be found under the following location: `public/src/order/components/order-details.ts`.

The full source can be found in the repository, but I'll try to explain what we did there.

Building the Storefront

As we discussed at the beginning of the chapter, we are going to try something different. Instead of building a single-page app for our Storefront, we are going to implement server-side-rendered pages.

Technically, we are going to build a classical web page. The pages are going to be dynamic, rendered using a view engine to render our templates.

We want to truly leverage the benefits of our headless core application and see how we can integrate it with different client applications, so we are going to experiment a little bit with server-side-rendered pages using a third-party package.

We can easily build this using Angular, but I wanted to add a twist, to see more complex solutions in action.

Storefront micro app

As we have seen before in the admin section of our application, we decoupled it from the main application into a micro app. So technically, we can just pull out the necessary code for the storefront from this application at any time, add it to a whole new Express app, and make all the calls across the network.

At first, this might seem a little strange, but as soon as your application starts growing and you need to scale your application, this will give you the upper hand to differentiate what part needs to be scaled or moved to a separate application for better scalability.

It is always a good thing to think ahead, but also, I'm not a big fan of early optimization. You cannot be certain from the beginning how your application will grow in time, but it is wise to plan ahead.

The Storefront application is going to showcase how we can integrate different techniques in the same application. The focus is purely educational, and this was added to the book to show different approaches to building Express apps.

Let's talk about the technologies used to build our Storefront. We are going to use nunjucks, which is a nice templating engine for JavaScript. It can be used both on the server side and the client side.

Before we get to the templates part, we need to make some preparations:

1. Create a new apps folder under apps/storefront.

2. Add a new file, apps/storefront/index.js.

3. Define the micro app's class:

```
'use strict';

const express = require('express');
const nunjucks = require('nunjucks');
const router = express.Router();
const ProductController = require('./controllers/products');

class Storefront {
  constructor(config, core, app) {
    this.config = config;
    this.core = core;
    this.app = app;
    this.router = router;
    this.rootUrl = '/';
    this.productCtrl = new ProductController(core);
    this.configureViews();
    this.regiterRoutes();
    this.app.use(this.rootUrl, this.router);
  }
}
```

4. Configure the view engine:

```
configureViews() {
  let opts = {};

  if (!this.config.nunjucks.cache) {
    opts.noCache = true;
  }

  if (this.config.nunjucks.watch) {
    opts.watch = true;
```

```
      }

      let loader = new
      nunjucks.FileSystemLoader('apps/frontstore/views',
      opts);

      this.nunjucksEnv = new nunjucks.Environment(loader);
      this.nunjucksEnv.express(this.app);
    }
```

5. Register routes:

```
      registerRoutes() {
        this.router.get('/', this.productCtrl.home);
      }
```

For this micro app, we started using a view engine to render our templates on the server side. The `configureViews()` method will initialize the `nunjucks` environment and load the template files from the filesystem. Also we are checking whether we should activate the cache and watch functionality from `nunjucks`. You can read more about this in the project's documentation.

Finally, we register the application's routes as for each of our previous Express applications we built together. For easier reading, I've only added the home location and only instantiated `ProductController`.

In case you are wondering what the `ProductController` is, we just use a class approach for our controller files so that we can instantiate it, and pass the core of the application. Let's take a look at a section of the code from `apps/storefront/controllers/product.js`:

```
    'use strict';

    let productCatalog;

    class ProductsController {
      constructor(core) {
        this.core = core;
        productCatalog = new core.services.ProductCatalog();
      }

      home(req, res, next) {
        productCatalog.list({}, 10, 0, (err, products) => {
          if (err) {
            next(err);
```

```
      }

      res.render('home', { products: products });
    });
  }
}

module.exports = ProductsController;
```

So basically, we are exporting a controller class, and in the `home()` method, we are retrieving products from the persistent storage — in our case, MongoDB — using our `ProductCatalog` service. After successfully getting all the products, we use the `render()` method from the response object to render an HTML response from our templates.

Storefront pages

We are not going to get into the details; you can check out the whole project and see how things are glued together.

Main layout

To have a single layout definition, almost every template will extend a master template file. This master template file will contain all of the necessary markup of a full HTML document. The master layout file can be found under `apps/storefront/views/layout.html`:

```html
<!DOCTYPE html>
<html>
  <head>
    <meta charset="utf-8">
    <title>ecommerce</title>
    {% include "includes/stylesheets.html" %}
  </head>
  <body>
    <div class="container">
      <div class="app-wrapper card whiteframe-z2">

        {% block header %}
        <header>
          <div class="row">
            <div class="col">
              <h1><a href="#">Awesome store</a></h1>
              <span class="pull-right">{{ currentUser.email
              }}</span>
```

```
            </div>
          </div>
        </header>
        {% endblock %}

        <div class="row">
          {% block content %}{% endblock %}
        </div>

      </div>
    <div>
    {% block footer %}
    <footer></footer>
    {% endblock %}
  </body>
</html>
```

The main `layout.html` file defines blocks to inject content inside them. Because we have a `Shared` micro app, all the necessary assets are available to us, so we can import these assets using a separate file, `apps/storefront/views/includes/stylesheets.html`:

```
<link href='https://fonts.googleapis.com/css?family=Work+Sans'
rel='stylesheet' type='text/css'>
<link rel="stylesheet" type="text/css"
href="/assets/css/style.css">
```

List products

To have full integration, let's see how we can list our products. Create a new template file called `apps/storefront/views/home.html` and add the following:

```
{% extends "layout.html" %}

{% block content %}
  <div class="product-list row">
    <div class="col">
    {% for product in products %}
      {% include "partials/product.html" %}
    {% endfor %}
    </div>
  </div>
{% endblock %}
```

We just extend the `content` block with the preceding code, iterate through the products list, and create a new product using a partial view.

Let's take a look at that partial view, `apps/storefront/views/partials/product.html`:

```html
<div class="col col-25 product-item">
  <a href="{{ baseUrl }}/products/{{ product.slug }}">
    <img src="http://placehold.it/208x140?text
    =product+image&txtsize=18" />
  </a>
  <h2>
    <a href="{{ baseUrl }}/products/{{ product.slug }}">{{
    product.title }}</a>
  </h2>
  <p>{{ product.summary }}</p>
  <p>price: {{ product.price.display }} {{
  product.price.currency}}</p>
  <p><button class="button">add to cart</button></p>
</div>
```

The static HTML markup is turned into a dynamic view. We are using the same structure as in our `Admin` micro application built with Angular 2.

If you are interested in the rest of the code, go ahead to the project's repository at `https://github.com/robert52/mean-blueprints-ecommerce` and find out more details. This part of the application was only for showing a different approach that you can integrate into your MEAN stack. You can always extend your stack with different technologies and see what works for you better.

Sometimes, you need to combine things, but having a solid base can make your life easier in the long run. We could have built everything using Angular, but it's always great to see how we can extend our horizons.

Summary

This chapter was about building an e-commerce application. From the beginning of the chapter, we started experimenting with new application architecture, one that can be easily extended in the future, and also used for server-side rendering in the implementation of our storefront.

Although this was much different from the previous chapters, it served well for educational purposes and opened doors to new possibilities. Keep your architecture modular and only experiment with small portions first to see how things work out in your favor.

In the next chapter, we'll try to extend our existing e-commerce application with an auction application.

6
Auction Application

This chapter will focus on building an auction-like application that will rely on the previously built e-commerce application's API. It is going to be a small proof-of-concept application. The backend solution of our application is going to consume the backend API of our e-commerce application. I want the last chapter to be a playground for us, so we can go through some interesting technologies used in this book, and also have some fun with a smaller but interesting app.

Setting up the base app

We are going to start with our classic boilerplate for an Express application. Follow these steps to set up the base project:

1. Clone the project from GitHub at `https://github.com/robert52/express-api-starter`.

2. Rename your boilerplate project `auction-app`.

3. If you want, you can stop pointing to the initial Git remote repository by running the following command:

   `git remote remove origin`

4. Jump to your working directory:

   `cd auction-app`

5. Install all dependencies:

   `npm install`

6. Create a development configuration file:

   `cp config/environments/example.js config/environments/development.js`

Your configuration file, `auction-app/config/environments/development.js`, should look similar to the following:

```
'use strict';

module.exports = {
  port: 3000,
  hostname: '127.0.0.1',
  baseUrl: 'http://localhost:3000',
  mongodb: {
    uri: 'mongodb://localhost/auction_dev_db'
  },
  app: {
    name: 'MEAN Blueprints - auction application'
  },
  serveStatic: true,
  session: {
    type: 'mongo',
    secret: 'someVeRyN1c3S#cr3tHer34U',
    resave: false,
    saveUninitialized: true
  },
  proxy: {
    trust: true
  },
  logRequests: false
};
```

What we are building

We are going to build an English auction site. The previous e-commerce application is going to serve us with products, and an admin can create auctions using those products. Auctions have different features; we are not going to discuss each of them, but instead we are going to describe an English auction.

The most common auction is the English auction; it's a single dimensional auction, and the only thing considered is the bid price offered for the goods. Usually it's seller oriented, meaning it's one-sided.

Normally, a starting price is set for the auction; it's called the **reserve price**, under which the seller won't sell the goods. Each buyer makes a bid and everyone knows every bid, so it's open-cry. The winner pays the winning price.

No lower bid is called than the current winning bid. Usually, the auction ends when no one is interested in paying the latest price. Also, an end time could be set for the auction.

The end time could be an absolute time, in our case a standard datetime, or a time relative to the last bid, such as 120 seconds. Later in the chapter, we are going to discuss the benefits of relative time.

Data modeling

In our application, an auction is a special event in which users—or more precisely, bidders—can bid on an item available for sale. An item is a product from the e-commerce platform, but one that retains only the necessary information to be displayed to the user. Let's discuss each model in more detail.

Auction

An auction is going to hold all the necessary information about the event. As discussed earlier, we are going to implement an English auction, in which we are going to sell goods from our main e-commerce application.

An English auction is open-cry, which means that everyone is aware of each bid. The winner will pay the winning price. Each bid is going to increase the price of the goods, and the next bidder has to pay more in order to win the auction.

All auctions will have a reserved price, a starting value below which we are not going to sell our product. In other words, it is the lowest acceptable price by the seller.

To simplify things, we are going to set an end time for our auction. The last bid closer to the end time will be the winning bid. You could go with a relative time, which means that you can set a time limit from the last bid (that is, 10 minutes) and just call the winner if no bids were made in that time frame. This could be very useful to prevent bid sniping.

For example, say you bid the starting price of 39 USD on a product. Normally, you have the highest bid. Now imagine that the auction is ending, but before the end with just few seconds another bidder attempts a bid at 47 USD. This will leave you with no time to react, so the last bidder wins the auction. This is how usually bid snipping works.

Let's see the Mongoose auction schema:

```
'use strict';

const mongoose = require('mongoose');
const Money = require('./money').schema;
const Schema = mongoose.Schema;
const ObjectId = Schema.ObjectId;
const Mixed = Schema.Types.Mixed;

var AuctionSchema = new Schema({
  item:            { type: Mixed },
  startingPrice:   { type: Money },
  currentPrice:    { type: Money },
  endPrice:        { type: Money },
  minAmount:       { type: Money },
  bids: [{
    bidder:        { type: ObjectId, ref: 'Bidder' },
    amount:        { type: Number, default: 0 },
    createdAt:     { type: Date, default: Date.now }
  }],
  startsAt:        { type: Date },
  endsAt:          { type: Date },
  createdAt:       { type: Date, default: Date.now }
});

module.exports = mongoose.model('Auction', AuctionSchema);
```

Besides the information discussed earlier, we embedded all the bids in our auction document. This would not be a good idea if there are going to be many bids in an auction, but since we are going to have a fixed-time auction, there are only going to be a few of them. For popular auctions, you could just move the bids to a separate collection and have a reference to the auction document.

Bidder

We are using the backend API from our e-commerce application, so we don't need to store users in our database. But we can store additional data about our bidding users. For this we can create a new model, called app/models/bidder.js, and add the following:

```
'use strict';

const mongoose = require('mongoose');
```

```
const Money = require('./money').schema;
const Schema = mongoose.Schema;
const ObjectId = Schema.ObjectId;
const Mixed = Schema.Types.Mixed;

const BidderSchema = new Schema({
  profileId:      { type: String },
  additionalData: { type: Mixed },
  auctions: [{
    auction:      { type: ObjectId, ref: 'Auction' },
    status:       { type: String, default: 'active'},
    joinedAt:     { type: Date, default: Date.now }
  }],
  createdAt:      { type: Date, default: Date.now }
});

module.exports = mongoose.model('Bidder', BidderSchema);
```

profileId stores the _id of the user in order to have a reference to the user document from the e-commerce platform. You could also store additional data in this model and store the auctions in which the bidder is present.

Auction backend

In the previous chapter, we added a service layer to our architecture. We are going to follow the same pattern. Also, we are going to add an extra component called Mediator, which will serve as a single point of entry to assist us in communicating with different modules.

We will follow the mediator design pattern in the construction of our modules, which is a behavioral design pattern. This is going to be a single central point of control, through which communication flows.

The Mediator

Our Mediator is going to be an object that will coordinate interaction with different modules through channels. A module can subscribe to a given event and get notified when that event occurs. All this event-related discussion pretty much makes us think about using the events core module from Node.js, which is used to emit named events that cause execution of the functions to be called.

This is a good starting point. One thing we need to solve is that our `Mediator` needs to be a single point of entry, and only one instance can exist at the execution time of our application. We could just use a singleton design pattern. With all this in mind, let's implement our mediator:

```
'use strict';

const EventEmitter = require('events');
let instance;

class Mediator extends EventEmitter {
  constructor() {
    super();
  }
}

module.exports = function singleton() {
  if (!instance) {
    instance = new Mediator();
  }

  return instance;
}
```

This should give us a solid start for our module; for now this should be enough. Because we are using the ES6 features, we can just extend the `EventEmitter` class. Instead of exporting the whole `Mediator` class, we are exporting a function that checks whether there is already an instance, and if not, we just create a new instance of our `Mediator` class.

Let's take a look at an example of how we are going to use this technique:

```
'use strict';

const mediator = require('./mediator')();

mediator.on('some:awesome:event', (msg) => {
  console.log(`received the following message: ${msg}`);
});

mediator.emit('some:awesome:event', 'Nice!');
```

We just require the `mediator` instance, and using the `.on()` method, we subscribe to events and execute a function. Using the `.emit()` method, we publish the named event and pass a message as an argument.

Remember when using `arrow` functions in ES6 that the `this` keyword in the listener function no longer points to `EventEmitter`.

Auction manager

Instead of implementing all the business logic in the application's controller layer, we are going to build another service, called `AuctionManager`. This service will have all the necessary methods for correct execution of an auction.

Using this technique, we can easily decide later how we are going to export our application's business logic: using traditional endpoints or through WebSockets.

Let's follow a few steps to implement our auction manager:

1. Create a new file called `/app/services/auction-manager.js`.

2. Add the necessary dependencies:

    ```
    const MAX_LIMIT = 30;

    const mongoose = require('mongoose');
    const mediator = require('./mediator')();
    const Auction = mongoose.model('Auction');
    const Bidder = mongoose.model('Bidder');
    ```

3. Define the base class:

    ```
    class AuctionManager {
      constructor(AuctionModel, BidderModel) {
        this._Auction = AuctionModel || Auction;
        this._Bidder = BidderModel || Bidder;
      }
    }
    module.exports = AuctionManager;
    ```

4. Getting all auctions method:

    ```
    getAllAuctions(query, limit, skip, callback) {
      if (limit > MAX_LIMIT) {
        limit = MAX_LIMIT;
      }

      this._Auction
      .find(query)
      .limit(limit)
      .skip(skip)
      .exec(callback);
    }
    ```

5. Joining an auction:

```
joinAuction(bidderId, auctionId, callback) {
  this._Bidder.findById(bidderId, (err, bidder) => {
    if (err) {
      return callback(err);
    }

    bidder.auctions.push({ auction: auctionId });
    bidder.save((err, updatedBidder) => {
      if (err) {
        return callback(err);
      }

      mediator.emit('bidder:joined:auction',
      updatedBidder);
      callback(null, updatedBidder);
    });
  });
}
```

As you can see, we started using our mediator to emit events. At this point, we are emitting an event when a bidder joins the auction. This does not add much value for us right now, but it will come handy when we start playing around with our real-time communication solution.

6. Placing a bid:

```
placeBid(auctionId, bidderId, amount, callback) {
  if (amount <= 0) {
    let err = new Error('Bid amount cannot be
    negative.');
    err.type = 'negative_bit_amount';
    err.status = 409;
    return callback(err);
  }

  let bid = {
    bidder: bidderId,
    amount: amount
  };

  this._Auction.update(
    // query
    {
      _id: auctionId.toString()
```

```
  },
  // update
  {
    currentPrice: { $inc: amount },
    bids: { $push: bid }
  },
  // results
  (err, result) => {
    if (err) {
      return callback(err);
    }

    if (result.nModified === 0) {
      let err = new Error('Could not place bid.');
      err.type = 'new_bid_error';
      err.status = 500;
      return callback(err);
    }

    mediator.emit('auction:new:bid', bid);
    callback(null, bid);
  }
);
}
```

When placing a bid, we just want to add it to the list of bids on our auction, and for that, we are going to use atomic operators to update the currentPrice and add the current bid. Also, after successfully placing a bid, we are going to emit an event for that.

Auctioneer

We are going to give a fancy name for our upcoming module, and we are going to call it Auctioneer. Why this name? Well, we are building an auction application, so we can add a touch of old-school feeling and add an auctioneer, which will call out new bids and who joins the auction.

As you must have already guessed, this will be our real-time communication module. This module will use SocketIO, and we are going to do something similar as in *Chapter 4, Chat Application*, where we used the module for real-time communication.

We'll go only through the most important parts from our module to see different concepts in action. Let's create a file called `app/services/auctioneer.js` and add the following content:

```
'use strict';

const socketIO = require('socket.io');
const mediator = require('./mediator')();
const AuctionManager = require('./auction-manager');
const auctionManager =  new AuctionManager();

class Auctioneer {
  constructor(app, server) {
    this.connectedClients = {};
    this.io = socketIO(server);
    this.sessionMiddleware = app.get('sessionMiddleware');
    this.initMiddlewares();
    this.bindListeners();
    this.bindHandlers();
  }
}
module.exports = Auctioneer;
```

So basically, we just structured our class and called a few methods in the constructor. We are already familiar with a few lines of code from the constructor; for example, the `.initMiddlewares()` method looks similar to *Chapter 4, Chat Application*, where we use middlewares to authorize and authenticate users:

```
initMiddlewares() {
  this._io.use((socket, next) => {
    this.sessionMiddleware(socket.request, socket.request.res,
    next);
  });

  this.io.use((socket, next) => {
    let user = socket.request.session.passport.user;

    // authorize user
    if (!user) {
      let err = new Error('Unauthorized');
      err.type = 'unauthorized';
      return next(err);
    }
```

```
    // attach user to the socket, like req.user
    socket.user = {
      _id: socket.request.session.passport.user
    };
    next();
  });
}
```

We made a clear split between our `SocketIO` handlers that are initialized when we call the `.bindHandlers()` method, and attached the listeners to our mediator by calling the `.bindListeners()` method.

So, our `.bindHandlers()` method will have the following structure:

```
bindHandlers() {
  this.io.on('connection', (socket) => {
    // add client to the socket list to get the session later
    let userId = socket.request.session.passport.user;
    this.connectedClients[userId] = socket;

    // when user places a bid
    socket.on('place:bid', (data) => {
      auctionManager.placeBid(
        data.auctionId,
        socket.user._id,
        data.amount,
        (err, bid) => {
          if (err) {
            return socket.emit('place:bid:error', err);
          }

          socket.emit('place:bid:success', bid);
        }
      );

    });
  });
}
```

Remember that this is only partial code, and the final version will have more handlers. So, when a new client connects, we attach a few handlers to our socket. For example, in the preceding code, we listen to the `place:bid` event, which will be called when a user places a new bid, and the `AuctionManager` service will persist that bid.

Now, obviously we would need to notify other clients about the occurred changes; we are not going to handle that here. Our .placeBid() method emits an event through the Mediator each time a new bid is successfully recorded. The only thing we need to do is listen for that event, which we already did when we called .bindListeners() in the Auctioneer's constructor method.

Let's take a look at a partial code sample from the .bindListeners() method:

```
bindListeners() {
  mediator.on('bidder:joined:auction', (bidder) => {
    let bidderId = bidder._id.toString();
    let currentSocket = this.connectedClients[bidderId];
    currentSocket.emit.broadcast('bidder:joined:auction',
    bidder);
  });

  mediator.on('auction:new:bid', (bid) => {
    this.io.sockets.emit('auction:new:bid', bid);
  });
}
```

In the preceding code, we are listening when a bidder joins an auction, and we broadcast a message to each client, expecting only the triggering socket client. When a new bid is placed, we emit an event to each socket client. So basically, we have two similar broadcast functionalities but with a major difference; one sends a message to each client expecting the one that triggered the event, and the second emits to all connected clients.

Using the service from controller

As we discussed earlier, our services can be consumed from any module and exposed in different ways to clients. Earlier, we used AuctionManager and exposed its business logic through WebSockets. Now, we are going to do the same using simple endpoints.

Let's create a controller file called app/controllers/auction.js with the following content:

```
'use strict';

const _ = require('lodash');
const mongoose = require('mongoose');
const Auction = mongoose.model('Auction');
const AuctionManager = require('../services/auction-manager');
const auctionManager = new AuctionManager();
```

```
module.exports.getAll = getAllAuctions;

function getAllAuctions(req, res, next) {
  let limit = +req.query.limit || 30;
  let skip = +req.query.skip || 0;
  let query = _.pick(req.query, ['status', 'startsAt', 'endsAt']);

  auctionManager.getAllAuctions(query, limit, skip, (err,
  auctions) => {
    if (err) {
      return next(err);
    }

    req.resources.auctions = auctions;
    next();
  });
}
```

We have already done this many times throughout the book, so there's nothing new here. The controller exports a function that will attach all the auctions returned from the service, and later on the response will be transformed into a JSON response.

Accessing data from the e-commerce API

When creating auctions, we need additional information about the item we add to the auction. All the info about the product item is stored on the e-commerce platform built in the previous chapter.

We didn't cover the creation of auctions in this chapter, but we can discuss the underlining communication layer with the e-commerce API. In the data modeling phase, we didn't discuss storing users in the database.

The reason for not including user management is that we are going to consume a third-party API to manage our users. For example, authentication and registration will be handled through the e-commerce platform.

E-commerce client service

To communicate with the third-party API, we are going to create a service to proxy the requests. As we don't consume many endpoints from the API, we can create a single service to handle everything. As your application grows, you could easily group your files by domain context.

Let's create a new file called app/services/ecommerce-client.js, and follow these steps:

1. Declare the constants used in the service and include the dependencies:

```
'use strict';

const DEFAULT_URL = 'http://localhost:3000/api';
const CONTENT_HEADERS = {
  'Content-Type': 'application/json',
  'Accept': 'application/json',
};

const request = require('request');
```

2. Define a custom RequestOptions class used to configure the request object:

```
class RequestOptions {
  constructor(opts) {
    let headers = Object.assign({}, CONTENT_HEADERS,
    opts.headers);

    this.method = opts.method || 'GET';
    this.url = opts.url;
    this.json = !!opts.json;
    this.headers = headers;
    this.body = opts.body;
  }

  addHeader(key, value) {
    this.headers[key] = value;
  }
}
```

To reduce the necessary code structure used to make calls with request, we defined a custom class to instantiate a default request option.

3. Add the EcommerceClient class:

```
class EcommerceClient {
  constructor(opts) {
    this.request = request;
    this.url = opts.url || DEFAULT_URL;
  }
}
```

The EcommerceClient class is going to be our main entry point to the third-party API. It's more of a facade to not know the underlining data source used in our application.

4. Specify how to authenticate users:

```
authenticate(email, password, callback) {
  let req = new RequestOptions({
    method: 'POST',
    url: `${this.url}/auth/basic`
  });
  let basic = btoa(`${email}:${password}`);

  req.addHeader('Authorization', `Basic ${basic}`);

  this.request(req, function(err, res, body) => {
    callback(err, body);
  })
}
```

The API server will handle the authentication for us; we are just using the token returned when making calls to the API. Our custom `RequestOptions` class permits us to add extra header data, such as the `Authorization` field.

5. Append the `getProducts()` method:

```
getProducts(opts, callback) {
  let req = new RequestOptions({
    url: `${this.url}/api/products`
  });
  req.addHeader('Authorization', `Bearer ${opts.token}`);

  this.request(req, function(err, res, body) => {
    callback(err, body);
  })
}
```

As you can see, with the same principle, we can retrieve data from our e-commerce application. The only thing is that we need to add a token to our calls. We are not going to discuss how we consume our service, as we have done this many times throughout the book.

It should be fairly simple to use it in a controller and configure a router to expose the necessary endpoints to the client application.

Frontend services

As we are touching only the most significant part of our application, we are going to discuss the implementation of our services used in the Angular application. I think it's important to understand the underlying communication layer with the backend application.

Auction service

`AuctionService` will handle all communications with the backend API to get info about a specific auction, or simply get all the available auctions. To do that, we are going to create a new file, `public/src/services/auction.service.ts`:

```
import { Injectable } from 'angular2/core';
import { Response, Headers } from 'angular2/http';
import { Observable } from 'rxjs/Observable';
import { Subject } from 'rxjs/Subject';
import { BehaviorSubject } from 'rxjs/Subject/BehaviorSubject';
import { AuthHttp } from '../auth/index';
import { contentHeaders } from '../common/headers';
import { Auction } from './auction.model';
import { SubjectAuction, ObservableAuction, ObservableAuctions } from
'./types';

const URL = 'api/auctions';

@Injectable()
export class AuctionService {
}
```

We imported our dependencies, and we've added an URL constant for better code readability, but you may handle your base URL configuration as you desire. A few things are missing before we can add the necessary methods, so let's define the constructor and class props:

```
public currentAuction: SubjectAuction = new
BehaviorSubject<Auction>(new Auction());
public auctions: ObservableAuctions;
public auction: ObservableAuction;

private _http: Http;
private _auctionObservers: any;
private _auctionsObservers: any;
private _dataStore: { auctions: Array<Auction>, auction: Auction };
```

```
constructor(http: Http, bidService: BidService) {
  this._http = http;
  this.auction = new Observable(observer =>
  this._auctionObservers = observer).share();
  this.auctions = new Observable(observer =>
  this._auctionsObservers = observer).share();
  this._dataStore = { auctions: [], auction: new Auction() };
}
```

We are exporting an Observable for a single auction and a list of auctions. Also, we are interested in the current auction. Besides all the familiar definitions, we added a third service to be used internally.

When getting a single auction or all auctions, we'll update the next value of the observers, so that subscribers get notified by the occurrence of changes:

```
public getAll() {
  this._authHttp
  .get(URL, { headers: contentHeaders })
  .map((res: Response) => res.json())
  .map((data) => {
    return data.map((auction) => {
      return new Auction(
        auction._id,
        auction.item,
        auction.startingPrice,
        auction.currentPrice,
        auction.endPrice,
        auction.minAmount,
        auction.bids,
        auction.status,
        auction.startsAt,
        auction.endsAt,
        auction.createdAt
      );
    });
  })
  .subscribe(auctions => {
    this._dataStore.auctions = auctions;
    this._auctionsObservers.next(this._dataStore.auctions);
  }, err => console.error(err));
}
```

To get a single auction, we can use the following method:

```
public getOne(id) {
  this._authHttp
  .get(`${URL}/${id}`)
  .map((res: Response) => res.json())
  .map((data) => {
    return new Auction(
      data._id,
      data.item,
      data.startingPrice,
      data.currentPrice,
      data.endPrice,
      data.minAmount,
      data.bids,
      data.status,
      data.startsAt,
      data.endsAt,
      data.createdAt
    );
  })
  .subscribe(auction => {
    this._dataStore.auction = auction;
    this._auctionObservers.next(this._dataStore.auction);
  }, err => console.error(err));
}
```

So, this service is going to communicate with our Node.js application and store all the received data in an internal store. Besides getting data from the server, we also want to eventually store the current auction, so this piece of code should handle it:

```
public setCurrentAuction(auction: Auction) {
  this.currentAuction.next(auction);
}
```

The socket service

The socket service is going to handle the communication with the SocketIO server. The benefit is that we have a single point of entry and we can abstract the underlying logic to the rest of the application.

Create a new file called `public/src/common/socket.service.ts`, and add the following:

```
import { Injectable } from 'angular2/core';
import * as io from 'socket.io-client';
import { Observable } from 'rxjs/Rx';
import { ObservableBid } from '../bid/index';
import { ObservableBidder } from '../bidder/index'

export class SocketService {
}
```

We just import the SocketIO client and all the rest of the data types. Also, don't forget to add the rest of the necessary code for your class:

```
public bid: ObservableBid;
public bidder: ObservableBidder;
private _io: any;

constructor() {
  this._io = io.connect();
  this._bindListeners();
}
```

An interesting thing we are doing here is to expose Observables—and the rest of the application can just subscribe to the stream of data—using the following technique:

```
private _bindListeners() {
  this.bid = Observable.fromEvent(
    this._io, 'auction:new:bid'
  ).share();
  this.bidder = Observable.fromEvent(
    this._io, 'bidder:joined:auction'
  ).share();
}
```

The nice part about RxJs is that we can create Observables from events. As the socket emits events, we can just create an Observable from that. With the preceding code, we can subscribe to incoming data from the backend.

In order to send information to the backend through SocketIO, we can expose an `.emit()` method that would be just a wrapper around the `.emit()` method on the socket client:

```
public emit(...args) {
  this._io.emit.apply(this, args);
}
```

The bid service

To get the big picture, we can take a look at the `BidService` found under the following path: `public/src/bid/bid.service.ts`. The class will have a similar structure:

```
@Injectable()
export class BidService {
  public bid: any;
  public currentAuction: any;
  private _socketService: SocketService;
  private _auctionService: AuctionService;

  constructor(
    socketService: SocketService,
    auctionService: AuctionService
  ) {
    this._socketService = socketService;
    this._auctionService = auctionService;
    this.currentAuction = {};
    this._auctionService.currentAuction.subscribe((auction) => {
      this.currentAuction = auction;
    });
    this.bid = this._socketService.bid.filter((data) => {
      return data.auctionId === this.currentAuction._id;
    });
  }

  public placeBid(auctionId: string, bid: Bid) {
    this._socketService.emit('place:bid', {
      auctionId: auctionId,
      amount: bid.amount
    });
  }
}
```

`BidService` will interact with `SocketService` in order to place bids, which will be pushed to all connected clients through the Express backend application. We also filter each incoming bid by the currently selected auction.

When the currently selected auction changes, we want to update our local copy by subscribing to `currentAuction` from `AuctionService`.

The bidder service

`BidderService` is going to be the first one to use `SocketService` and subscribe to changes on the `bidder` object. It will store all the incoming data from the backend Node.js server.

Let's create a new file called `public/src/services/bidder.service.ts`, and add the following base content:

```
import { Injectable } from 'angular2/core';
import { Observable } from 'rxjs/Observable';
import { Subject } from 'rxjs/Subject';
import { BehaviorSubject } from 'rxjs/Subject/BehaviorSubject';
import { contentHeaders } from '../common/headers';
import { SocketService } from './socket.service';
import { Bidder } from '../datatypes/bidder';
import { ObservableBidders } from '../datatypes/custom-types';

@Injectable()
export class BidderService {
}
```

Now that we have a starting point, we can define our constructor and declare all the necessary properties:

```
public bidders: ObservableBidders;

private _socketService: SocketService;
private _biddersObservers: any;
private _dataStore: { bidders: Array<Bidder> };

constructor() {
  this.bidders = new Observable(observer =>
  this._biddersObservers = observer).share();
  this._dataStore = { bidders: [] };
}
```

In this proof of concept, we are not going to do any HTTP calls from this service, and mostly we are going to store information inside the data store. The following `public` methods will come in handy:

```
public storeBidders(bidders: Array<Bidder>) {
  this._socketService = socketService;
  this._dataStore = { bidders: [] };
  this.bidders = new Observable(observer => {
    this._biddersObservers = observer;
```

```
    }).share();
    this._socketService.bidder.subscribe(bidder => {
      this.storeBidder(bidder);
    });
  }

  public storeBidder(bidder: Bidder) {
    this._dataStore.bidders.push(bidder);
    this._biddersObservers.next(this._dataStore.bidders);
  }

  public removeBidder(id: string) {
    let bidders = this._dataStore.bidders;

    bidders.map((bidder, index) => {
      if (bidder._id === id) {
        this._dataStore.bidders.splice(index, 1);
      }
    });

    this._biddersObservers.next(this._dataStore.bidders);
  }
```

The preceding logic was used in a similar form in earlier chapters. To keep it short, we just store the bidders or a single bidder in our data structures and update the next value of the observer, so that every subscriber gets notified to get the latest values.

Earlier, we used a `Bidder` custom data type—or a model if it sounds more familiar to you. Let's take a quick look at it, found under the following path—`public/src/datatypes/bidder.ts`:

```
export class Bidder {
  _id:            string;
  profileId:      string;
  additionalData: any;
  auctions:       Array<any>;
  createdAt:      string

  constructor(
    _id?:            string,
    profileId?:      string,
    additionalData?: any,
    auctions?:       Array<any>,
    createdAt?:      string
  ) {
```

```
        this._id = _id;
        this.profileId = profileId;
        this.additionalData = additionalData;
        this.auctions = auctions;
        this.createdAt = createdAt;
    }
}
```

The Auction module

We have taken the initial steps and implemented our services. Now we can start to use them in our components. There are many moving things in our `Auction` application. The most demanding part of the app will be the auction detail page.

The preceding code will list the details about a specific auction and also list the current bids. When a new bid is placed, it will be pushed to the `bids` list.

Earlier in our services, we used the `Auction` model. Let's take a look at it first. It can be found under `public/src/auction/auction.model.ts`:

```
import { Money } from '../common/index';

export class Auction {
  _id:             string;
  identifier:      string;
  item:            any;
  startingPrice:   any;
  currentPrice:    any;
  endPrice:        any;
  minAmount:       any;
  bids:            Array<any>;
  status:          string;
  startsAt:        string;
  endsAt:          string;
  createdAt:       string

  constructor(
    _id?:            string,
    item?:           any,
    startingPrice?:  any,
    currentPrice?:   any,
    endPrice?:       any,
    minAmount?:      any,
    bids?:           Array<any>,
```

```
    status?:        string,
    startsAt?:      string,
    endsAt?:        string,
    createdAt?:     string,
    identifier?:    string
  ) {
    this._id = _id;
    this.item = item || { slug: '' };
    this.startingPrice = startingPrice || new Money();
    this.currentPrice = currentPrice || this.startingPrice;
    this.endPrice = endPrice || new Money();
    this.minAmount = minAmount || new Money();
    this.bids = bids;
    this.status = status;
    this.startsAt = startsAt;
    this.endsAt = endsAt;
    this.createdAt = createdAt;
    this.identifier = identifier || `${this.item.slug}-
    ${this._id}`;
  }
}
```

It has a long list of properties. We are doing some initializations when we instantiate the model. We use a custom `Money` model, which reflects our custom monetary type from the backend.

If you remember, in the `Job Board` application, we used nice URLs to access a company. I wanted to have the same aspect but add a little bit of a twist to experiment with a different structure. We have the same concept but a different identifier for an auction.

We are using the product's slug in combination with the auction's `_id` for our `identifier` property. Now let's take a look at the `Money` model, `public/src/common/money.model.ts`:

```
export class Money {
  amount: number;
  currency: string;
  display: string;
  factor: number;

  constructor(
    amount?: number,
    currency?: string,
    display?: string,
```

```
        factor?: number
    ) {
      this.amount = amount;
      this.currency = currency;
      this.display = display;
      this.factor = factor;
    }
}
```

As you can remember, we are using these techniques to have initial values for our objects and to make sure we have the necessary properties. To fresh up our memories, the `amount` is obtained by multiplying the `display` value with the `factor`. This is all done on the server side.

The base component

We are going to add a base component that configures our routes. Our base component is usually pretty basic, without much logic; it has only routing-related logic. Create a new file called `public/src/auction/components/auction-base.component.ts`, and add the following code:

```
import { Component } from 'angular2/core';
import { RouteConfig, RouterOutlet } from 'angular2/router';
import { AuctionListComponent } from './auction-list.component';
import { AuctionDetailComponent } from './auction-detail.component';

@RouteConfig([
  { path: '/', as: 'AuctionList', component: AuctionListComponent,
  useAsDefault: true },
  { path: '/:identifier', as: 'AuctionDetail', component:
  AuctionDetailComponent }
])
@Component({
    selector: 'auction-base',
    directives: [
      AuctionListComponent,
      AuctionDetailComponent,
      RouterOutlet
    ],
    template: `
      <div class="col">
        <router-outlet></router-outlet>
      </div>
    `
```

```
})
export class AuctionBaseComponent {
  constructor() {}
}
```

The auction list

To display a list of currently available auctions, we are going to create a new
component, called `public/src/auction/components/auction-list.component.ts`:

```
import { Component, OnInit } from 'angular2/core';
import { AuctionService } from '../auction.service';
import { Router, RouterLink } from 'angular2/router';
import { Auction } from '../auction.model';

@Component({
    selector: 'auction-list',
    directives: [RouterLink],
    template: `
      <div class="auction-list row">
        <h2 class="col">Available auctions</h2>
        <div *ngFor="#auction of auctions" class="col col-25">
          <h3>
            <a href="#"
               [routerLink]="['AuctionDetail', { identifier:
               auction.identifier }]">
               {{ auction.item.title }}
            </a>
          </h3>
          <p>starting price: {{ auction.startingPrice.display }}
          {{ auction.startingPrice.currency }}</p>
        </div>
      </div>
    `
})
export class AuctionListComponent implements OnInit {
  public auctions: Array<Auction> = [];
  private _auctionService: AuctionService;

  constructor(auctionService: AuctionService) {
    this._auctionService = auctionService;
  }

  ngOnInit() {
```

```
    this._auctionService.auctions.subscribe((auctions:
    Array<Auction>) => {
      this.auctions = auctions;
    });
    this._auctionService.getAll();
  }
}
```

From this component, we'll link to the auction detail. As you can see, we used the `identifier` as a router param. The value of the property was constructed inside the `Auction` model.

The detail page

The detail page will have the most moving parts in this application. We are going to display the auction's details and list all new bids. Also, the user can bid from this page. To implement this component, let's follow these steps:

1. Create a new file called `public/src/auction/components/auction-detail.component.ts`.

2. Add the dependencies:

    ```
    import { Component, OnInit } from 'angular2/core';
    import { AuctionService } from '../auction.service';
    import { RouterLink, RouteParams } from 'angular2/router';
    import { Auction } from '../auction.model';
    import { BidListComponent } from '../../bid/index';
    import { BidFormComponent } from '../../bid/index';
    ```

3. Configure the `Component` annotation:

    ```
    @Component({
        selector: 'auction-detail,
        directives: [
          BidListComponent,
          BidFormComponent,
          RouterLink
        ],
        template: `
          <div class="col">
            <a href="#" [routerLink]="['AuctionList']">back to
            auctions</a>
          </div>
          <div class="row">
            <div class="col sidebar">
              <div class="auction-details">
    ```

```
        <h2>{{ auction.item.title }}</h2>
        <p>{{ auction.startingPrice.display }} {{
        auction.startingPrice.currency }}</p>
        <p>{{ auction.currentPrice.dislpay }} {{
        auction.startingPrice.currency }}</p>
        <p>minimal bid amount: {{
        auction.minAmount.display }}</p>
      </div>
    </div>
    <div class="col content">
      <bid-list></bid-list>
      <bid-form></bid-form>
    </div>
  </div>
  `
})
```

4. Add the class:

```
export class AuctionDetailComponent implements OnInit, OnDestroy {
  public auction: Auction;
  private _routeParams:RouteParams;
  private _auctionService: AuctionService;

  constructor(
    auctionService: AuctionService,
    routeParams: RouteParams
  ) {
    this._auctionService = auctionService;
    this._routeParams = routeParams;
  }
}
```

5. Implement ngOnInit:

```
ngOnInit() {
  this.auction = new Auction();
  const identifier: string =
  this._routeParams.get('identifier');
  const auctionId = this.getAuctionId(identifier);
  this._auctionService.auction.subscribe((auction:
  Auction) => {
    this.auction = auction;
  });
  this._auctionService.getOne(auctionId);
}
```

6. Add `ngOnDestroy`:

```
ngOnDestroy() {
  this._auctionService.setCurrentAuction(new Auction());
}
```

When the component is destroyed, we want to set `currentAuction` to be empty.

7. Define the private `getAuctionId` method:

```
private getAuctionId(identifier: string) {
  const chunks = identifier.split('-');
  return chunks[chunks.length -1];
}
```

We are using `RouterParams` to get the identifier. Because we have the nice URI we need to strip only the necessary information from the identifier. For that, we used a private method that splits the URL component into chunks and gets only the last portion.

The last part of the URL is the auction's `id`. After we have the necessary `id`, we can retrieve the information from our API.

This component uses two other components, `BidListComponent` and `BidFormComponent`. The first is used to display a list of bids, listen to the bids' data stream, and update the bids list.

The second, `BidFormComponent`, is used to make bids. It's easier to encapsulate all the functionalities into separate components. This way, each component can focus on its domain requirements.

The bid module

We are going to close our chapter with the `bid` module, as we used many of its components in the previous `auction` module. Only the `bid listing` will be discussed, as it implies working with the underlining socket stream.

Listing bids

From the previous `AuctionDetailComponent`, we can see that this component will have the bids as input. This data comes from the `auction` entity, which holds previously placed bids.

Create a new file called `public/src/bid/components/bid-list.component.ts`:

```
import { Component, OnInit, OnDestroy } from 'angular2/core';
import { BidService } from '../bid.service';
import { Bid } from '../bid.model';
import { BidComponent } from './bid.component';

@Component({
    selector: 'bid-list',
    inputs: ['bids'],
    directives: [BidComponent],
    template: `
      <div class="bid-list">
        <div *ngIf="bids.length === 0" class="empty-bid-list">
          <h3>No bids so far :)</h3>
        </div>
        <bid *ngFor="#bid of bids" [bid]="bid"></bid>
      </div>
      `
})
export class BidListComponent implements OnInit, OnDestroy {
  public bids: Array<Bid>;
  private _bidService: BidService;
  private _subscription: any;

  constructor(bidService: BidService) {
    this._bidService = bidService;
  }

  ngOnInit() {
    this._subscription = this._bidService.bid.subscribe((bid) => {
      this.bids.push(bid);
    });
  }

  ngOnDestroy() {
    if (this._subscription) {
        this._subscription.unsubscribe();
    }
  }
}
```

We subscribe to the `bid` data stream from `BidService` to push all the new incoming bids and display them using `BidComponent`. The subscription is also stored so that we can unsubscribe from the stream when the component is destroyed.

The bid component

Our bid component is going to be fairly simple. It will have a `bid` input, and after the view is initialized successfully, we are going to scroll to the bottom of the bid listing view. Let's create the following component under `public/src/bid/components/bid.component.ts`:

```
import { Component, AfterViewInit } from 'angular2/core';
import { Bid } from '../bid.model';

@Component({
    inputs: ['bid'],
    selector: 'bid',
    template: `
      <div class="bid-item">
        <div class="">
          <span class="">{{bid_id}}</span>
          <span class="">{{bid.amount}}</span>
        </div>
      </div>
    `
})
export class BidComponent implements AfterViewInit {
  public bid: Bid;

  constructor() {}

  ngAfterViewInit() {
    var ml = document.querySelector('bid-list .bid-list');
    ml.scrollTop = ml.scrollHeight;
  }
}
```

Also let's take a look at our `bid` model, `public/bid/bid.model.ts`:

```
export class Bid {
  _id:          string;
  bidder:       any;
  amount:       any;
  createdAt:    string

  constructor(
    _id?:       string,
    bidder?:    any,
    amount?:    any,
```

```
    createdAt?:    string
  ) {
    this._id = _id;
    this.bidder = bidder;
    this.amount = amount;
    this.createdAt = createdAt;
  }
}
```

Now we have a full round trip from the backend to our frontend components. Data is streamed from the WebSocket server to our Angular 2 application.

This application had the purpose of going through all the techniques used in the book, and we had a chance to put together a proof of concept. The main focus of the chapter was to see the underlining modules, how they will be combined, and how data will be modeled and transmitted between each module.

Summary

This is our final chapter, and we created a small proof-of-concept application. The purpose was to go through some of the most interesting parts and methods used in the book and see how we can combine exciting ideas to create something small but powerful.

Also, we used our existing e-commerce API to retrieve information about product items and manage our users. There was no reason to go through this process again as we can rely on third-party APIs for faster prototyping.

Through most of the chapters, we only touched the most important parts. All the necessary code can be found on the Packt Publishing website (https://www.packtpub.com/) for each chapter.

Index

www.ingramcontent.com/pod-product-compliance
Lightning Source LLC
Chambersburg PA
CBHW080927060326
40690CB00042B/3160